Islamic Conversion and Christian Resistance on the Early Modern Stage

Jane Hwang Degenhardt

Edinburgh University Press

For James and Minjoo

© Jane Hwang Degenhardt, 2010

Edinburgh University Press Ltd
22 George Square, Edinburgh

www.euppublishing.com

Typeset in Sabon and Futura
by Servis Filmsetting Ltd, Stockport, Cheshire, and
printed and bound in Great Britain by
CPI Antony Rowe, Chippenham and Eastbourne

A CIP record for this book is available from the British Library

ISBN 978 0 7486 4084 3 (hardback)

The right of Jane Hwang Degenhardt
to be identified as author of this work
has been asserted in accordance with
the Copyright, Designs and Patents Act 1988.

Contents

Acknowledgments

This book has been fostered by many wonderful teachers and mentors who have shaped my thinking over the years. While they are not responsible for any of the book's shortcomings, they certainly deserve thanks for any strengths it may have. Most of all, I am grateful to Jean Howard for offering a model of excellence. I deeply value her honest appraisals and her shared appreciation for the imaginative potential of the theater. For their inspired and rigorous training, I thank Margreta de Grazia and Peter Stallybrass. Together, they made the study of Renaissance literature irresistible. I thank as well my other mentors from the University of Pennsylvania, especially Ania Loomba, Phyllis Rackin, Barbara Fuchs, and David Wallace. Earlier in my academic career I benefited from a wealth of teachers who influenced me in ways they may never know. I would not be doing what I am today if it were not for Agha Shahid Ali, John O'Neill, Austin Briggs, Vincent Odamtten, Ama Ata Aidoo, James Thompson, Mae Henderson, Catherine Belsey, and Houston Baker.

If I have been fortunate in my teachers, I am just as fortunate in my many colleagues and students at the University of Massachusetts, Amherst, who have supported me in the completion of this book. Arthur Kinney has made Renaissance Studies a rich communal experience in western Massachusetts. In addition to a department full of supportive colleagues, I have benefited from two wonderful chairs who have looked out for my interests: Anne Herrington and Joseph Bartolomeo. The Five-College Renaissance Seminar, the Interdisciplinary Seminar in the Humanities and the Fine Arts, and the English Department Colloquia offered occasions at UMass to share my book-in-progress. I am particularly grateful to my research assistants, Phil Palmer and Tim Zajac, as well as to Sandra Williamson, without whom this book would have taken much longer to complete. I also want to thank my colleagues in the four colleges who have gone out of their ways to make me feel welcome and supported – lending their offices, their sympathetic ears, and their critical eyes: Brown Kennedy, Peter Berek, Sharon Seelig, Ann Jones, Lise Sanders, Marisa Parham, John Drabinski, Anston Bosman, and Barry O'Connell.

As my closest friends know, writing this book has involved a complicated juggling act, and I can say without a doubt that my act would not have been possible without the help of these friends. For being there for me in so many ways, I thank Suzanne Daly, as well as Julia Lee, Deb Aaronson, Asha Nadkarni, Haivan Hoang, and Jen Adams. Before starting my job I was incredibly lucky to be part of a supportive community of graduate students who continue to foster my intellectual life. I am especially grateful to Elizabeth Williamson for her constant faith. She is brilliant in every way. I also thank Jean Feerick, Marissa Greenberg, Cyrus Mulready, and Clare Costley King'oo for their wealth of expertise that is so freely shared. This book has also benefited in direct ways from scholars who have gone out of their way to share their work with me or offer feedback: Amanda Bailey, Jonathan Burton, Valerie Forman, Julia Reinhard Lupton, Susannah Brietz Monta, Michael Neill, Holly Crawford Pickett, Debora Shuger, and Sarah Wall-Randell.

I am extremely grateful to Wendy Lochner for her immediate encouragement and for shepherding my manuscript through the review process at Columbia. And my heartfelt thanks go to Jackie Jones at Edinburgh University Press for so unhesitatingly taking the book on when Columbia decided to refocus their publishing program. I am fortunate to have worked with two such humane and professional editors.

Finally, I thank those in my family whose love and good humor have been constants throughout this long process. My mother and brother are among my closest friends and have always supported my intellectual pursuits. My husband Jim has provided both spiritual and material support, as well as essential doses of irony. I thank him for honoring my love for my work. My children, James and Minjoo, help to put everything into perspective. I am grateful to them for the time they sacrificed for me to complete this work as well as for the time that they refused to sacrifice. It is to them that I dedicate this book and everything good that I do.

Versions of Chapters Two and Three have appeared in *ELH* and *The Journal for Early Modern Cultural Studies*. I am grateful to the editors of these publications for permission to reprint these materials here. I also thank UMass for supplying a pre-tenure research leave, as well as a Faculty Research/Healy Endowment Grant and a Mellon Mutual Mentoring Micro-Grant. Earlier versions of the book were presented at the University of Connecticut and Harvard University.

Figures

Seduction, Resistance, and Redemption: "Turning Turk" and the Embodiment of Christian Faith

> Nay, if the flesh take hold of him, he's past redemption.
> He's half a Turk already; it's as good as done.
>> Robert Daborne, *A Christian Turned Turke* (c.1610)[1]

Could anything be worse than being captured by Turks, stripped, beaten, and mercilessly killed? In the minds of early modern English people, there was one thing even worse than dying at the hands of Turks: conversion. Whereas a death by martyrdom offered the chance for salvation, converting to Islam set one on a path of irredeemable damnation. In addition, "turning Turk" implied not just a religious conversion, but also the complete undoing of all things constitutive of an English Christian identity.

It was a threat that was oddly familiar to those living in and around London in the late sixteenth and early seventeenth centuries. The Ottoman empire may have been halfway across the globe, but its influence was increasingly present in the daily lives of English Christians – in the foods they ate, the clothes they wore, the sermons they heard at church, the stories they read in the news, and the fears and fantasies that filled their imaginations. In particular, English awareness of the Ottoman empire heightened as the result of England's growing participation in Mediterranean trade. Commerce brought eastern imports into English spaces and drew increasing numbers of English citizens to the waters and ports of the eastern Mediterranean. But commerce depended upon certain risks, which included not only the dangers of seafaring and the economic risks of piracy and foreign investment, but also the personal risk of losing English bodies and souls to Islamic conversion. The more general threat of Ottoman imperialism – of course linked to commerce in various ways – also raised the specter of conversion. Stories of Muslim conquest and forced conversion in places such as Greece,

Hungary, and the Balkans were well known to the English, and by the early seventeenth century Turkish ships had ventured as far west as the English Channel. Indeed, there were numerous real-life Christian, even English, converts to Islam during this period, many of whom had been captured by Turks in the pursuit of trade.[2] But just as powerful was the *imagined* threat of conversion that emerged in English stage plays and in other popular media. Within this context, the collective (and interrelated) commercial, imperial, religious, and cultural threats of the Ottoman empire were condensed into a single, personalized threat that centered upon the individual Christian body and soul. This book interrogates the ways that Christian-Muslim conversion was conceived in the popular imagination, focusing in particular on the theater both as a receptacle for popular beliefs and as an influential force in shaping them. In the following chapters, I seek to uncover the particular terms by which conversion to Islam, as well as Christian resistance and redemption, were imagined to take place, and what these embodied terms might tell us about the threshold of difference that divided Christians from Muslims.

If conversion to Islam transformed one's earthly identity and damned the soul, it did so by targeting the Christian body. Naturally, the stage would make conversion a matter of bodies and outward materiality, but there were important ways in which the physical technologies of the theater accorded with beliefs about the nature of Islam's particular threat of conversion. Numerous news pamphlets and travel books from the period offer graphic accounts of the physical tortures used to coerce Islamic conversion and the permanent bodily mark that conversion left in the form of circumcision. In *The famous and wonderfull recoverie of a ship of Bristoll*, a news pamphlet published in 1622, John Rawlins describes his experience as a Turkish captive by emphasizing its physical ramifications. As he explains, "the first newes [he] encountered" upon his arrival as a newly captured man in Ottoman Algiers concerned the excruciating methods of torture used to force Christian slaves to turn Turk:

> They commonly lay them on their naked backs, or bellies, beating them so long, till they bleed at the nose and mouth, and if yet they continue constant, then they strike the teeth out of their heads, pinch them by their tongues, and use many other sorts of tortures to convert them; nay, many times they lay them on their whole length in the ground like a grave, and so cover them with boords threatening to starve them, if they will not turn, and so many even for feare of torment, and death, make their tongues betray their hearts to a most fearful wickednesse, and so are circumcised with new names, and brought to confesse a new religion. [. . .] and this was the first newes we encountered with at our coming first to Algiers.[3]

In addition to indulging the physical details of bodily torture, this description invokes conversion as a literal turn of the body, conjured through its visualization of Christian bodies being laid "on their naked backs, or bellies" or "in the ground like a grave" and then threatened "if they will not turn" as if on a skewer. In addition, Rawlins attests, conversion is coerced through the body despite or against the inner intentions of the victim's heart, in that "feare of torment, and death" makes the captives' "tongues betray their hearts." The immediate consequences of voicing an acceptance of Islam are also manifestly physical: the converted Christian is circumcised and receives a new name. Thus, after being laid in the ground "like a grave" and buried with boards, the convert is in effect reborn to a fate construed to be worse than death. As Rawlins suggests, conversion to Islam threatens a complete and permanent undoing of Christian identity. Manifested in external terms such as a change of name and an indelible mark upon one's body, this transformation may or may not mirror the intentions of one's heart or soul.

In fact, depending upon one's assumptions about the spiritual dimensions of religious conversion, it may seem striking that the word "soul" is completely absent from Rawlins's description. Certainly, the soul is affected by conversion, but according to the logic that Rawlins presents, the soul's transformation is driven by the physical pain (or fear) of torture, the physical betrayal of the tongue, and the physical mark of circumcision, rather than the convictions of the soul driving the body. At the very least, Rawlins's description of conversion reveals the intertwined nature of confessional identity and physical embodiment.

The body's sway over the soul may seem to apply most clearly to involuntary converts. Of course, not all converts were won against their wills, and Rawlins acknowledges another category of apostates who willingly shed their Christian identities and embraced Islam. But even these converts are driven by an impulse that seems to originate in the body:

> Others again, I must confess, who never knew any God, but their owne sensuall lusts, and pleasures, thought that any religion would serve their turnes, and so for preferment or wealth very voluntarily renounced their faith, and became *Renegadoes*, in despite of any counsel which seemed to intercept them.[4]

Drawing upon an already longstanding tradition of associating Islam with "sensuall lusts, and pleasures," Rawlins describes the temptation to convert as a sexual one.[5] Again, the embracement of Islam as a religious choice comes secondary to that which it affords: easier access to sexual pleasures and monetary wealth. Doctrinal persuasion appears to

be as irrelevant to these individuals as Christian attempts to "intercept" them from renouncing Christianity. Indeed, in the case of these renegades, "any religion would serve their turnes," and thus conversion to Islam is not really construed to be a "religious" choice. What is more, the sexual connotation of "serving a turn," invoking both the "turn" of conversion and "screwing," as well as referring to the fulfillment of one's sexual desires, underscores the carnal motivations for Islamic conversion.[6] According to Rawlins, Islam also attracts those who are susceptible to the superficial rewards of "pleasures," "preferment," and "wealth," which again are implicitly defined against the less immediate and tangible rewards of a Christian soul.

Conversion and Theatricality

The stage was the perfect medium for capitalizing on the visceral appeal of forced conversions and physical resistance. Because of its visual and aural orientations, theater could bring these things to life like no other medium. Dramatic counterparts to the tortures described by Rawlins included Thomas Shirley's torture on the rack in *The Travails of the Three English Brothers* (*c.*1607), Ariana's condemnation to the scaffold in *The Knight of Malta* (*c.*1618), and Vitelli's imprisonment in biting chains in *The Renegado* (*c.*1624), as well as plays that established a resonance between early Christian martyrs and the persecution of Christian captives by Turks. Stories adapted from the news as well as from medieval romance, involving travel to faraway places, dangerous exploits in foreign settings, shipwreck, captivity and rescue, torture, and of course conversion and resistance, provided wonderful opportunities for grand spectacles and exotic costuming and props. As I will go on to discuss, depictions of cross-cultural encounters in the Mediterranean and of Turks and the Ottoman empire were particularly topical because of England's commercial interests at the time. Jonathan Burton estimates there were "over sixty dramatic works featuring Islamic themes, characters, or settings," and certainly many more plays registered England's pervasive awareness of the Turks through brief or allusive references.[7] Given this fascination with Islam, it is not difficult to understand the dramatic appeal of stories of threatened conversion, or why they lent themselves so well to theatrical performance.

At its most basic level, the stage itself functioned as a technology of illicit conversion: it converted male actors into gentlemen and women, Christians into Turks, Moors, and Jews, and audiences into

believers. Thus when Hamlet asks his friend Horatio whether his successful production of "The Mousetrap" might earn him "a fellowship in a cry of players" should "the rest of [his] fortunes turn Turk," he invokes an analogy between the mechanism of theatrical production and the complete unmaking of identity that was associated with turning Turk (3.2.269–72).[8] By linking the conditions of becoming an actor, joining a "fellowship," and "turning Turk," Hamlet also alludes to the ways in which actors like Ben Jonson were marked with the brand of indebtedness and disreputability, sometimes associated with physical cuts or brands to the nose and ear. The dramatic nature of conversion, in which a subject is seduced, forced, or driven by desperation to abandon the most fundamental aspects of his or her identity, and "turn" into that which is most feared, loathed, or perceived to be essentially different, not only provided immense theatrical appeal but was itself essentially theatrical. Depending on how they were enacted, staged conversions between Christianity and Islam could be harrowing, humorous, shocking, appalling, or miraculous.

In beginning a book about the imaginative contours of Islamic conversion with an example from a news pamphlet, I want to stress the close relationship between the stage and the popular news press in early modern England. Targeting what was often the same popular audience, plays and news pamphlets tapped into topical interests and borrowed material from one another. And just as the stage shaped and embellished content from real life, pamphlets like that of Rawlins shaped the meaning of conversion through their particular stylistic and narrative choices, including the use of diction, tone, structure, and metaphor. By analyzing these textual details, we move beyond the basic facts of a narrative to its more nuanced local texture and the unspoken implications of metaphor, gaining a closer sense of the more intangible ways in which English culture understood the threat of turning Turk. As Rawlins's accounts illustrate above, Islamic conversion is compelled and manifested through the body. The events Rawlins reports upon may well be based on "truth," but it is a mistake to impose too strict a binary opposition between printed publications like news pamphlets or travel narratives, presumed to be factual, reliable, and authoritative, and more "fictional" texts like popular plays. By the same token, the dramatic stage featured numerous characters and incidents that were based on real-life events, though these "factual" reports were clearly filtered through the imagination. Together, news pamphlets and the public theater participated in a bilateral conversation mediated by popular tastes and interests. Although my study focuses primarily on stage plays, I necessarily set the public theater in the context of a larger popular

culture of exchange, facilitated by travel, commerce, the printing press, and performance.

Whereas a number of literary critics have addressed the multifarious signification of the "Turk" on the Renaissance stage, I focus on how conversion reveals on a more immediate and personal level the complex stakes of difference and sameness that pertain to Muslim and Christian identities. In analyzing the mechanism that threatened to turn Christians into Muslims, I observe how it enlisted various logics of sexuality and gender, manipulating them within and against the conventions of dramatic genre. In particular, I interrogate the tragic stakes of conversion and its comic aversions by looking at how conversion to Islam was often represented as a sexual threat, and what it meant that its aversion was rooted in physical chastity and temperance. What did these imaginative stakes reveal about how English culture was grappling with differences between Christians and Muslims? In other words, if conversion to Islam represented a fate worse than death, what did it mean that its tragic stakes were directly associated with interfaith sexual intercourse? Why was a religious, or spiritual, conversion represented on the stage in not just physical, but sexual terms? These imaginative negotiations, I argue, offer a window on the elusive and uneven process by which confessional identities fused into categories that we now associate with racial differences. In establishing particular terms for conversion (as well as for its resistance and redemption), the stage attempted to instate an apprehensible, if permeable, threshold of difference between Christians and Muslims. This book seeks to uncover the particular logics of gender, sexuality, and genre that informed this imagined threshold.

Religious Turnings

In addition, my study addresses how these negotiations were performed in terms specific to the history of Protestant reform, revealing how the threat of conversion was importantly framed by a culture of domestic religious unrest. Conversion was already a vexed issue in England given the culture of conversion created by the Reformation and its instabilities. Moreover, the foreign threat of Islam exacerbated existing cultural controversies over the material or immaterial basis of Christian faith and its proper forms of expression. In the decades following England's break from Catholicism, Protestant reformers not only rejected material objects such as icons, relics, rosary beads, and crucifixes, but also eschewed certain embodied expressions of Christian faith. These

included practices such as vowed virginity, fasting, and self-flagellation; outward signs of devotion such as genuflection and making the sign of the cross; the veneration of saints' body parts; the idea that priests could serve as human proxies for God; and even the emphasis on Jesus's corporeality and the notion of consuming his flesh that were implicit in Catholic understandings of transubstantiation. In place of these embodied practices, Protestant reformers attempted to emphasize a more spiritualized and intangible notion of Christian faith that was not driven by bodily or material expression. But because Islamic conversion was understood in the popular imagination to be a physical threat, it drew attention to the untenable nature of such an ideal and pointed up the need for more tangible methods of Christian resistance and redemption, including materials and practices recently devalued by the Reformation. In response to the terrifying specter of Islamic conversion, the stage turned to the embodied and ceremonial forms of England's Catholic past, reinvesting the talismanic qualities of relics and crosses, the mediating powers of the priest, and the redemptive magic of the sacraments.

Thus, the early modern stage shows us how English ambivalence about Protestant disembodiment and immateriality was brought to a particular crisis by Islam. When pitted against the specter of Islamic conversion, the spiritualized expressions of faith championed by Protestant reformers could not offer convincing enough methods of Christian defense, and required supplementation by embodied and material forms of resistance. Certainly, the endurance of embodied and material religious practices haunted Protestantism even outside the threat of Islam. A culture forcibly converted from Catholicism to Protestantism did not easily relinquish the devotional habits to which it had been long accustomed, and English Protestantism retained many elements of Catholic practice.[9] As Elizabeth Williamson has persuasively shown, the theater's frequent use of stage props that included (or looked like) Catholic objects exploited the layers of meaning and complex emotional responses that were attached to these objects in the wake of the Reformation.[10] That these objects could be both derided and venerated within the fictions of early modern plays reflects the "ongoing contradictions between post-Reformation theory and practice."[11] In this book I demonstrate how Islam, and in particular the embodied consequences associated with conversion to Islam, helped to fuel these ongoing contradictions. I interpret the stage's use of Catholic forms to combat Islam not as evidence of Catholic sympathies per se, but as one way in which the threat of conversion forced differences of faith into the physical realm. In producing a new model of Christian faith that physically

resisted conversion, the stage established a boundary between Christian and Muslim identity that was not merely religious and spiritual in nature, but also embodied, sexual, and increasingly racialized. Not only did Islam compel Protestants to re-embrace some of their discarded ideas about the materiality of faith, then; it also drove them to perceive religious differences in racial terms. In short, this book maps a certain conjunction between an early modern history of race and that of post-Reformation controversy over the nature of Christian faith.

To the extent that my study addresses the relationship between theater and religious culture, it engages a current critical dialogue surrounding the recent "turn to religion" in early modern English studies. In an important 2004 article Ken Jackson and Arthur Marotti chart this critical turn and also identify a splintering of scholarly approaches.[12] In particular, they critique a tendency among some New Historicist critics to translate the "alterity" of early modern religion too quickly into other struggles of social, economic, or political power.[13] My approach seeks to avoid this tendency by emphasizing how, in its attempts to apprehend conversion to Islam, the stage intimately engaged with early modern religious culture and exposed – and even promulgated – ruptures in the conceptual application of Protestant models of faith. These ruptures reveal not simply that religion should be read as race, but rather an imaginative process whereby religious identities became fused with national, embodied, and proto-racial categories. Thus, I call attention to how the stage's exploration of conversion directly engaged a religious concern while also revealing the limitations of existing religious categories and concepts. While I view the theater as an imaginative and ultimately secular institution, I am distinctly interested in how the stage drew upon religious language and structures, responded to religious controversies, and even recreated religious experiences through its multiple sensory effects. I would not want to overestimate the theater's investment in religious doctrine, but by the same token I do not believe that the stage necessarily evacuated doctrinal allusions of their religious significance. As Michael O'Connell puts it, while not inherently religious in nature, the public stage was an important "site of religious contestation" insofar as it was the place "where the deepest preoccupations of the culture found expression and representation."[14] My book demonstrates how the stage's engagement of Islam was directly informed by a backdrop of domestic religious controversy, as well as how the threat of conversion imaginatively impinged upon domestic religious controversies. But, as Anthony Dawson observes, religion was just one of the languages that the theater engaged, and in its redeployment of this language the theater often

"shifted and transformed" religion through the very fact of performance and its commercial context.[15] As I hope my analysis bears out, it is important to acknowledge how the theater not only demystified but also *remystified* religious content through its imaginative renegotiations and because of its particular goals of entertainment and profit. Religion on the stage was not necessarily a screen for other power struggles, but neither was the theater a transparent screen for religion.

Commercial and Imperial Backdrop

Recent historians, seeking to redress the long-overlooked influence of eastern trade on early modern English culture, have well established the historical backdrop of increased English awareness of the Ottoman empire.[16] During the late sixteenth and early seventeenth centuries, England underwent a marked shift in its commercial orientation.[17] Increasingly less reliant on their cloth export trade with northern Europe, the English began in the late sixteenth century to pursue commercial opportunities in the Near and Far East opened up to them by the collapse of the Antwerp and Iberian entrepôts and the weakening holds of Portugal and Spain within the eastern territories. With the chartering of the joint stock companies, including the Levant Company in 1592 and the East India Company in 1599, the English forged monopolies on eastern Mediterranean trade.[18] They began to import large quantities of raw silks and spices for domestic manufacturing, broad home consumption, and re-export within Europe. Yet, as many critics have acknowledged, the English were far from an imperial power in this period, and their early commercial intercourse in the Mediterranean was colored by their profound awareness of the far larger, wealthier, and more powerful Ottoman empire. For English seamen venturing into the foreign and largely unpoliced territories of the southeastern Mediterranean, the dangers were many. Because maps and navigational technology were unreliable, English seamen frequently got lost or shipwrecked, and starvation and sickness were common. Perhaps most menacingly, English ships were constantly threatened by attacks from other merchant ships, including Barbary pirates and Turks, as well as Spanish and other Christian competitors in the region.

In addition to confronting the perils of maritime commerce, the English were repeatedly reminded of the Ottoman empire's imperial ambitions and its increasing incursions on European territories. Ottoman territorial threats continued a long history of Christian-Muslim warfare, including the Crusades as well as more recent sixteenth-century struggles over the Mediterranean islands of Rhodes, Malta, Crete, Sicily, and Cyprus. As texts such as *The Estates, Empires, and Principallities of the World* (1615) ominously reported, the Ottoman empire's imperial dominion now extended 3,000 miles "from Buda to Constantinople," as well as across the northern coast of Africa from Alexandria to the border of Morocco.[19] In taking up the rhetoric of the Crusades many early modern writers interpreted Ottoman imperialism as a religious threat to all Christendom, lamenting the loss of a united Christendom due to the fracturing effects of the Reformation. Together, the threats of Turkish imperial expansion, piracy, and, by extension, conversion set the scene for a proliferation of Muslim characters on the English stage as well as the production of numerous plays featuring intercultural conflicts between Christians and Turks in Mediterranean settings.

Given the imperial dominance of the Ottoman empire in the early modern period, the majority of existing studies on representations of Islam in English literature and culture share an interest in undoing assumptions about western supremacy that characterize later periods. Edward Said's *Orientalism* offers a theoretical model around which these recent studies converge and from which they depart.[20] Whereas Said's model is premised on the Christian West's dominance over the Islamic East, studies of the early modern period address the implications of England's pre-imperial status. Accordingly, Richmond Barbour's *Before Orientalism* (2003) begins with an acknowledgment of England's belatedness in the realms of overseas exploration, trade, and colonization, and, in taking account of "the disparities between dominant representations and foreign negotiations," seeks to expose the unequal power dynamic that popular representations often occluded or distorted.[21] Similarly, Nabil Matar (1998, 1999), Daniel Vitkus (2003), and Jonathan Burton (2005) emphasize the ways in which the relationship between early modern England and the Ottoman empire does not accord with the Orientalist paradigm.[22] In particular, they draw attention to a rich archive of early modern writings on Turks, and to the diverse ways that Turks were represented on the stage. Recent studies by Matthew Dimmock, Linda McJannet, Benedict Robinson, and Bernadette Andrea build upon these introductions to the "Turk" plays by focusing on more specific time periods, generic influences, or thematic concerns; in doing so, they continue to weigh in on the Orientalism debate, but also steer it in new directions.[23] For example, Andrea considers how hierarchies of gender complicated the power dynamics between England and the Islamic world. And Robinson offers a useful qualification to the critical consensus that rejects Said's model; recognizing that Orientalism is not just a question of empire but also of the cultural and intellectual dispositions that helped to enable empire, he reminds us of the dangers of overstating "the firm line drawn between early modern and postcolonial studies."[24]

I share Robinson's view that the history of English imperialism begins prior to its absolute realization and that there are important ways in which imperial logic is rooted in the cultural desires and fantasies that find their expression on the stage in other imagined forms. In my reading, the negotiations of the imagination that took place in the popular theater helped to establish a grammar of the Orient even in the face of geopolitical realities that suggested Ottoman imperial dominance. Thus, I address the Orientalism debate not by reading geopolitical realities onto the early modern stage, or even by observing how the stage challenged geopolitical realities, but by looking at how theatrical representations of conversion betray a dynamic power struggle that played out on the level of religious identity and its destabilization. Attending to the imaginative function of conversion as a site where the terms of religious identity start to bleed into something akin to racial identity offers a more nuanced, if admittedly more narrow, understanding of these broader power struggles (between East and West, England and the Ottoman empire, or Christendom and Islam).

Historicizing Race

The question of whether race is a valid category for talking about Muslim Turks in early modern England – if it applies at all to the period – has been vigorously debated by critics. In particular, critics have questioned whether Turks were distinguished by phenotypical differences that could be suggestive of racial markings. Visual representations of Turks ranged from serious portraits in chronicles such as Richard Knolles *Generall Historie of the Turkes* (1603) and commemorative portrait medals to the derogatory caricatures of the "Turk's head" on tavern signs and archery targets. Philip Henslowe's inventory of the costumes and stage properties owned by the Admiral's Men in March of 1598 included an unspecified number of "Turckes hedes" as well as an "owld Mahemetes head," suggestive of identifiable facial features.[25] In addition, Muslims shared with Jews the physical stigma of circumcision, which, as critics such as James Shapiro, Julia Reinhard Lupton, and Janet Adelman have argued, may have signified in ways more threatening than taxonomies of color.[26] We might be tempted to conclude that the mark of circumcision approximated modern formulations of race more accurately than early modern understandings of skin color, though as I discuss in Chapter 1 it is important to bear in mind the difference between physical and physiological traits, as well as between inherited ones and environmentally produced ones. Drawing primarily on English Ottoman histories, Linda McJannet has concluded that "The 'swarthy Turk' is an entirely modern construction."[27] At the same time, references from dramatic dialogue reveal that at least some Muslim "Turks" were depicted on the stage with dark complexions and subsequently demonized or ridiculed on this basis.[28] Thus, it is important to consider how phenotypical differences may have figured differently in different genres and cultural media. Moreover, it is necessary to realize that skin color was not always understood in terms of an inherited phenotypical difference: it was also linked to environmental effects on the body's humors, to the biblical curse of Ham, and to the work of the devil. Thus blackness was not necessarily a condition of race in the same way that it is today. Disagreements over whether circumcision and skin color amounted to distinctions of race, and which if either was the more pertinent sign, seem to reflect an irresolvable lack of consensus over how to define racial criteria in the period. And of course, phenotypical difference, or physical difference rooted in genetic and environmental factors, is not the only way to identify the presence of race. As Jonathan Burton and Ania Loomba assert in their recent documentary companion on early modern race, racial logic necessarily encompasses not only distinctive combinations of physical traits, "but also the eclectic range of cultural differences that are used to explain, manage, or reorganize relations of power."[29]

One of the difficulties of talking about race in early modern England is the lack of a contemporary term for it. It does not help matters that the term "race" was in fact abundantly used in early modern discourses, but with a meaning quite distinct from our own.[30] As Jean Feerick has pointed out, whereas modern definitions emphasize distinctions like skin color, the structural logic of early modern "race" was more proximate to social "rank."[31] The distinction between early modern (or pre-modern) and modern usages of the term has led critics to either deny the presence of anything akin to modern race in the early modern period or too easily conflate the earlier and later meanings. Feerick rightly points out that such critical responses have "discouraged careful consideration of the ways a singular semantic unit – race – can describe quite distinct social formations across the historical divides that anchor its meaning."[32] She offers a necessary corrective to these dehistoricizing tendencies by bringing into view a blood-based social hierarchy that somatically anchored early modern differences of race/rank, showing how modern racial formations were predicated upon the decline of this earlier blood system. Feerick's insistence that the significance of "blood" as an inheritable condition of rank and a precursor to modern race should not simply be translated as "class" underscores her interest in exposing the interrelationship between the two racial systems – the earlier one unraveling as the later one emerged.

Clearly, to speak of racial difference in the early modern period is not to reference the same kinds of distinctions and historical conditions that characterize modern understandings of race. At the same time, the absence of a term to describe even a fuzzy category of difference linking "natural" distinctions with cultural hierarchies does not mean that the category itself did not exist in some form. When I use the term "race" in this study I am referring neither to the same term as it functioned in the early modern period nor to an unnamed concept of race that is exactly equivalent to our own. Rather, I refer to an unstable and newly emerging category whose dynamic presence could only be apprehended through the increasing insufficiency of existing terms or concepts, such as "religious identity," to contain it. Whereas Feerick uncovers a crucial discursive phase in the genealogical history of race by calling attention to a system of blood, I offer a different window on this process. Attending to the embodied and sexual logic of conversion and its somatic anchoring of Protestant faith, I capture a point of transition between constructions of religious and racial identity. If race may be seen to spill over from categories of religious identity, I argue that the categorical excess of race came into view inadvertently on the public stage through representations of Islamic conversion. Taking a cue from Ania Loomba, I locate cultural hierarchies not in their absolute and full-fledged realization, but in the subtle negotiations of imagined forms. Moreover, I identify moments of transition in the cultural ruptures produced by the body's anxious and insistent intrusions on the spiritual process of conversion – betraying a racial logic that exposes itself not directly but in spite of itself. In plain terms, conversion reveals an imaginative rupture where race breaks away from religious identity.

Critics such as Kim Hall, Joyce Green MacDonald, Mary Floyd-Wilson, and Lara Bovilsky have similarly used the stage to explore the cultural history of race by analyzing how the stage reappropriated tropes of darkness and fairness, refigured classical humoral traditions, and revealed parallels between race and gender.[33] Other critics such as Dympna Callaghan, Virginia Mason Vaughan, and Andrea Stevens have focused more explicitly on the evolving material technologies of face paint to draw conclusions about constructions of racial difference in specific plays.[34] While there are limits to what we can know about the staging of Islamic figures in the early modern theater, we can discern something about the use of turbans and other costuming, as well as technologies of face paint, through surviving inventories of stage props and cues from dialogue and stage directions in the playtexts. Although my own approach complements the work of these scholars, I focus not on racial materiality itself, but on what we can learn about the nature of racial embodiment through the process of conversion. Approaching race from this angle forces us to understand race itself as a dynamic and unstable process. Accordingly, I uncover the hidden stakes of Islamic conversion and Christian redemption. In other words, what did it take to render a conversion complete, and by what means could conversion be reversed? How did factors such as gender, setting, and genre play into these equations?

Seduction and the Stage

As the plays I discuss in this book reveal, sexual seduction functions as a crucial vehicle for linking conversion to a racial logic. Rawlins's harrowing description of the fate of Christian captives in Algiers alludes to the sexual motivations of renegades, but the sexualized element of conversion was even more overt on the public stage, where turning Turk was often presented as the inevitable consequence of interfaith seduction or rape. Part of the way the stage racialized Muslims was by casting them as sexual predators, the Muslim woman an exotic temptress in need of taming, and the Muslim man a lust-controlled rapist, contained best through annihilation. What is more, in closely associating conversion with sexual intercourse between a Christian and a Muslim, the stage represented conversion's effects in terms that involved the reproductive physical body. The stage's heightened anxiety around the sexual penetration of a Christian woman by a Muslim man suggested that conversion followed a patriarchal logic which rendered the female body and its offspring more vulnerable than Christian men to reinscription by a Muslim sexual partner.

Robert Daborne's *A Christian Turned Turke* (c.1610) offers a vivid illustration of the stage's representation of Christian-Muslim conversion as a consequence of sexual seduction. As a number of critics have by now brought to our attention, the play fictionalizes the exploits of John Ward, a real-life English pirate based in Tunis, who converted to Islam and lived the remainder of his life as an Ottoman subject. Two contemporary news pamphlets that describe the piratical activities of

John Ward (along with another notorious Christian renegade named
Simon Dansiker) suggest that the play's performance joined other
ventures aimed at capitalizing on Ward's popularity.[35] Crucial differences between the play and the pamphlets' representations of Ward,
however, reveal the stage's unique commitment to telling Ward's story
as a story of conversion. And more specifically, the play illustrates
the stage's unique tendency to link Christian-Muslim conversion to
interfaith sexual attraction and intercourse. Whereas other critics
have drawn attention to the play's fabrications of Ward's biography
to reveal Daborne's moral commitment to denouncing Ward's piracy
and holding him up as a cautionary lesson, I hope to reveal the more
particular ways in which the play establishes the implications of conversion as well as the hidden logics of sexuality, gender, and genre that
underpin it.[36]

It is perhaps worth underscoring the great pains to which this play
goes to link Ward's conversion exclusively to sexual desire and intercourse. Prior to his conversion, Ward explicitly and repeatedly rejects a
wide variety of pressures to persuade him to convert, including promises of material wealth, status, and protection, as well as arguments of
logic that flatter his intelligence, proclaim the righteousness of Islam,
or emphasize Islam's supposed freedoms and tolerance of carnal pleasures. Having repeatedly failed with such strategies to entice Ward, the
captain of the Janissaries whispers to his associate, "Work in my sister
presently" (7.80). Only when confronted with this beautiful Turkish
temptress does Ward's former resolve fall to pieces. At first sight of her,
he is deeply moved, and confesses, "I am no more mine own . . . Here
is an orator can turn me easily. / Where beauty pleads, there needs no
sophistry. / Thou hast o'ercome me" (7.159, 164–6). Thus, the play
insists that Ward's sole motivation for conversion is his uncontrol-
lable sexual desire for a Muslim woman – a desire that completely
"overcome[s]" him and transforms him from his former self. Burton
also draws attention to the overdetermined way in which this play
insists upon female seduction as the impetus for Ward's conversion. But
whereas Burton reads this as a collapsing of domestic anxieties about
"unruly English women and overruled English men" onto a foreign
context, I am interested in the collapsing of conversion itself onto an
act of sexual intercourse.[37]

In addition to establishing a causal relationship between sexual
intercourse and conversion, the play understands Islamic conversion to
be a permanent, one-way process: whereas the Christian can become
Muslim through the transgression of his sexual body, he cannot return
to the Christian fold. I argue that it is by virtue of the sexual act that

is seen to facilitate Ward's conversion that the play cannot imagine an alternative to a tragic ending. As Benwash, a former Jew turned Turk, says of Ward's seduction by Voada, "Nay, if the flesh take hold of him, he's past redemption. / He's half a Turk already; it's as good as done" (6.442–3). Notably, Benwash's phrasing emphasizes the agency of Ward's "flesh," rather than Voada's agency as a temptress: it is not Voada, but Ward's own "flesh" that "take[s] hold of him." Thus, in a sense, Ward's "flesh" functions as a metonym for the Muslim that threatens to convert him, implying that the alien Turk is always already a part of him, resident in the sinful sexual desires of his flesh. As Benwash suggests, in giving in to the "flesh" by having sex with a Muslim woman, Ward chooses a path that is irreversible, "past redemption," the inevitable precursor to a tragic ending. Accordingly, the play reveals the extraordinary stakes of interfaith sexual intercourse. By contrast, the news pamphlets, which do not mention a Muslim love interest, acknowledge that the real-life Ward continues to thrive and enjoy a pleasant life of luxury in Tunis even at the time of the play's performance. Whereas real life rewarded Ward for his conversion to Islam, Daborne's play construes his sexual and religious transgression to be the automatic precursor to a tragic downfall punctuated by hopeless repentance, suicide, and eternal damnation. Thus, this play shows us how the sexualized body serves as an anchor for mediating convertibility as well as redemption, and how conversion to Islam sets into motion a certain inevitable collusion between sexual contamination and tragedy.

Another significant way in which Daborne's play establishes the terms of Islamic conversion is through its negotiation of gender. In foregrounding a male protagonist, the play, like Rawlins's pamphlet, reflects the reality of most actual Christian renegades, who were male merchants and professional seafarers. But what would happen if the Christian protagonist seduced by a Muslim lover or threatened with conversion were female? Did the stage imagine the terms and stakes of female conversion to Islam in the same way? *A Christian Turned Turke* gestures toward the possibility of female conversion through its portrayal of a Christian virgin who is captured as booty by Ward's crew and must cross-dress in order to protect her sexual chastity from the predatory lust of Turks and Christian renegades alike. Unable to imagine the possibility of a female conversion that results from voluntary sexual congress with a Muslim, the play suggests a possible distinction between the stakes of male and female conversion. In addition, it ensures that the Christian heroine not only avoids being raped by a Turk, but also dies a martyr's death with her virginity intact.

This book identifies a similar pattern of female resistance in a number of other plays and reveals how female sexual constancy served as an important model for Christian resistance to Islam. It also links the greater anxiety surrounding sexual penetration and conversion of the female body to the patriarchal logics that make women more susceptible than men to racial reinscription. If the interpenetration of religion and race is a central concern of this book, then gender is the key variable that exposes this interpenetration. Specifically, the factor of gender – the difference between a Muslim man's pursuit of a Christian woman and a Muslim woman's pursuit of a Christian man – was crucial in mediating the sexual facilitation and effects of conversion, revealing the stage's literal interpretation of sexual intercourse, and by extension, its racialized implications.

In plotting out the worst-case scenario – the protagonist's seduction, conversion, suicide, and eternal damnation – Daborne's play provides an object lesson in what course to avoid. By contrast, a host of other plays depicted an alternative course for would-be converts in the form of miraculous Christian resistance or reversals, or as Burton has argued, confined conversion to the realm of comedic clowns and fools.[38] The terms by which these alternative outcomes were made possible reveal the embodied nature of conversion, its complex gendered and racialized logic, and the measures that were necessary to portray convincingly its aversion or reversal. In other words, the orchestration of a comic outcome (resistance, redemption) in place of a tragic one (conversion, damnation) also tells a story about what means are necessary to avoid or redeem an embodied transformation, pitting the intangible spirit up against the polluted body.

Christian Resistance

More popular and pleasing than Ward's tragic demise were narratives that transformed Islam's seductions and persecutions of the body into opportunities for Christian triumph. Rawlins's narrative, for example, exhibits a tragicomic arc, increasingly common both on the stage and in popular prose narratives of the early seventeenth century, wherein the threats and dangers of Turkish captivity are overcome through Christian fortitude and miraculous deliverance. Rawlins in fact refers to his narrative as a "Comick Tragedie" and emphasizes from the start its triumphant conclusion, in which he manages to overpower his captors by leading a successful mutiny of Christian slaves.[39] Notably, his organization of the mutiny is predicated upon his earlier ability to resist the physical pressure to convert – an achievement that stresses bodily over spiritual resistance – and both acts of resistance are carried out against nearly impossible odds. As Rawlins's narrative bears out, a sustained posture of constancy and resistance is essential to bring about any successful Christian outcome against Turkish persecution. He frames his triumph as a testimony not only to God's support, but also to his own human agency – his abilities to withstand the tortures and temptations to convert, and his initiative in organizing a mutiny even though he and the other captives are grossly outnumbered. Thus, the narrative functions as an example of how one can successfully resist the overpowering forces of Turkish persecution: if one practices a strategy of bodily and spiritual resilience, carried out with human initiative, ingenuity, and persistence, one's efforts will be rewarded by God.

In other narratives, Christian triumph against impossible odds is more explicitly predicated on a logic of miracle, which was often revealed through physical manifestations. A pamphlet optimistically entitled *Good Newes to Christendome* (1620) suggests that the best defense against the power of Islam might be a good offense, and boldly predicts the impending conversion of the Turkish sultan and all Muslims thereafter to Christianity.[40] This prophesy is based upon a miraculous vision that appeared over Muhammad's tomb, followed by the spontaneous extinguishing of 3,000 lamps around the tomb and the eruption of a rainstorm of blood over the city of Rome. A woodcut on the pamphlet's title page depicts the vision in all of its sensational aspects (see Figure 0.1). On the right, a floating woman in white extends an open book to a retreating army of Muslim "Turks, Persians, Arabians, and Moors," who appear to float away on clouds on the left side of the page; under the clouds, a "rayning of blood" falls upon the buildings of Rome.[41] The arresting possibility of a rainstorm of blood associates the miracle with a physical violence connected to the body, evoking Christ's incarnation and crucifixion.[42]

In demonstrating the extreme and improbable lengths that were necessary to imagine a Christian triumph over Islam, the narrative and its accompanying woodcut expose the virtual impossibility of such an outcome. But like Rawlins's narrative, the pamphlet illustrates English audiences' investment in imagining a happy conclusion to Christian-Muslim opposition and their attraction to the drama of surmounting impossible odds. Perhaps most striking about the 1620 pamphlet are its authorization and visual depiction of a Catholic miracle, illustrating how the threat of Islam compelled a Catholic response characterized by supernatural, material effects in order to convincingly portray Islam's defeat. English Protestants knew they were not meant to place credence

Figure 0.1: "Prophetic Visions," from Ludovico Cortano, *Good newes to Christendome* (London, 1620), title page woodcut. Reproduced by permission of the Folger Shakespeare Library.

in miraculous visions such as a rainstorm of blood, and often mocked the tales of talismanic relics, divinely preserved virginity, and spontaneous conversions associated with Jacobus de Voragine's *The Golden Legend*. And yet, the Christian conversion of the Turkish sultan, not to mention all of Islam, was so improbable that it could only be imagined through the Catholic rhetoric of miracle. According to its anonymous English translator, the narrative originated as a letter written by a Venetian merchant named Lodovico Cortano who traveled to Arabia to visit Mahomet's tomb. In his Prologue and Epilogue, the English translator explains that the manuscript was brought to England "by some of the last Venetian company" and expresses his initial discomfort with the content and his reluctance to undertake the translation.[43] He changes his mind, however, in the hope that readers will find it of some use even if they "cannot beleeue it as truth," by virtue of its exemplary illustration of how God punishes the "obstinate sinner" and sheds mercy on the "penitent soule."[44] In other words, English Protestant readers can appreciate the narrative not for its literal truth but for its figurative message.

But if the translator's paratextual frame suggests a Protestant way to read the miracle by distilling its figurative message, the narrative itself plays up the literal elements of the miracle. The repackaging of the Italian manuscript for an English audience by publisher Nathaniel Butter included his commission of the customized woodcut, which made its sole appearance in this 1620 pamphlet. What this suggests is that the miraculous elements of the narrative were both constitutive of the pamphlet's public appeal and warranted by its subject matter. While English Protestants might express some discomfort in identifying with a Catholic subject position, there were ways in which such a position became acceptable – even necessary – when articulating an oppositional position between Christianity and Islam. As I argue throughout this book, the threat or fantasy of conversion provided a catalytic site around which Protestant and Catholic interests were often renegotiated and consolidated. It was through the narrativization of conversion threats – and particularly because of the narrative compulsion to turn these threats into happy stories of Christian resistance and redemption – that Protestant figurative metaphors fused into a more Catholic language of miracles, rituals, material forms, and embodied practices.

Of course, it is important to recognize that news pamphlets, like the theater, were a commercial, profit-seeking enterprise; their content was oriented around popular interests and what was saleable. What we can conclude from *Good Newes* and Rawlins's narrative, both produced by the same publisher, who apparently identified a niche for Christian-Turk encounters in the market, is that part of what made stories of Christian conversion and resistance so sensational and entertaining was their visceral appeal.[45] Rawlins's harrowing description of bodily torture, as well as his plotting of a dangerous mutiny, drew readers' empathy and sense of suspense. The sadistic physical nature of the tortures and the threat of physical punishment that loomed over Rawlins as he planned his mutiny added to the immediate and suspenseful appeal of the narrative. In the case of *Good Newes*, the woodcut on the title page achieves a similar visceral effect; it is shocking, sensational, engrossing. To some extent, the Catholic aspects of the woodcut were secondary to these effects. It was not the Catholicity of the woodcut and miraculous vision, per se, that made the pamphlet entertaining and attuned to popular tastes, but rather the sensational, visual, and sensual nature of this material that constituted its appeal and happened to resonate with Catholic modes. Perhaps similarly, part of what made narratives of Turkish persecution like Rawlins's so entertaining were the same things that made Catholic saints' tales and virgin martyr legends popular in medieval England – their graphic descriptions of sadistic bodily torture and miraculous Christian resistance.[46]

But the entertainment value of this material did not mitigate the real threat that the Ottoman empire constituted for the English. Thus, in addition to entertaining audiences, the stage provided an important means by which the English negotiated their relationship to the overwhelming presence of the Ottoman empire. One important way that plays diffused tension was by turning threats of conversion into opportunities for Christian triumph. Plays such as Thomas Kyd's *Soliman and Perseda* (*c.*1589), John Fletcher, Nathan Field, and Philip Massinger's *The Knight of Malta* (*c.*1618), and Massinger's *The Renegado* (*c.*1624) established a common pattern: threats of Muslim seduction were resolved through Christian resistance and redemption. And, crucially, tales of triumph were dependent upon certain forms of embodied resistance. Like the news pamphlets, they idealized Christian constancy through physical resistance to torture. They also played up the sexual nature of conversion by deploying irresistible Muslim temptresses or raging male Turks who lusted after Christian virgins. To combat these threats, the plays modeled strategies of sexual resistance, including temperance for men and miraculously preserved virginity for women. They attempted to mount an offensive stance by extending the miracle of Christian conversion to Muslim women through marriage to Christian men. Finally, they considered the question of what happens when a Christian crosses the line and succumbs to the pressures or seductions of Islam. Could he or she ever be brought back into the Christian fold? Was redemption possible, and if so, for whom and on what conditions?

Narrative Models

To devise plots of Christian-Muslim encounter, English playwrights drew upon, recycled, and refigured narrative models from the past that were distinctly invested in an embodied Christian self. They appropriated older narratives of Christian persecution from saints' tales, martyrologies, and histories of the Roman empire. In doing so, they resuscitated Catholic models of martyrdom and miracles, and embodied ideals such as immunity to physical torture and inviolable virginity. In addition, playwrights turned to a rich tradition of medieval romance that adapted the long history of the Crusades into stories of seduction and conversion.[47] This material included a wide body of Spanish, Italian, and French prose sources, some of which had been translated into English. The stage's tendency to associate conversion with sexual intercourse extended and reappropriated a tradition of linking conversion with seduction in medieval romance.[48] This romance convention in turn resonated with the linking of sexual and religious infidelity in the Hebrew scriptures, whose injunctions against intermarriage warned against the dangers of "whoring after other gods."[49] But English playwrights did not merely reproduce older narrative traditions in the theatrical medium. Rather, they took great liberties in adapting older narrative models and making them current by reframing them with contemporary commercial contexts and settings, or integrating real-life figures like John Ward and the Shirley brothers. One might say that they not only adapted older models, but *converted* them into something new, infusing them with new functions that responded to an evolving cultural context. Ultimately, as my discussions of individual plays bear out, this process of conversion was extremely complex and sophisticated. It was by means of this complex process that older embodied models of Christian resistance became imbued with a new significance that understood Islam to be a racialized threat.

To a large degree, triumphant dramatizations of Christian resistance and redemption represented the work of cultural fantasy and creative imagination. But in order to imagine the ramifications of conversion, as well as the specific terms of resistance and redemption, the stage assimilated the Turkish threat to cultural memories and printed histories of former kinds of Christian persecution. Not coincidentally, plays featuring early Christian persecutions by Roman pagans and Vandals became popular around the same time that turning Turk emerged as a popular theme on the stage. For example, Thomas Dekker's *The Virgin Martyr* (1620) and Henry Shirley's *The Martyred Soldier* (1619), depicting the fourth-century Diocletian and fifth-century Vandal persecutions, respectively, shared stage time in the Red Bull Theatre with topical plays about Mediterranean travel and trade, such as Thomas Heywood's *Fortune By Land and Sea* (c.1609); John Day, George Wilkins, and William Rowley's *The Travails of the Three English Brothers* (c.1607); and John Webster's *The Devil's Law-case* (c.1619). Collectively, these plays participated in an active conversation with plays both inside and outside their own repertories, revealing shared tropes and resonances that included depictions of captivity, renegadism, forced conversion through torture, miraculous conversions to Christianity, and sexual persecution and resistance.

Early Christian martyr plays offered alternative ways of capitalizing on the theatrical appeal of religious persecution and conversion, as well as opportunities for working out anxieties about Turks or identifying exemplary Christian precedents by foregrounding other settings and time periods. These martyr plays afforded audiences the pleasure of experiencing the exotic distance of the past as well as the recognition of a contemporary resonance with the present. Moreover, they point up the ways in which plays about Islamic persecution drew upon models that were invested in the embodiment of identity, and how these models could be refunctioned to address the integration of a religious and racial threat of conversion.

A Culture of Religious Unrest

As I suggested earlier in this introduction, dramas of conversion not only drew upon narrative religious models from the past, but were shaped by a present culture of highly charged domestic religious unrest. Post-Reformation England was characterized by controversial Protestant reforms, lingering Catholic practices and sympathies, and compulsory as well as unauthorized conversions across the Christian confessional divide. The ecclesiological and doctrinal compromises that gave the post-Reformation English church its characteristic if unstable identity were the subject of ongoing negotiation, debate, and at times heated controversy throughout the later sixteenth and early seventeenth centuries.[50] In turn, the popular stage reflected, reproduced, and commented upon England's shifting ecclesiological and doctrinal positions. For example, in its depiction of Christian resistance and redemption for its protagonists, the stage drew upon contemporary theological understandings and debates about such topics as predestination, valid assurances of grace, and regeneration. Similarly, the terms of conversion were negotiated in relation to a culture of evolving Protestant reform and enduring Catholic traditions and residual habits.

Shifting doctrinal interpretations had structural as well as generic implications. Playwrights assimilated the structures of miracle, conversion, resistance, and redemption – all of which were framed within specific, though fluctuating doctrines – into the generic structures of tragedy, comedy, or tragicomedy. Sometimes, a play offered a clear citation of a specific religious doctrine or responded to a particular moment in religious politics. For example, *A Christian Turned Turke* expresses overt Calvinist sympathies. Its particular view of renegadism as indicative of one's predestined reprobation to hell speaks to heightened concerns about containing Barbary piracy,[51] as well as to contemporary efforts to buttress the tenets of English Calvinism against a resurgence of Catholic apologetics in the years following the Gunpowder Plot and during the beginnings of the Arminian controversy.[52] Such a doctrinal positioning accorded well with a tragic plotline. By contrast, Massinger's tragicomic *The Renegado* assumes a position on doctrinal points such as lay baptism, penance, and the significance of good works in ways that seem either distinctly Catholic or proto-Arminian.[53] Accordingly, it may reflect James's public self-fashioning as peacemaker and his relative openness toward ecumenical Christian politics, or even the relative tolerance for Catholics that characterized foreign policy in the later part of his reign, as he negotiated a Spanish match for his son and sought a mutually supportive alliance with Spain against Ottoman piracy.[54] As Michael Questier has persuasively argued, religion and politics were inextricably linked in early modern England, and popular religious sentiments were often tied to historical shifts in royal policy.[55]

In a country that itself had undergone conversion three times in a twenty-five-year period – first from Catholicism to Protestantism under Henry VIII (and Edward VI), then back to Catholicism with Queen Mary I's reign, and finally back to Protestantism during the reign of Queen Elizabeth – conversion was a heated subject. England's denominational instability provided an important context for the kinds of anxieties that conversion evoked on the stage. Compulsory conversions raised questions about effective methods of enforcement and how to determine whether a true conversion had taken place. If faith was spiritual and salvation predetermined, as Protestants tended to argue, what might constitute a reliable assurance of someone's faith? As Molly Murray and Holly Crawford Pickett have shown, the English government faced the problem of serial converts – individual subjects like William Alabaster, Anthony Tyrrell, and Marco Antonio De Dominis, who repeatedly converted back and forth between Catholicism and Protestantism, though each time they changed religious affiliation they swore it was a sincere and final recognition of the true path to salvation.[56] The ease and invisibility of conversion made sharp distinctions between confessional identities difficult, perhaps impossible, to sustain in practice, despite the fierce polarity of religious rhetoric.

Anxieties about conversion and its resistance to verification were exacerbated by Protestant attempts to distinguish true faith from Catholic idolatry. While modern critics have questioned the practical reality of an unmitigated binary opposition between Protestant spirituality and Catholic materiality, Protestant polemicists often sought to cast it in absolute terms.[57] Ecclesiastical reforms emphasized the intangibility of Christian faith by targeting the use of iconography, outward ceremonies associated with the sacraments, and sacred material objects, such as relics, crucifixes, rosary beads, and altars. The reforms also targeted certain embodied rituals and practices, ranging from physical forms of devotion to vowed virginity to transubstantiation. As I discuss in Chapter 1, Protestant reformers distinguished Protestant spirituality from Catholic materiality by drawing upon St. Paul's distinction between the Jewish practice of circumcision and the notion of a "circumcision of the heart," embracing an understanding of conversion that bound Christians in a spiritual rather than bodily fellowship. For English Protestants, St. Philip's baptism of an Ethiopian eunuch (Acts 8.36–8) – an event that directly precedes the baptism of St. Paul himself – served as a powerful symbol of the spiritual powers of baptism. The extreme physical alterity of the black eunuch is relevant only insofar as it underscores the extraordinary universalizing potential of Christian faith. As Protestant sermons on the passage emphasize, it is the faith behind the sacrament that renders the eunuch's physical difference inconsequential. For example, Samuel Hieron's three sermons on Acts 8, preached in 1613, forcefully distinguish the Protestant understanding of baptism from the outward sacrament itself: "It is the beleeuing and receiuing of the word that maketh the Sacrament to be effectuall."[58] The distinction between inward faith and outward ceremony continues to emerge throughout the sermon, as when Hieron insists, "Faith is the tenure by which we hold heauen, Baptisme is but the seale to confirme it."[59] In some sense, the outward ceremony that marks conversion assumes a secondary importance analogous to the specificity of the Ethiopian eunuch himself.

This study aims to address what happens when the visible difference of the Ethiopian eunuch is brought back into the equation, when, through his physical embodiment on the stage, he ceases to be a metaphor and inhabits a form that we are forced to look at. It addresses what happened when, as the result of cross-cultural trade and exploration, figures with similar kinds of eastern and North African alterity entered the English imagination and began to assume particular geographical, religious, and cultural significance. It was at this critical juncture that the post-Reformation turn to spirituality intersected with competing cultural imperatives to attach specific meaning to non-Christian identities. The English drama explored the implications of such a powerful notion of Christian spiritual faith for figures outside the Christian fold by testing the feasibility of Christianized Muslims. In *Othello*, Iago casually references the fact of Othello's baptism as a way of illustrating Desdemona's hold on him: Desdemona could "win the Moor," he suggests, even "were't to ask him to renounce his baptism" (2.3.338).[60] The implication is that Desdemona's power over Othello is so strong that she could convince him *even* to renounce his own baptism; of course, both Desdemona's persuasions and Othello's Christian identity turn out to be fallible in the end. In so matter-of-factly presuming the security of Othello's Christian faith, Iago draws attention to the actual leap of faith that such a presumption requires. The play seems to ask whether indeed there might be limitations on who is eligible for the saving powers of Christian faith. Did the mark of someone's outward appearance have something to do with their inner spiritual capacity after all?

The Stage and Tangible Forms

The early modern stage responded to the problem of faith's invisibility by embracing more tangible religious models in order to forge effective forms of resistance to Islam. Thus, it played up the visual and performative elements of miracles, ceremonies of conversion, the use of talismanic objects, and embodied forms of resistance to counter Islam's sexual seductions and bodily threats of conversion. In addition, playwrights reverted to Roman Catholic models of chastity, martyrdom, and sacramental ritual in order to physically anchor Christian bodies against conversion. These tendencies may be explained in multiple ways. The stage's reliance on material and embodied religious expressions was partly a function of theatrical entertainment, including the material aspects of the stage and its visual reliance on the spectacle of bodily movements and objects. It was also partly a function of the rich body of Catholic source material and older models that the stage drew upon in order to imagine efficacious forms of resistance to religious persecution. The stage reflected and exploited contradictions in Protestant practice including a continued reliance on the physical accoutrements of faith. Positive depictions of Catholic forms may also be explained through specific political shifts and alliances, particularly those associated with King James's religious politics, his softening attitude toward Spain and other Catholic countries, and hardening opposition to the Ottoman empire, which rendered certain Catholic content more acceptable.

But the early modern stage helps us to understand on an immediate, conceptual level as well the ways that English Protestant identity fused into a more ecumenical Christian identity. Something about the very intangibility of Protestant faith prompted an embrace of more Catholic forms when Islam was thrown into the mix. For one, immaterial expressions of faith created a conceptual problem in mounting a convincing defense to Islam. In addition, the ease of conversion and its imperviousness to verification fueled a desire to mark it in observable ways and to stabilize confessional identity. The stage addressed these anxieties by anchoring Christian resistance through embodied practices and the use of material objects; through rendering conversion visible by playing up the importance of outward ceremonies; and through establishing the difficulty of reversing conversion by associating it with permanent marks like circumcision or irreversible bodily conditions like the loss of virginity.

Thus the English stage brought to the surface Protestant reformers' continuing ambivalence about the role of embodiment and the material aspects of Christian faith. In particular, it revealed how Islam exacerbated uncertainties about the intangible nature of conversion and brought these uncertainties to a head. The drama's emphasis on the body, rather than the spirit, as a means of avoiding Islamic conversion and contamination not only illustrates the continuing sway of Catholic models of faith, but affords unique insights into the process by which racial distinctions emerged between Christians and Muslims in the early modern period. Ultimately, I offer a new way of understanding the emergence of race by identifying the ways that Catholic-Protestant tensions between spirit and body took on a racial inflection in the face of Islam. The stage's reliance on outward and bodily forms to resist, mark, and reverse the effects of turning Turk was specifically necessitated by the sexual and bodily threats that were associated with Islam. In effect, the threat of turning Turk frequently compelled a complex fusing together of Catholic and Protestant models, resulting in a notion of Christian faith that was both spiritually and materially determined.

***

Each of the following chapters focuses tightly on localized readings to understand how the stage depicts interfaith sexual contact and conversion through gendered models of seduction, resistance, and redemption. I attend closely to issues of narrative and generic convention, including playwrights' appropriation of earlier narratives and genres, as well as the significance of dramatic generic categories and their structural implications. Also, in taking account of the repertory system, rather than privileging individual playwrights, I include discussions of less canonical plays that were nonetheless popular and influential in their time. This approach illuminates ways in which early modern plays cited one another, shared common tropes, and participated in mutual conversations that are now obscured by the literary canon's organization around individual authors and its marginalization of many non-Shakespearean plays. For example, my second chapter uncovers a small group of martyr plays performed at the Red Bull Theatre that resonate in important ways with "turning Turk" plays performed around the same time. Similarly, my fourth chapter examines the appearance of characters who are Knights of Malta in a range of plays performed between the late 1580s and the 1620s, revealing a connection between Christopher Marlowe's canonical *Jew of Malta* and four other plays that have largely escaped critical attention. Recognizing the value of identifying these commonalities while also attending to their individual historical specificity, I take an approach that is both local and general.

In addition, my readings emphasize how the material and visual orientations of the stage lend themselves to representations of threatened conversion and its aversion in ways that play up its embodied nature. In particular, I observe the sometimes surprising ways in which the stage drew explicitly upon a Catholic history of material objects (relics, crosses, etc.), rituals and ceremonies (the magic of the sacraments), and embodied practices (vowed virginity) in order to dramatize Christian resistance to Islam. Finally, I address the complicated question of what this investment in outward forms meant in a post-Reformation culture, revealing not just a holdover of Catholic practices, but the ways in which Islam reshaped Protestant culture and resignified certain Catholic practices as "Christian."

My first chapter focuses on how Shakespeare's *Comedy of Errors* (*c.*1594) and *Othello* (*c.*1604) provide a prehistory for the tensions between spiritual faith and bodily distinction that I argue are brought to the forefront in later plays by the explicit threat of Islamic conversion. These two plays seem to present an odd pairing: *Othello* is a tragedy of difference, while *Errors* is a comedy of sameness. However, I argue that the assimilation of a baptized Moor in *Othello* and the reunion of two sets of identical twins in *The Comedy of Errors* have more in common than one might assume. Both plays are set in eastern Mediterranean territories (Ephesus and Cyprus) that were central to St. Paul's travels and later became important commercial centers and sites of imperial contest between Christians and Muslims. Drawing upon this layered history, the plays explore the Pauline ideal of a universal fellowship of faith, but simultaneously fall back on the tangible materiality of physical differences to stabilize identity against conversion.

Chapter 2 turns to plays performed in the early decades of the 1600s, after England had established a significant trading presence in the eastern Mediterranean and turning Turk had become a familiar theme on the stage. I identify a resonance between early Christian martyrdom and strategies for resisting Islam in Thomas Dekker's *The Virgin*

Martyr (1620). Two contemporary plays also performed at the Red Bull Theatre – Henry Shirley's *The Martyred Soldier* (1619) and the anonymous *Two Noble Ladies* (1622) – reinforce these temporal resonances. Given the geographical correspondence between these plays' ancient settings and the contemporary Ottoman empire, I demonstrate how the early modern stage invoked histories of former pagan persecution in order to depict the threat of Muslim persecution. Moreover, these plays' idealization of embodied chastity as a strategy of resistance to conversion addresses the particular vulnerability of the female Christian body to sexual contamination by the Turk. In modeling Christian resistance through miraculously preserved female virginity, the plays make visible the Catholic models that informed English imaginative responses to Islam, as well as the ways in which Islam's religious and imperial threats were transfigured on the stage into sexual and bodily threats.

Chapter 3 further interrogates the gendered implications of Islamic conversion by considering the stakes of sexual seduction, repentance, and redemption in Philip Massinger's *The Renegado* (c.1624). Reading this play against Daborne's *A Christian Turned Turke* (c.1610), I identify a tension in *The Renegado* between spiritual redemption and embodied resistance that divides along the lines of gender. Whereas the Christian protagonist's sexual transgression with a Muslim woman is redeemable through spiritual repentance, the Christian heroine's chastity is protected with the aid of a magical relic, revealing her greater vulnerability to racial reinscription. In other words, the reversibility of the male's transgression suggests its receptiveness to a spiritual remedy, whereas the permanent, embodied consequences of female sexual contamination compel the use of a Catholic prophylactic. While Catholic objects and rituals may no longer be authorized in Protestant England, they reattain authority in the play's North African setting. I argue that *The Renegado*'s selective supplementation of Christian faith with Catholic materials and rituals speaks not only to the political benefits of merging Catholic and Protestant interests against the Muslim enemy but, more specifically, to the ways in which the embodied and sexualized threat of Islamic conversion necessitated material forms of resistance.

My fourth chapter focuses on the revival of the Knights of Malta in five plays performed between 1589 and 1621 that allude to territorial battles between Christians and Muslims on the islands of Rhodes, Malta, and Sicily. Despite the dissolution of the English *langue*, or national branch, of the Knights of Malta after the Reformation and the tarnished reputation of the Knights due to their corsair activities, the stage resurrects these figures as crusading Christian heroes. I argue that a range of English plays model the redemption of Christian renegades by re-embracing the Knights' Catholic vow of chastity. On the one hand, the vow of chastity helped to cement a commitment to pan-Christian brotherhood, which symbolized the strategic alliances between Christian subjects and nations (Catholic and Protestant) against the common Muslim enemy. But more importantly, this vow came to signify masculine self-control and gentility in a world of new cross-cultural challenges. The figure of the chaste Knight of Malta cultivated a model of English masculinity that could both resist and carry out imperialism in honorable ways. The shared tropes that repeatedly emerge in these plays also have startling generic implications, reversing the expected outcome of comedy by substituting homosocial brotherhood for heterosexual marriage.

In the concluding Epilogue, I turn directly to a discussion of genre as another way of assessing the gendered and racial stakes of Christian-Muslim conversion. Foregrounding a crucial deviation between Ludovico Ariosto's epic romance *Orlando Furioso* (1516) and Robert Greene's stage adaptation (*c.*1591), I examine what happens when a romance plot is forced into a tragicomic structure. In Ariosto's epic romance, the Indian heroine Angelica forsakes the Christian Orlando and marries the Muslim Medor, whereas in Greene's stage adaptation, the heroine is ultimately reunited with the Christian hero. The tragicomic structure of the play seems to facilitate a trajectory of sexual and religious transgression followed by redemption. However, closer inspection reveals that the play's comic resolution is achieved not through the heroine's redemption but through the revelation that her sexual union with Medor never took place. This elision in turn reveals the early modern stage's inability to imagine Christian redemption for a female character following Islamic sexual contamination. In ultimately resisting the fungibility of religious conversion, the plays I explore reveal a slippage between spirituality and embodiment, or religious and racial identity, which is crucially mediated through their generic structures.

To return to the question of whether there was a fate worse than death for a Christian captured by Turks, we need to realize that a number of unarticulated questions proceed this one. How did the stage reveal a complex logic of conversion? What role did gender, sexuality, and genre play in this imagined logic? What were the ties between sexuality, conversion, and race? How did the embodied and racial threat of Muslims impact Christian fears of conversion? And how were these fears exacerbated by understandings of Christian faith that emphasized its spiritual nature?

Examining these questions may help us to perceive unexpected links as well as important differences between our own world and the early modern past. In today's world, anxieties about the invisibility of religious faith are particularly pronounced in relation to Islamic "fundamentalists" and the possibility that even white Americans such as John Walker Lindh (the young Californian captured in 2001 and renamed Abdul Hamid, or "the American Taliban") could undergo such an extreme conversion while not manifesting any outward changes that a superficial makeover could not reverse.[61] In this sense, the fact that the perpetrators of the 9/11 terrorist attacks were all dark-skinned Arab men was a comfort to some Americans, providing a sense of security that inner faith might correspond to a detectable outward difference. This discernible correlation helped foster a stereotype in which Arab racial features became equated with Islam, which in turn became equated with Islamic "fundamentalism" – thus discounting Muslims who are "non-fundamentalists" and Arabs who are Christian. Ironically, it is the invisibility of religious faith and identification that often leads to racialization of religious identity and its obfuscations.

Certainly, there is no direct equation between understandings of race today and centuries earlier, and my point is not to dilute the specificity of the historical conditions that inform the meaning of race in any given historical moment. Rather, my interrogation of a racial logic that emerged from the particular confluence of England's commercial encounter with the Ottoman empire, the religious instability of the Reformation, and early modern theater reveals a set of distant conditions that enables us to see how the invisibility of religious faith might fuel a desire for outward distinctions. Both in early modern England and today, the problem with conversion stems not from the invisible differences that it obscures, but rather from the frightening fungibility of human identity that it too readily reveals.

Chapter 1

Dangerous Fellowship: Universal Faith and its Bodily Limits in *The Comedy of Errors* and *Othello*

There is neither Iewe nor Greeke, there is neither bond nor free, there is neither male nor female: for ye are all one in Christ Iesus.

Galatians 3.28[1]

St. Paul's famous statement of universal fellowship radically proposes that Christian faith renders indifferent the distinctions of ethnicity, caste, and gender. His contention that Israel's covenantal bonds were illegitimately dividing the early Christian church suggested that all people were eligible for conversion regardless of their earthly stations. Relegating the rite of circumcision to local custom, St. Paul replaced the Jewish covenant with a broader universalism whose basis for inclusion was faith – an intrinsically internal state. As Julia Reinhard Lupton explains, "Once spiritualized, [God's covenant] can also be infinitely extended: No longer the singular badge of Jewish men, this new circumcision of the heart joins both sexes, all peoples, and all classes into common fellowship with Christ."[2] This spiritual ideal was a particular source of tension in early modern England during a time when the reverberations of the Reformation were still strongly felt and expanding Mediterranean trade was shifting England's worldview. On the one hand, St. Paul's assertion that outward rituals like circumcision held no value, that "the only thing that counts is faith which worketh by loue" (Galatians 5.6), constituted an important touchstone by which Protestants distinguished themselves from Catholics. It was an ideal frequently alluded to in English sermons by preachers such as John Donne, William Attersoll, and William Perkins, who embraced the notion of a "circumcision of the heart" as the true mark of Christianity.[3] On the other hand, however, spiritualized notions of Christian faith and their promise of effortless conversion created substantial unease in the decades surrounding the start of the seventeenth century: not only was England's own religious identity still in flux – its spirituality still very much rooted in material and embodied expressions of faith – but unprecedented commercial contact between English Protestants and people of other religious, national, and ethnic origins called into question the desirability of a Christian faith that was so undiscriminating and resistant to verification.

In this chapter I explore early modern tensions associated with Pauline universalism and cross-cultural contact by juxtaposing two Shakespearean plays that dramatize the implications of a Christian faith powerful enough to annul bodily distinctions. *The Comedy of Errors* tests the practical ramifications of a universal spiritual fellowship through its attempts to reunite two sets of brothers who are physically indecipherable. What happens, the play asks, if bodily differentiation is relinquished altogether under the presumption that universal fellowship nullifies such marks of difference? Can such a notion of Christian identity and fellowship exist in a setting where social hierarchies are informed not only by local cultural norms but by cross-cultural influences and multiple temporalities? By contrast, *Othello* explores the prospect of a subject who is converted to Christianity by baptism and yet singularly marked by his irreducible physical difference. Does spiritual faith have the power to embrace all bodies within a Christian fellowship, and how can its conversion of a black body be assured?

My focus on these two plays, associated with approximate performance dates of 1594 and 1604 respectively, specifies a historical period around the turn of the century when in the words of religious historian R. T. Kendall, "Protestant ecclesiological controversy . . . was at its height."[4] Even putting aside the influences of international politics and interfaith conflict, the difficulty of defining English Protestantism constituted a profound problem within England's own ecclesiological circles. Leading into the turn of the century, English clergymen avidly debated the central Calvinist doctrine of divine predestination, which held that all humans were divided between election to heaven and reprobation to hell, and that both fates were completely reliant on the will of God, impervious to good works or other deeds performed on earth.[5] Such controversy reveals that Calvinism's division of souls was a source of contention decades before the more organized Arminian opposition of the mid-to-late 1620s. Spurred by debates at Cambridge University in the 1590s, the Hampton Court Conference of 1604 and subsequent disputes pertaining to the Lambeth Articles reflect on some level a compulsion to control the universal pretenses of faith by scrupulously nailing down the terms of Calvinist predestination to differentiate the elect from the reprobate. Disagreements centered on a wide range of issues, including the relationship between baptism and election (and who could administer baptism), the doctrine of perseverance (whether election and reprobation were absolute), the problem of temporary faith (and how it meant that a reprobate soul could be mistaken for a saved one), and the proper method of assurance (or how one could be assured of one's status as saved or damned).[6] Nicholas Tyacke has influentially identified the Hampton Court Conference as a watershed event in that it brought anti-Calvinist and predestination disputes into a national arena, whereas prior to 1604, these disputes had not fully escaped the confines of universities.[7]

In both direct and indirect ways, Shakespeare's plays engage these topical religious debates: *The Comedy of Errors* through its symbolic thematization of baptism and *Othello* through its negotiation of a converted soul's damnation. For my purposes, however, the value of these two plays lies not in their allegorical rendering of contemporary religious debates, but rather in their imaginative exploration of more general tensions surrounding the terms for inclusion within the Christian faith. Shakespeare explores these tensions by testing the limits of Pauline universalism. Of course, Paul's theology lay at the root of many Protestant controversies, and it also offered a powerful rhetorical framework for articulating these controversies. As John S. Coolidge observed in his 1970 volume *The Pauline Renaissance: Puritanism and the Bible*, the ecclesiastical controversies between Elizabethan Puritans and their conformist opponents were importantly centered on exegetical interpretations of Paul.[8] In many ways, English Puritans understood their challenge of reconciling the fundamentally mixed body of the church – comprised of clergy and laypeople, Puritans and Conformists, elected souls and recipients of a merely common grace – as mirroring Paul's challenge of attempting to unify Jews and Gentiles in the early church. The plays I examine extend Paul's challenge beyond the confines of the English church, asking how it might be possible to reconcile Christian universalism with an emerging global economy.

In addition to engaging the unstable climate of domestic religious politics, both plays engage contemporary global economics through their Mediterranean settings in Ephesus, Venice, and Cyprus – places of particular interest to the English because of their commercial aspirations and concerns about Islamic conversion and imperialism. As I outline in the Introduction, during the time that Shakespeare's plays were being performed in London, English commerce in the eastern Mediterranean was in the midst of rapid and unprecedented growth.[9] The business of trade brought the English increasingly into eastern territories, and into contact with a diverse range of religious, national, and ethnic others. Despite the biblical significance of Ephesus and Cyprus as places of central importance to the founding of the Christian church, these territories were both under the dominion of the Ottoman empire when *The Comedy of Errors* and *Othello* were first written and performed. As a result, religious conversion assumed a new significance in these geographical locations as a force that threatened to turn Christians into Muslims. English privateers' constant vulnerability to piracy, enslavement, and forced conversion in the dangerous territories of the eastern Mediterranean compelled a hardening of the limits of Christian faith, so as to demarcate more certain and permanent distinctions between English Protestantism and the far greater force of Islam.[10] In addition to the physical vulnerability of English privateers in the largely unpoliced waters and territories of the eastern Mediterranean, and the general threat posed by the commercial, territorial, and military dominance of the Ottoman empire, Islam's direct theological challenge to Christianity contributed to English concerns about conversion and related attempts to shore up religious boundaries.[11]

The English popular stage participated in the process of negotiating the physical and spiritual boundaries of faith by representing religious identity in relation to questions of embodiment. The very conjunction between religious conversion and sexual turning that is repeatedly put forward on the stage reflects a compulsion to link religious identity directly to bodily contamination and reproduction. Conversely, the stage depicted resistance to conversion by idealizing physical chastity, a bodily state that, while itself virtually unverifiable, appeared to offer a more tangible assurance of a subject's spiritual intactness and purity. As I go on to illustrate in this chapter, *The Comedy of Errors* and *Othello* respond to anxieties about conversion generated by Christian-Muslim commerce and imperialism by bolstering bodily distinctions against Pauline universalism to help regulate conversion. This theatrical impulse demonstrates how the universal pretenses of Pauline faith and its inherent reliance on conversion colluded with the coalescing of racial distinctions in the early modern imagination.

St. Paul's Legacy and Renaissance England

If Coolidge demonstrated the centrality of Pauline theology to the religious controversies of Renaissance England, more recent critics have mounted their own "Pauline Renaissance" by reassessing the significance of Paul's messianic convictions and their communal implications in the early modern period. In particular, such critics as Julia Reinhard Lupton and Gregory Kneidel approach Paul's legacy in the

Renaissance not in terms of interiority but in terms of communal identity.[12] Accordingly, they view Paul's challenge not as a contest of spirit against flesh, but as one of community against individuals. Lupton characterizes the Pauline struggle in terms of "citizenship," an initiation into a civic community that involves a "passage from the particular to the universal."[13] Both for Paul and for early modern England, this passage is not simply triumphal, but constitutes a kind of death experienced through the renunciation of one's claims to distinction. Kneidel takes up the problem of Christian universalism somewhat similarly, understanding its manifestation in the English Renaissance as an ongoing struggle "to conceptualize an enduring, collective, public ethic of all believers."[14] His identification of a "struggling universality" questions the "rejection-replacement" paradigm of biblical typology, proposing instead a "repetition-remainder" paradigm that emphasizes continuities.[15] For both Kneidel and Lupton, the Pauline struggle for universality was as vexed and finally unresolved in Renaissance England as it was in Paul's own time: Protestantism's break from the past was not triumphal or complete, and neither was Christianity's break from Judaism.

These critics' commitment to the messianic dimensions of Paul's thought puts them in dialogue with philosophers such as Giorgio Agamben and Alain Badiou who appropriate Paul's legacy for its modern applications, particularly to mount political critiques of global capitalism and liberal individualism.[16] Badiou emphasizes Paul's radical rupture with Judaism, but recasts it as a "militant, rather than an ontological thesis," serving as a model for modern political revolution.[17] For him, Christ's resurrection represents the opening of an epoch that is "neither Judeo-Christian nor Greco-Christian, nor even a synthesis of the two," but rather delineates a "third figure."[18] In that the figure of the resurrected son "filiates all humanity," it provides the basis for a universalism that "suspends difference."[19] By contrast, Agamben theorizes messianic time as the period in "between" the end of Jewish time (the resurrection) and the beginning of Christian time (the second coming).[20] For Agamben, this time in "between" is characterized as neither Jewish nor Christian, neither Hebrew nor Greek, because it designates a period of waiting or deferral. Messianic time, according to Agamben, does not denote a period of transition or a state of becoming, since no clear direction is revealed until the second coming. Similarly, we may live "as if" Jewish law remains, but Jesus's resurrection makes this not so.[21] Agamben sets out to re-examine Paul's questions concerning the structure of messianic time with the understanding that "these questions . . . must also be ours."[22]

In his own way, Shakespeare, too, interprets the messianic meaning of Pauline universalism for his own time and place. He responds to the way England's struggling universalism was informed by the particular cross-currents of domestic religious politics and global economics. More specifically, Shakespeare demonstrates how, if Paul's dream of universality is ultimately unfulfilled in the English Renaissance, its limits are revealed by the influx of religious others who must be barred from conversion because their convertibility threatens chaos. Drawing upon Protestantism's emphasis on spiritual faith in contradistinction to Catholic forms of materiality, Shakespeare's plays characterize England's struggling universalism partly as a contest between spiritualized faith and embodied difference. Kneidel usefully insists that Paul's own interest in spiritual interiority has been critically overdetermined – reflecting "the dualistic vocabulary derived from an Augustinian spirituality that was shared by most medieval and Reformation theologians."[23] This distinction is important: for Paul, the implications of spiritual faith were centered not in notions of interiority but in community. At the same time, English reformists were drawn to Paul in part because his rejection of circumcision and Jewish law resonated with their rejection of Catholic rituals and their struggle to empower a Christianity that was driven not by material expression but by faith itself. (Whether or not Protestant reformers succeeded in their attempts to disentangle faith from material forms and to what degree such a distinction is even possible is another question.) The spiritualized nature of faith was what made it such a difficult proposition, both for a figure such as Othello who is asked to place faith in something that eludes tangible proof and for an audience that is asked to believe that a Moor's spiritual conversion is possible. In focusing on how English Protestants turned to Paul to distinguish the spiritualized dimensions of faith from the Catholic forms and practices that they rejected, I emphasize spirituality not to talk about inwardness or subjectivity but to consider how faith might serve as the basis for universality.

Renaissance theologians were particularly drawn to Paul's notion of baptism, the means by which universalism could be carried out through a spiritualized conversion. In his letter to the Colossians, Paul describes baptism as "a circumcision made without hands" (2.11), indicating an act of faith that supersedes the bodily mark of inherited privilege. His vision of a universal Christian church relied on baptism's ability to extend Christian conversion to the Gentiles of the Roman empire, replacing the old law of genealogical inheritance with faith in Jesus Christ. In the Acts of the Apostles, baptism's capacity to override the outward differences between Gentiles and Jews is exemplified through

Philip's baptism of an Ethiopian eunuch – a figure distinguished by extreme physical alterity. When the eunuch requests to be baptized, Philip responds simply, "If thou beleuest with all thine heart, thou maist" (8.37). For English Protestants the baptism of the Ethiopian eunuch became a particularly loaded symbol. Because the Ethiopian's alterity was taking on new, experiential meaning as the result of travel and commerce, his Christian conversion tested the limits of Pauline universalism in a new way, illustrating the unfathomable miracle of faith's converting properties. As Kim Hall has noted, in the wake of England's Reformation, "The whitewashed Ethiopian [became] a ubiquitous image in Renaissance literature, appearing often in emblem books and proverbs as a figure of the impossible."[24]

Although strict English Calvinists shied away from the sacramental emphasis of baptism, they were drawn to St. Paul's interpretation of baptism as a spiritual replacement for outward marks like circumcision. Late sixteenth-century English sermons abound with references to baptism's capacity to convert even the most resilient souls. In a sermon entitled "The Sinners Conuersion" (1599), Henry Smith recounts from Luke 29 the story of Jesus's miraculous conversion of Zaccheus, a principal Gentile publican, to become "the childe of Abraham":

> Zaccheus was a Gentile, a meruaile to see a Gentile become a Iewe: that is, to beleeue in Christ. He was a principall Publican. A strange thing to see a chiefe Customer to giue ouer his office: and hee was rich also: a rare matter to see a rich man to enter into the kingdom of God: and therefore beholde a miracle, as if at this daie, the Turke, the Pope, and the King of Spaine, were at once perswaded to forsake their idolatry and superstition.[25]

In effect, the conversion of Gentile into (Christianized) Jew is here being compared to the seeming impossibility of converting Muslims and Catholics. In another sense, the passage replaces the extreme alterity of the Ethiopian eunuch with his late sixteenth-century equivalents: "the Turke, the Pope, and the King of Spaine." While the uncircumcised Gentile, the Ethiopian eunuch, and the Catholic or Muslim all constitute historically contingent embodiments of difference, they occupy positions analogous to one another in designating the absolute outer limits of Pauline universalism. The attempts of English Protestants like Smith to apply the tenets of Pauline baptism to their own increasingly global world brought home both the miracle of Christian faith and its potential limits.

Significantly, Smith demonstrates the miraculous power of baptism not just by positing its conversion of Muslims and Catholics, but by suggesting its capacity to correct a misguided faith in "idolatry and superstition." Thus, his formulation incorporates terms specific to

Protestant reform, drawing an implicit connection between idolatry (or an inability to distinguish material idols from true faith) and the physical alterity of the black Ethiopian eunuch. Despite Islam's actual repudiation of idolatry, Smith conflates Muslims and Catholics as idolaters. I want to suggest that his association of these religious others with the practice of idolatry plays up the impossibility of their conversion precisely by singling out their inability to apprehend a faith they cannot see – a logic that, as we will see, also inheres in *Othello*. Moreover, Smith's formulation implies through analogy an association between the Ethiopian eunuch's physical alterity and an incapacity to embrace the spiritual essence of Christian baptism.

In *Othello*, the irony of the protagonist's ultimate failure of faith – his desperate reliance on obtaining ocular proof – is conveyed through the fact that he is himself marked out by a physical difference that visually distinguishes him from other Christians. I want to suggest that this collusion between a reliance on outward proof in lieu of faith and outward bodily difference is not accidental, that together these conditions capture the very impossibility of Pauline conversion that makes Christian baptism a miracle. Smith's sermon helps us to see how the possibility of Othello's baptism into the Christian faith suggested a radical act of conversion that both epitomized the ideal of Pauline fellowship and performed an inversion of deep-rooted cultural associations. As Thomas Rymer sarcastically observed in the late seventeenth century, such a radical formulation exceeded the bounds of probability: "With us a Black-amoor might rise to be a Trumpeter: but Shakespeare would not have him less than a Lieutenant-General. With us a Moor might marry some little drab, or Small-coal Wench: Shakespeare would provide him the Daughter and Heir of some great Lord, or Privy-Councellor."[26] Somewhat similarly, these improbabilities prompted Samuel Coleridge to conclude in the early nineteenth century that Othello must not have been "a negro" after all.[27] A bearer of both incontrovertible blackness and a "perfect soul" (1.2.31), Othello is the exception that proves the rule of universal Christian faith.[28] His Christian conversion illustrates the extreme limits of Pauline fellowship, making him the essential Pauline subject – a physically differentiated body converted through spiritual baptism, joined by marriage to a Christian noblewoman, and even appointed to spearhead the Christian struggle against Islam. If the Ethiopian eunuch constituted the essential figure of Pauline conversion, Othello was his early seventeenth-century equivalent.[29]

By contrast, the physically indecipherable Antipholuses and Dromios of *The Comedy of Errors* project in both comic and frightening ways the practical implications of a universal Christianity that might efface all bodily difference through faith. While the identical bodies and names of the twins emphasize the injustice of their separation by demonstrating their inherent fellowship, the play also resists a principle of human fungibility by constantly depicting the botched or disproportionate exchanges that are caused by the doublings of identity. As much as the play struggles toward a Pauline reconciliation, it also struggles to disentangle the individual identities of bodies that lack outward distinction. That the two struggles – for reconciliation and differentiation – merge together and yet are inherently at odds constitutes a central paradox of the play. Revealing a pattern of chiasmus, this paradox exemplifies a form that according to Patricia Parker pervades the entire play, beginning with Egeon's emblematic description in the opening scene of the splitting of his family.[30] The only way to sort things out is to get all of the bodies together at once, and yet even when this is accomplished, it is still impossible to tell the twins apart. *The Comedy of Errors* ultimately reveals the need for a type of spiritual fellowship that forestalls bodily exchange by simultaneously allowing for some level of outward differentiation to persist. An excess of identical and indecipherable bodies demonstrates the dangers of a disembodied faith by revealing the erroneous exchanges and confusions that ensue in the absence of physical differentiation.

If Coolidge, Lupton, and Kneidel demonstrate how Renaissance writers adapted Paul's universalism to work out the relationships between election and common grace, clergy and laity, Catholic works and Protestant faith, Shakespeare adapts the logic of Paul's universalism to consider the question of how travel, trade, and emerging cosmopolitanism were brought to bear on the ideal of Christian universalism. Kneidel emphasizes a universalism that for both Paul and Renaissance writers attempted to bridge time and communities. By contrast, I want to demonstrate how in the early modern imagination Christian universalism was not all inclusive, how its very promise of universal faith depended on certain degrees of exclusion, and how Shakespeare reveals its limits in particularly canny ways.

Pauline Faith and Mercantile Exchange in *The Comedy of Errors*

Set in the Mediterranean port city of Ephesus, *The Comedy of Errors* is a play permeated with logics of conversion associated with both Pauline universalism and mercantile trade. In analogizing the conversions associated with universal faith and global commerce, the play exposes the dangers that emerge when human bodies are subsumed into these systems of exchange. Ephesus provides a particularly apt setting for overlaying these temporally and culturally distinct systems of exchange. In adapting Plautus's *Menaechmi*, which is set not in Ephesus but in Epidamnum, Shakespeare presents an Ephesus that signifies in multiple and inconsistent ways: it is both pre-Christian and post-Christian, classical and contemporary, familiar and foreign.[31] Perhaps most overtly, its biblical connection to St. Paul, who spent two years in Ephesus converting the Gentiles to Christianity, distinguishes it as a site of religious conversion. Crucial to St. Paul's, and later St. John's, project of enlarging the early Christian church through conversion, Ephesus became an important center for early Christianity and is one of the seven cities addressed in the Book of Revelation (2.1–7). Wayne Meeks surmises that St. Paul's letter to the Ephesians, written during his later imprisonment in Rome, "was intended to be read to new converts in a group of churches in the southwestern part of the province of Asia (modern Turkey), as a written substitute for a personal address by the apostle to the newly baptized."[32] While in Ephesus, St. Paul performed numerous baptisms and miracles in the name of Jesus Christ, though he also encountered considerable opposition from Greek idolaters and Jewish sorcerers (detailed in Acts 19). Such Pauline details re-emerge in *The Comedy of Errors* when, for example, the confusions created by the two sets of twins prompt Antipholus and Dromio of Syracuse to presume that Ephesus is overrun with witches and sorcerers. As Patricia Parker has observed, the play is virtually riddled with Pauline references, both in its language and in its story of two sets of brothers and a husband and wife who are violently separated and then reunited years later in a restorative fellowship.[33]

But, as critics including Linda McJannet and Jonathan Gil Harris have pointed out, the Ephesus of Shakespeare's time was also understood to be a Mediterranean port of the Ottoman empire, a place that Christian merchants valued for its rich trade but also entered with serious concerns about the safety of their bodies and souls.[34] *The Comedy of Errors* is explicitly framed within a global mercantile context that differs markedly from its Plautine sources. In Harris's estimation, the play is in fact "more rooted in the world of commerce than any other of Shakespeare's."[35] It explicitly alludes to contemporary commerce in the eastern Mediterranean through casual references to the "Turkish tapestry" in Antipholus of Ephesus's house (4.1.104) and to the pressing business of sea merchants, like the Second Merchant whose voyage to Persia is delayed (4.1.4).[36] As Arthur Kinney has pointed out, "the business of *The Comedy of Errors* is business"; every character in the play has some good or service to sell or trade, and the word "gold" occurs thirty times – far more than in any other Shakespeare play.[37] And in a larger sense, the plot is set in motion by a conflict of commercial trade. It begins with the ominous capture of Egeon, a merchant of Syracuse, who is ransomed in Ephesus for violating a mutual trade embargo between Syracuse and Ephesus. The Duke of Ephesus, Solinus, sentences Egeon to death unless he can come up with the sum of a "thousand marks" by five o'clock (1.1.21). For Shakespeare's audience, the ransoming of unlawful strangers was of pressing topical concern as the result of acts of piracy committed by both Muslim and Christian corsairs. In response to the epidemic of piracy in the Mediterranean, the English crown constantly renegotiated its trade relations to accommodate embargoes and shifting alliances with other European nations (most notably, the Spanish embargo of 1585–1604). The new chartering of the Levant Company in January of 1592 (two years prior to *The Comedy of Errors*' earliest recorded performance at Gray's Inn) sought to pre-empt confusions among rival merchants by incorporating the Turkey and Venice companies into a single body politic, but numerous reports of piracy, abuse, and human capture recorded between 1592 and 1603 indicate that English ships continued to be involved in frequent, mutually antagonistic relationships with both Christian and Ottoman corsairs.[38]

The contemporary location of Ephesus in the Ottoman empire meant that it was a place where English merchants and adventurers were putting their own baptisms to the test by trading and consorting with Muslims, Jews, and Catholics. If English parishioners were routinely preached to about St. Paul's notion of a "circumcision of the heart," they were also bombarded with prayers and collections taken up for the redemption of Christian captives enslaved in Muslim territories. Thus, for Shakespeare's audience, the significance of religious conversion in Ephesus was simultaneously informed by Paul's teachings on the conversion of Gentiles and by contemporary reports of Christians being captured and converted to Islam in the commercial port cities of the eastern Mediterranean. I argue that the juxtaposition of these temporal resonances – the Pauline and the contemporary Ottoman East – informs the bodily exchanges that permeate the play, ultimately revealing an uneasy conjunction between religious conversion and commodity exchange. While on the one hand, the play produces amusing physical comedy through its conflation of the fungibility of commodities with Pauline conversion, on the other hand, it taps into early modern anxieties about the possibility of conversions away from Christianity, and the extent to which eastern commerce provided the material conditions for such conversions to occur. As one early seventeenth-century merchant's notebook reveals, the kinds of commodities that an English merchant might encounter in an Ottoman port city ranged in diversity from "Raw and salted ffishe," "Barbary horses," "Wax Lonsy," and "Corrall" to "Christn Captives of all kindes."[39] The intercultural contact facilitated by maritime trade in the late sixteenth and early seventeenth centuries made Christian merchants personally vulnerable to captivity, commodification, and enforced conversion. The ransoming of "Christn Captives of all kindes" epitomized the dangers of human fungibility, constituting both a profitable human trade and a mechanism for conversions away from Christianity.

England's participation in Mediterranean trade also produced more general concerns about England's national economic transformation and engagement in a larger system of global mercantilism. As Daniel Vitkus has suggested, the threatening concept of conversion encompassed not only individuals, but also the "collective cultural and economic transformation that English society was undergoing . . . in adopting new procedures and identities based on Mediterranean experience."[40] Thus, in positing the fungibility of bodies, *The Comedy of Errors* exposes not only the potential effects of commerce on individual identity but also its damaging effects on the nation. In Harris's reading, the play incorporates a leitmotif of bodily disease, in particular syphilis, to address the question of individual/national agency within the global system of commerce: drawing on competing interpretations of syphilis as a disease that is both "internally generated and externally contracted," the play "vacillates between a traditional view of commerce as a subset of ethics in which the appetitive subject assumed moral responsibility for his or her transactions and an emergent conception of commerce as an amoral, global system to whose demands the subject and the nation have no choice but to submit."[41] The Duke of Ephesus's repeated invocation of the "laws" (1.1.4, 25) of international commerce that force his hand in sentencing Egeon to death at the opening of the play reflect his, and by extension Ephesus's and Egeon's, containment within a system of laws that eviscerate individual agency.

Crucially, of course, it is the cutting off of commerce between Ephesus and Syracuse, rather than its free-flowing operation, that puts a price on Egeon's head and sets the stage for potential tragedy. The play thus opens with the presumption that commercial exchange is positive and redemptive, raising the expectation that the recommencement of trade will resolve Egeon's immediate predicament and heal the various breaches that afflict his family. Ostensibly oriented against forces of separation and in favor of restored intercourse and reunion, the play implies a parallel between the trade embargo and the violent splitting of Egeon's merchant ship that separated his twin sons and their two twin servants, as well as Egeon and his wife, thirty-three years ago. The termination of commerce works to sustain the division of Egeon's family by compelling Antipholus and Dromio of Syracuse to suppress their Syracusan identities while in Ephesus – a precaution that repeatedly stalls their reunion with their brothers and their father. Thus, the play suggests that through the restoration of intercourse between Ephesus and Syracuse, Egeon's family can be reconciled and the play can end with comic resolution. In ostensibly aligning the flow of trade with familial reconciliation, the play suggests a relationship between economic and generic form that Valerie Forman argues is characteristic of tragicomedy; however, the play ultimately problematizes this alignment by revealing the social inversions (both hilarious and tragic) that ensue when human conversion follows a logic of economic exchange.[42]

The Comedy of Errors' linking together of commercial intercourse and familial reconciliation offers a clear example of how it analogizes – and elides – commercial exchange and Pauline fellowship. In imposing a boundary of "citizen" and "alien" among brothers, the trade embargo references the breach of faith that divided the early church between Jews and Gentiles, poignantly illustrating St. Paul's anguish at the unjustness of such a division through the severing of identical twin bodies. In addition, Egeon's narrative of the splitting of the ship that divides his family invokes the division of the church caused by Jewish adherence to the "weak and beggerly elements" of the law (Galatians 4.9). Egeon tells of how upon hitting rough waters, he and his wife sought to secure their newborn twins and the twin servants to the boat, when his wife "more careful for the latter-born [son] . . . fastened him unto a small spare mast" (1.1.78–9). The mother's prioritizing of care for the younger son may be seen to presage the violent splitting of the ship and its cargo, for no sooner do Egeon and his wife fasten themselves "at either end [of] the mast" (1.1.85) than they are

> encountered by a mighty rock,
> Which being violently borne upon,
> Our helpful ship was splitted in the midst;
> so that in this unjust divorce of us
> Fortune had left to both of us alike
> What to delight in, what to sorrow for. (1.1.101–6)

Egeon's characterization of the splitting of the boat "in the midst" (or at the "mast") and the separation of the twins as a most violent and "unjust divorce" suggests the sundering of the cross that St. Paul aspired to heal by unifying Jew and Gentile under one Christian faith. Just as St. Paul sought to unify the church by substituting the law of Jesus ("Loue thy neighbour as thyselfe," Galatians 5.14) for the old Jewish law that divides, the play seeks resolution by lifting the law of the embargo and reconciling the separation of brothers and husband and wife, reuniting them into one family.

And indeed, *The Comedy of Errors* concludes with an overt reference to Pauline reconciliation. The two sets of twins and Egeon and his wife are reunited in a priory, and in the final lines of the play, the two Dromios resolve to exit hand in hand, rather than eldest first: "We came into the world like brother and brother, / And now let's go hand in hand, not one before another" (5.1.424–5). Leading up to this point, however, the belief shared by all the characters that only one Antipholus and one Dromio exist in Ephesus, and the inadvertent exchanging or substitution of their bodies that ensues, creates considerable confusion and violence. In presenting a series of exchanged bodies and identities that lead not to harmony or reconciliation, but to chaos (comic for the audience, but torturous for the characters), the play exposes the social impracticalities of Pauline universalism, as well as its residual production of confusion and violence.

The multiple confusions of the twins' identities result in a series of uneven commercial exchanges in which the intended recipient winds up either short or vastly overcompensated. For example, Angelo the goldsmith mistakenly gives a chain to Antipholus of Syracuse, and then unsuccessfully seeks payment from Antipholus of Ephesus; Angelo is thus unable to pay his debt to another merchant. Adriana mistakenly gives money to Dromio of Syracuse for Antipholus of Ephesus' bail; Dromio of Syracuse then delivers this money to the wrong Antipholus, and as a result Antipholus of Ephesus cannot be ransomed. Antipholus of Ephesus beats Dromio of Ephesus for bringing him a rope instead of the 500 ducats he mistakenly ordered Dromio of Syracuse to retrieve from his house. In the end, Antipholus of Syracuse winds up with the chain, the 500 ducats, and dinner at the house of Antipholus of Syracuse, while Antipholus of Ephesus winds up in debt for a chain he did not receive, in debt to both his wife and the courtesan to whom he promised the chain, arrested and bound for his debt to the goldsmith, and locked out of his own house. In short, the physical misplacements of the gold chain illustrate the figuratively broken chain of exchange caused by the twins' indecipherability.

Over and over again, the play hypothesizes the satisfaction of unpaid debts through the ransoming of bodies. Antipholus of Syracuse and Antipholus of Ephesus are arrested and bound for failing to pay Angelo for the chain, and both of the Dromios receive repeated beatings, or "marks" upon their bodies, for appearing to carry out uneven exchanges. But in repeatedly exposing the insufficiency of bodies to satisfy debts, the play ultimately resists the conversion of bodies into exchange value. Foreshadowing Shylock's inability to extract exactly one pound of flesh from Antonio's body in *The Merchant of Venice* (1596), the physical bondage of the two Antipholuses does not adequately compensate for the payment of the chain, and neither do the "marks" upon the Dromios' bodies make up for the discrepancies in value for which they appear to be responsible. Indeed, in a play that centers so crucially on the activity of exchange, it is curious that nearly every debt remains unsatisfied in the end. Angelo never does receive his payment for the chain, and the merchant to whom he is indebted never makes it onto his ship; Egeon is forgiven his debt for trespassing in Ephesus; the arresting officer never receives payment for his captives' release; and Antipholus of Ephesus is never returned his gold.

Moreover, though the bodies and names of the twins are identical, their identities prove not to be fungible. The play's exaggerated portrayal of their physical similarities seems at first to emphasize the injustice of their separation and the inevitable force of their oneness. Even the marks that normally distinguish one identical twin from another are in the case of the Dromios identical, making their bodies indecipherable even to the most familiar set of eyes. As Nell the kitchen maid reveals, her lover who is Dromio of Ephesus bears the very same "privy marks . . . [including] the mark of [his] shoulder, the mole in [his] neck, the great wart on [his] left arm" that Dromio of Syracuse bears (3.2.126–7). However, the play ultimately argues for the value of physical distinctions, and the essential correlation between physicality and identity, by showing how such indecipherability enables all manner of 'unnatural' things to happen. The temporary undoing of the twins' individual identities results in a wife unable to recognize her own husband, a man being locked out of his own house, a lover unable to recognize her fiancé, masters who cannot recognize their servants, servants who cannot recognize their masters, and a rope that costs 500 ducats. In short, it results in a world *turned outside in*, creating a series of estrangements that the characters seek in vain to explain through sorcery or madness.

If St. Paul explicitly defined Christian universalism against the bodily distinctions and social divisions privileged by ancient Jewish laws governing diet, exogamy, and circumcision, *The Comedy of Errors* considers and ultimately resists the evisceration of contemporary social customs that divide individuals on the basis of such determinants as gender and class. Instead, it demonstrates the necessity of retaining the divisions that define identity, and grounding these divisions in bodily distinctions, precisely by dramatizing the unappealing consequences of mistaken identities and inverted social hierarchies. To do so, the play reappropriates biblical verses and commentaries intended to illustrate the universalizing power of Pauline fellowship. For example, it refigures the New Testament metaphor of a "knock upon the door" to expose the danger of allowing the wrong person to enter one's house. In the New Testament, this metaphor emphasizes the accessibility of Christian conversion or redemption to all willing parties: according to Matthew 7.7, "knocke, & it shalbe opened unto you"; and Revelation 3.20, "Behold, I stand at the doore, and knocke: if any man heare my voice, and open the doore, I will come in vnto him, and will Sup with him, and he with me." In turn, early modern sermons such as Thomas Jackson's *The Converts Happines* (1609) draw on these passages to emphasize the accessibility of conversion and redemption to all human souls and repentant sinners. Jackson references John's first vision and how it compelled him to write to the Gentile churches in Asia Minor, rather than the churches in Judea. According to Jackson, John chose to convey his message to the new converts in Asia Minor "to signify that now the kingdome of God was come to the Gentiles, and that the partition wall being broken downe, the Gentiles were admitted & adopted into the fellowship of God's people."[43] By contrast, in *The Comedy of Errors* Adriana's opening of her door to Antipholus of Syracuse results in the transgression of the "partition wall" by a stranger. That the rightful master has been displaced from his house by a stranger who is in Ephesus "but two hours old" directly alludes to the sacrament of baptism that indiscriminately converts strangers into citizens (2.2.139). The play thus illustrates how such access to conversion leads to the undoing of identity and social organization. In addition, the stranger's displacement of the master demonstrates how the "undividable, incorporate" union of marriage, referenced several lines earlier by Adriana, is vulnerable to infiltration (2.2.113).

Just as the play reappropriates the metaphor of "a knock upon the door" to illustrate the risks of indiscriminate access to conversion, it employs water as a metaphor in two separate instances to illustrate the dangers of a notion of identity that is not demarcated from that of others. This metaphor references both the water of baptism that in Paul's rendering washes away the blood of circumcision, erasing the bodily distinction between Jews and Gentiles, and the oceans that divide human beings into separate nations, religions, and ethnicities. In contrast to St. Paul's assurance to an audience of newly baptized Gentiles in his letter to the Ephesians that "There is one body and one spirit . . . One Lord, one Faith, one Baptisme" (4.4–5), *The Comedy of Errors* problematizes the anonymity and razing of individual identity conferred by baptism. After being confronted with the possibility that her own husband does not know her, Adriana compares the impossibility of depositing "a drop of water in the breaking gulf" and retrieving "unmingled thence that drop again" to the commingling of husband and wife in one body (2.2.117–18). In one sense, her use of this metaphor attests to and celebrates the notion of a husband and wife's inviolable union; but in another sense, the fluidity of identity that makes this commingling possible is also precisely what enables a stranger to displace her husband. That Adriana conceives of the union of marriage as not merely spiritual but distinctly physical is emphasized through her description of how she is physically contaminated by her (presumed) husband's failure to recognize her:

> I am possessed with an adulterate blot.
> My blood is mingled with the crime of lust;
> For if we two be one, and thou play false,
> I do digest the poison of thy flesh,
> Being strumpeted by thy contagion. (2.2.131–5)

What begins in her speech as a positive celebration of the inseparable union of marriage devolves into images of bodily contamination and contagion.

Similarly, Antipholus of Syracuse employs the metaphor of water to describe how his pursuit of fellowship leads to the tragic loss of his own identity:

> I to the world am like a drop of water
> That in the ocean seeks another drop,
> Who, falling there to find his fellow forth,
> Unseen, inquisitive, confounds himself.
> So I, to find a mother and a brother,
> In quest of them unhappy, lose myself. (1.2.35–40)

Like Adriana's invocation of water as a metaphor for the unity of marriage, Antipholus' description of questing for his "fellow" leads to unhappiness and loss. Both Adriana and Antipholus describe the merging of a drop of water with a larger body of water as a "fall": in Adriana's terms, "as easy mayst thou fall / A drop of water in the breaking gulf" (2.2.116–17). Thus, while the play opens by identifying familial separation as the source of tragedy that must be righted, it maps a quest for reconciliation that produces as much sadness and loss as it does laughter. In comparing his identity to "a drop of water," fungible, anonymous, and inseparable from the billions of other drops in the ocean, Antipholus of Syracuse describes the hazards of bodies without distinction, and a world without borders. While the play's Pauline resonances suggest that its resolution lies in the merging of brothers into one Christian body, it clearly exposes the dangers of such unification. Until the individual identities of the Antipholuses and Dromios are sorted out, the identical bodies in Ephesus create havoc and discord, rather than harmony and fellowship.

The ending of the play is in some ways far less settled than it might appear. Debts remain unpaid and mistaken identities prevail. Antipholus of Ephesus fails to recognize his father, and even Egeon himself cannot tell his sons apart. Wouldn't everyone be better off if Antipholus and Dromio of Syracuse simply returned to Syracuse? In effect, the splitting of Egeon's ship upon the rock that separated his family served a useful purpose by rendering the two Antipholuses and the two Dromios singular within their own respective communities. Contrary to its rhetoric of reconciliation, the play concludes by re-establishing this separation: its final denouement consists of untangling the four separate identities that are imposed on two bodies. Ultimately, the reunion of the brothers leads to comic resolution, but the practical significance of their reunion is not a merging of identity but the exposure of the twins' separate and distinct identities. Thus, it is the recognition of the differences that distinguish one twin from another, rather than their sameness, that resolves the play. In insisting upon the impracticality of razing human distinctions, *The Comedy of Errors* counteracts the logics of Pauline universalism and transnational commerce that converge in late sixteenth-century Ephesus.

Shakespeare's Leap of Faith? Othello's Unconvertible Difference

First performed around 1604, *Othello* presupposes the Christian conversion of a black Moor, who then goes on to transgress a variety of cultural boundaries by marrying a Christian woman, commanding trust and respect from the Venetian Senate, and leading a Christian army against the Muslim enemy. I argue that this representation raises, rather than answers, the question of whether a Moor can be converted and assimilated into Christianity, and in doing so, exposes the profoundly unsettled relationship between faith and the body in early modern England. In imagining the scope and limits of Christian faith, *Othello* explores whether Christian faith can spiritually transcend a black body and explicitly links conversion to embodiment by positing a conjunction between inner faith and outer difference. In recent years, critics have been divided over whether *Othello* is a play about race or whether such an interpretation reflects understandings of race anachronistically imposed by modern readers. In focusing not on Othello's racial difference, but on the question of his Christianity, I sidestep this debate to some degree while at the same time considering how questions of religious conversion might themselves reveal an early coalescing of racial categories. If *Othello* ultimately racializes its black protagonist, it does so in part by negotiating relationships between sight and belief, tangible proof and intangible essence, outward difference and inner faith. Simply put, the play asks: is a black body eligible for Christian redemption?

In an article entitled "Shakespeare's Leap" Stephen Greenblatt suggested that *Othello* reflects a leap of faith through its complex and multidimensional portrayal of the Moor – a portrayal that exemplifies the "touch of the real" by fusing representation with "the vivid presence of actual lived experience."[44] His linking of *Othello* with a leap of faith is apt, but it is a leap that ultimately fails, straining early modern belief precisely by pushing the boundaries of who can exist among the believers. In Renaissance England, Moors were frequently the subjects of literary fables, travelers' tales, and stage plays, and were at least occasionally present on the streets of London, though as Queen Elizabeth's 1596 and 1601 edicts for the expulsion of "negars and blackmoors" suggest, they were neither inconspicuous nor fully integrated into English culture.[45] And yet, *Othello* posits an assimilation of the Moor into Christian society that is in some ways remarkably seamless. The play's initial setting in Venice, a vital European trading port and home to many non-Christian foreigners including Moors, Turks, and Jews, provided a site through which to imaginatively project London's own future, given its growing participation in transnational trade and its increasingly porous borders. However, even in the context of Venice's comparatively cosmopolitan culture, Othello's assimilation seems exceptional. Unlike Shylock, who remains a social outsider despite his forced conversion to Christianity at the end of his trial, Othello's conversion appears to go unquestioned.

As observed in the Introduction to this book, *Othello* acknowledges its protagonist's baptism in a way that takes for granted both its unremarkable nature and its efficacy. Specifically, Iago offers the hyperbolic example of undoing Othello's baptism as a way to describe Desdemona's immense power over him. Desdemona could "win the Moor," he suggests, even "were't" to ask him

> to renounce his baptism,
> All seals and symbols of redeemed sin,
> His soul is so enfettered to her love
> That she may make, unmake, do what she list,

Even as her appetite shall play the god
With his weak function. (2.3.338–43)

In drawing a parallel between the "seals and symbols" that confirm Othello's baptism and the "love" that makes Othello's "soul" "enfettered" to Desdemona, Iago suggests an equation between Othello's conversion to Christian faith and his faith in Desdemona's love. As the play progresses, Desdemona's love comes to stand in for Othello's Christian faith: his sustained faith in her mutual love and fidelity – later equated with her "chastity" – constitutes an index of the authenticity of his conversion. But crucially, both Othello's Christian faith and Desdemona's chastity are entities that elude visual corollary. While Iago's point above is to acknowledge the security of Othello's Christian identity by equating the great unlikelihood of its undoing with Desdemona's immense power over him, it is significant that the play does not allow us to *see* Othello's baptism, but rather asks us to accept it as a matter of faith. Similarly, we do not get to see the courtship that prompts Desdemona to fall in love with Othello. Instead, Othello narrates the details of their courtship in answer to Brabantio's charge that Desdemona could not possibly fall in love with a man such as he. Specifically, what defies belief is the possibility that Desdemona could "fall in love with what she feared to look on" (1.3.99).

The play's refusal to supply visual evidence of both Othello's Christian conversion and Desdemona's seduction by Othello is offset by the constant visual reminder of the thing that makes both conversions so difficult to believe – Othello's physical difference. While we must simply have faith in Othello's conversion through baptism and in Desdemona's conversion from "a maiden" "of spirit so still and quiet that her motion / Blushed at herself" (1.3.95–7) to one who "falls in love with what she feared to look on," the thing we unequivocally *do* get to see is the outward difference of Othello's black body. Thus, in implicitly appropriating a Pauline notion of universal faith that eschews an outward corollary, the play simultaneously uses the visual element of performance to exploit the audience's reliance on sight as an index of belief.

Seeing (Beyond) the Black Body

Compounding the dramatic impact of Othello's bodily presence on the stage are the graphic descriptions of his offensive blackness and its sexual threat to Desdemona that visually mark him even before his first entrance. These threatening images of bestiality and miscegenation conjured by Iago and Roderigo – "an old black ram / Is tupping your white ewe!" (1.1.87–8); "the devil will make a grandsire of you" (90); "you'll have your daughter covered with a Barbary horse" (110) – offer stark visual contrasts to Othello's declaration of his "perfect soul" in the following scene. Upon being warned of Brabantio's intention to accuse him before the Senate of stealing his daughter, Othello both refuses to hide his body and makes a case for the persuasive force of his intrinsic virtues:

> Not I, I must be found.
> My parts, my title and my perfect soul
> Shall manifest me rightly. (1.2.30–2)

His explicit willingness to "be found" calls attention to the visual presence of his physical body, and his repetition of "I, I" emphasizes how he in fact distinguishes himself from others ("not I") by his very refusal to conceal his body ("I must be found"). At the same time, he suggests that despite the evidence of this conspicuous body – the only black body among many white bodies – his "parts," his "title," and his "perfect soul" shall exonerate him from blame. These components of his identity refer respectively to personal "qualities and attributes," social "rights or claims," and a "faultless" or "immaculate" spiritual status.[46] In effect, they express his merits in intrinsic, social, and salvational terms. Thus, Othello's lines suggest that his intangible qualities will outweigh the more tangible effects of his bodily presence. In defending himself against Brabantio's charges, Othello asks that both the Venetian Senate and the audience of the play make a leap of faith, as Desdemona has, by valuing his unseen virtues over the blatant spectacle of his physical difference.

Although the negative images of blackness propounded throughout the play by Iago, Roderigo, and Brabantio were not the only characteristics associated with Moors in the early modern period, I want to suggest that their visual force directly contributed to the theatrical challenge of representing a Moor with a "perfect soul" (1.2.31). These visual descriptions become inseparable from the constant reminder of Othello's physical difference whenever he appears on the stage. The play references this effect when, upon Othello's entrance to the Senate, along with Brabantio, Cassio, Iago, Roderigo, and officers, the Duke immediately greets Othello before turning apologetically to Brabantio to say, "I did not see you" (1.3.51). The Duke's remark simultaneously registers the fact of Othello's physical conspicuity *and* his respected authority (at the expense of Brabantio), the combination of which constitutes a paradox that is returned to throughout the play. Writing in 1812, Charles Lamb drew attention to how the impact of Othello's blackness manifests itself in the difference between reading the play and seeing it performed: "I appeal to everyone that has seen *Othello* played whether he did not, on the contrary, sink Othello's mind in his colour; whether he did not find something extremely revolting in the courtship and wedded caresses of Othello and Desdemona; and whether the actual sight of the thing did not overweigh all that beautiful compromise which we make in reading."[47] While Lamb certainly speaks from a position informed by his own cultural racism, I suggest that even in 1604 Shakespeare's play was not innocent of the way the performed spectacle of Othello's blackness could be used to exploit a distinction between sight and belief.

Desdemona's own explanation for her attraction to Othello acknowledges the perceived contradiction between his external and internal qualities. Making her case to the Senate to accompany her husband to war, she soberly explains,

> I saw Othello's visage in his mind,
> And to his honours and his valiant parts
> Did I my soul and fortunes consecrate (1.3.253–5)

She thus proposes a crucial opposition between sight and belief, which informs her perception of inner virtue over outer body. Whereas a person's "visage" refers to their "face" or "assumed appearance" (*OED* 1, 8), the "mind" refers to a "mental faculty," which is "regarded as being separate from the physical" (*OED* 19a). In addition, Desdemona's description of "consecrat[ing]" her "soul and fortunes" to Othello's "honours and valiant parts" – explicitly disembodied rather than embodied entities – emphasizes the spiritual aspects of marriage rather than its union of two bodies. At the same time, Desdemona certainly does not disavow her physical attraction to Othello, and even boldly prefaces her case to accompany him to war by insisting, "I did love the Moor to live with him" (1.3.249). But I want to suggest that Desdemona's ability to see "Othello's visage in his mind" is all the more remarkable because of her simultaneous willingness to embrace his physical self. Desdemona's ability to see beyond Othello's black body to his inner virtue is testimony to her faith in that which cannot be seen, a capacity that directly contrasts with Othello's ultimate demand for ocular proof.

Huston Diehl has similarly observed how the play's exploration of the relationship between blind faith and ocular proof resonates with the religious controversies of the Reformation.[48] She explains,

"By demonstrating both the insufficiency of visible evidence and the difficulty of sustaining faith in what cannot be seen, Shakespeare's play thus addresses fundamental questions about seeing, knowing, and believing, questions that are at the heart of sixteenth-century religious reforms."[49] But whereas Diehl interprets Othello's demand for ocular proof as "a typical response to the renewed emphasis in reform culture on faith" (reflecting Protestantism's continued reliance on material forms), I suggest that Desdemona's way of seeing establishes a corrective counter to Othello's inability to distinguish between misleading materiality and the truth of an essence unseen. In this way the play models a contrast between proper and improper forms of belief. Robert N. Watson has made a similar point about the contrast between Desdemona's faith and Othello's faithlessness, arguing that in allegorizing a doctrinal dispute over the necessity of faith, the play amounts to "Protestant propaganda."[50] What I am suggesting is not that Othello should be read as Catholic (or that the play should be read as Protestant), but rather that the play draws on distinctions of sight and belief made pertinent by the Reformation to consider whether subjects outside the Catholic-Protestant divide are eligible for conversion. Othello's failure of faith, I argue, is singled out by his blackness. By contrast, Desdemona's undying faith is distinguished by her ability to see beyond the black body. As I go on to demonstrate, the significance of blackness as the subject and object of the faith being tested is crucial here.

Of course, Othello does not spontaneously lose his faith in Desdemona's love and develop an incapacity for faith in the intangible, but is explicitly converted by Iago. And, in contrast to the invisibility of his baptism and seduction of Dedemona's love, Othello's seduction and conversion by Iago are explicitly staged. By communicating a series of disturbing inferences, Iago undoes Othello's faith in Desdemona's love and substitutes in its place his own false loyalty and devotion. The exchange of "sacred" vows between Othello and Iago in 3.3 simulates not only a marriage ceremony but also a reconversion ceremony in which Othello withdraws his faith in Desdemona's love and recommits his faith to Iago (3.3.464). As the agent of Othello's conversion, Iago turns Othello's faith precisely by convincing him that his blackness matters, a condition that, in turn, "turn[s]" Desdemona's "virtue into pitch" (2.3.355). Iago's persistent inferences about Desdemona's infidelity rely on the presumption that Othello's blackness obviously precludes the possibility of her genuine love. While Othello initially dismisses the suggestion, saying, "she had eyes and chose me" (3.3.192), this shift in his attention quickly leads him to an authorization of visual proof as the only reliable index for truth: "No, Iago, / I'll see before I doubt, when I doubt, prove" (3.3.192–3). In this way, Iago helps facilitate a connection between somatic difference and reliance on visual proof that is progressively reinforced throughout the play. Ultimately, of course, Othello is converted to doubt not by means of ocular proof but by Iago's conjuring of images through spoken words. Nonetheless, Othello's vow to rely on ocular proof stands in stark contrast to the intangible nature of Desdemona's love and, by extension, her chastity. Thus, Iago's reconversion of Othello consists of converting him from a reliance on intangible faith to a reliance on tangible proof.

In addition, Iago convinces Othello that he cannot trust the things he thinks he sees, while simultaneously reminding him of the evidence of his physical difference. He points, for example, to the deceptive way that Desdemona first responded to his looks: "When she seemed to shake, and fear your looks, / She loved them most" (3.2.210–11). Again, Iago implies that Desdemona's response to Othello's outward difference cannot be trusted, but what is certain is that this difference is not insignificant. By linking Othello's blackness to an incapacity to properly interpret signs, Iago destabilizes Othello's sense of Christian identification. His undoing of Othello's faith in his own ability to read Desdemona reveals, through Othello's very susceptibility to such conversion, the failure or impermanence of his initial conversion to Christianity. Indeed, Iago persuades Othello to doubt his fellowship with the Christian community by casually inferring his outsider status as though it were a foregone conclusion, and appoints himself as a reliable translator of Venice's "country disposition" (3.3.204). This suggestion of Othello's insecure place in the Christian society starkly contrasts with his prior sense of confidence in his position as not just the military but the moral leader of the Christian army. Such confidence is casually exemplified when Othello reprimands his brawling men, "Are we turn'd Turks?" (2.3.166), clearly aligning himself with their Christian identity. In short, Iago convinces him that his blackness constitutes an insuperable difference that bars him from both Christian fellowship and Desdemona's genuine love.

Ambiguous Origins

Significantly, Othello's native origins are never definitively established in the play; at various times he is tenuously linked to the eastern and African geographies of Turks and Muslims, and at other times to the New World and its pagan cannibals. In fact, the "travailous history"

(1.3.140) that Othello narrates before the Senate suggestively ties him to a range of discursive histories, including that of the romance or renegade adventurer, passing "battles, sieges, [and] fortunes" (131) and negotiating "hair-breadth scapes" (137);[51] that of biblical Exodus, characterized by "flood and field" (136), "antres vast and deserts idle, / rough quarries, rocks, and hills whose heads touch heaven" (141–2); that of the noble African convert and Leo Africanus's *Historie of Africa*;[52] that of a Christian captive "taken by the insolent foe / And sold into slavery" (138–9); and that of classical and medieval travelers' tales such as Pliny's *History of the World* and Mandeville's *Travels*, featuring "cannibals that each other eat" (144), "the Anthropophagi" (145), and "men whose heads / Do grow beneath their shoulders" (145–6). In turn, these discursive histories suggest a range of geographical, ethnic, and religious identities, including the Israelite Judean, the Muslim or pagan African, and the pagan "cannibal."

Othello's identification as a Moor lends further complication, rather than clarity, to his identity. Throughout the play, his Moorishness persists as the single most prevalent means of his identification by others, often superseding the use of his name. He is occasionally referred to as "general" or "lord," but far more frequently as "the Moor." Despite the consistency of this label, as critics have shown, the specific meaning of Moorish identity was highly unstable in early modern England in that it designated numerous, often incongruous categories of geographical, national, religious, and embodied distinction.[53] As Emily Bartels incisively sums up, "The 'notorious indeterminacy' that seems to mar the Moor's story is, in fact, essential to its core . . . the Moor is first and foremost a figure of uncodified and uncodifiable diversity."[54] Dramatic representations of Moors reflected a variety of characteristics and origins.[55] The characteristics attached to Othello alone suggest a wide range of positive and negative stereotypes: he is referred to as "lascivious Moor," "valiant Moor," "brave Moor," "warlike Moor," "lusty Moor," "noble Moor," "dull Moor," and "cruel Moor." Despite their diversity, none of these modifiers for Moorishness is considered unfamiliar or beyond the pale.

In addition, the figure of the Moor evoked specific concerns about conversion, and straddled the line of distinction between legitimate Christian conversion and insincere or chronic turning. Such ambiguity was partly informed by the legacy of the Spanish Moriscoes – a discursive history associated with chronic illegitimate or superficial conversions – and the (complexly related) literary idealization of the "noble Moor" in the romance and classical traditions.[56] Iago draws on this range of extremes as they suit his own agenda when appealing to

Othello and other characters. For example, when first warning Othello of Desdemona's infidelity, Iago expresses concern for Othello's "free and noble nature," which makes him particularly vulnerable to abuse (3.3.202). Echoing his previous remark to Roderigo in which he alludes to Othello's "free and *open* nature" (1.3.398, italics mine), Iago's substitution here of "noble" for "open" reflects the unstable nature of Moorishness – its enduring "noble" integrity versus its changeable "openness." This instability pervades Othello's characterization throughout the play. He remains a figure impossible to pin down: "a wheeling stranger / Of here and everywhere" (1.1.134–5), and yet simultaneously the "Moor *of Venice*" (italics mine), both black and Christian, a foreign imposter and a privileged officer of the state.[57]

The unstable meaning of "Moor" and the play's lack of specificity about Othello's origins have led critics to consider the implications of reading Othello as a Muslim Turk as opposed to an African pagan. Most notably, Julia Reinhard Lupton and Daniel Vitkus have exposed the long-held critical assumption of Othello's pagan African roots – often implicitly conflated with his blackness – by calling attention to the possibility of his Muslim origins and his reversion to Turkish tyranny at the end of the play.[58] For Lupton, Othello's possible religious origins as a Muslim constitute a separate and unrelated threat from that of his skin color. She suggests that the notion of a circumcised, Muslim Othello was in fact much more threatening for early modern audiences than that of a darker-skinned, pagan Othello, because of the imperial threat associated with the Ottoman empire and the theological links between Christianity and Islam. Whereas paganism was understood to be pre-Christian, Islam stemmed from the "same Abrahamic lineage as Christianity," and was thus perceived by English audiences to be more resistant to conversion.[59] This recognition of Othello's possible Muslim origins importantly complicates our understanding of his difference and of the complexities attendant upon his Christian conversion.

Nonetheless, it is important to recognize that the play is explicitly ambiguous about its protagonist's origins and refuses to associate him with any one religion or geography. This ambiguity may suggest that the spiritual conversion of baptism renders indifferent the particular specificity of Othello's past, or that the opposition critics have constructed between paganism and Islam is overdetermined. As Ania Loomba asserts, "It is impossible, but also unnecessary, to decide whether Othello is *more* or *less* 'African/black' than 'Turkish/Muslim.'"[60] For one thing, "African" did not necessarily mean non-Muslim, as these binary oppositions imply. But more significantly, the play refuses to offer conclusive evidence of Othello's origins and, in thus sustaining the possibility that he could have been either pagan or Muslim, reveals how both religious identities could be associated with dark skin. Blackness did not foreclose the particular threat associated with a circumcised Muslim and in some cases reinforced it. Even though, as Burton puts it, "Othello's skin color" could potentially "distract us from the possibility of his more significant religious difference," it is also the case that skin color could function as an indication of religious difference in the early modern period.[61] Considering the vast range of geographies and histories to which Othello is attached throughout the play, perhaps the only thing constant or unequivocal about his identity is the very fact of his blackness – a quality that in the words of Dympna Callaghan had the capacity "to intensify, subsume and absorb all aspects of otherness."[62]

Skin Color and Marking Faith

It is worth underscoring the point that whereas Othello's potential circumcision is not directly evidenced in the play, the fact of his blackness is repeatedly evidenced through multiple verbal allusions as well as by the visual spectacle of his body. I intend this not as an argument for reading Othello as black/pagan *instead of* Muslim, but rather to draw attention to the difference between locating religious alterity in the sign of blackness and in that of circumcision. In effect, the play privileges an undeniable and visible marker of difference rather than an uncertain and, for all intents and purposes, invisible marker. Clearly, the stage could not easily allow (if at all) for circumcision to be visibly apparent, but even if it could, it seems important to recognize that the mark of circumcision is categorically distinct from that of skin color. Whereas Othello could not hide his blackness without concealing his entire body, the mark of circumcision is always (under normal circumstances) concealed from public view. Moreover, as Lupton points out, circumcision symbolized a covenant rather than a biologically inherited trait: "physical yet not physiological, genealogical yet not genetic, circumcision marks the Jews off as a distinct people without becoming a 'racial' indicator in the modern sense."[63] In assiduously avoiding the question of whether Othello is circumcised or not, the play in effect substitutes a mark of inherited (racial) difference for a mark that is inscribed onto the body (which could conceivably be inscribed onto *any* male body).

Othello's reliance on skin color to mark his alterity is significant, I argue, not only because it privileges a spectacle of difference that is indisputable, but because it forces a consideration of whether a difference conceived as natural and inherited can be rendered indifferent by Christian faith. The fact of Othello's blackness also opens the possibility that his original faith (prior to his baptism) was not merely inscribed onto his body but bred into it. Of course, blackness in the period was not understood exclusively in terms of a heritable condition, but was also understood to be produced by environmental influences such as the sun or diet (acted upon the body, somewhat like circumcision). In this sense, the production of blackness was analogous to the stage's use of prosthetics or makeup to conceal or darken an actor's white skin. At the same time, competing discourses of blackness – such as those implicit in Iago's invocation of a "black ram . . . tupping . . . [a] white ewe" – understood it to be indelible, innate, and tied to sexual reproduction. As Jonathan Burton puts it, "In *Othello* Shakespeare stages an early modern contest of contemporaneous notions of race."[64] Bound up with these competing understandings of how blackness was embodied was the distinction between Muslims and pagans and their varying susceptibility to conversion. Thus, the question of whether a black body could be converted to the Christian faith seems to return to the distinction between the more threatening, and hence unconvertible, Muslim and the more easily converted pagan. However, if the religious difference between Muslims and pagans directly impinged upon the ontological significance of blackness, these differences also collapsed under the sign of blackness – a contradiction that Othello's ambiguous origins neatly illustrate.

Richard Eden provides an example of how blackness elides Muslim/pagan differences (even as it is called into service to distinguish them) in the preface to his English translation of Peter Martyr d'Anghiera's *The Decades of the Newe Worlde* (1555). Seeking to encourage colonization and conversion in the New World, Eden attempts to link the dark skin of pagans to their relative susceptibility to Christian conversion. Of course, it is important to realize that the conclusions Eden draws for New World pagans do not necessarily apply to African pagans, though the very use of the same term ("pagan") to denote the religions of these two groups reflects their status as western constructions that presume their equivalence. What I hope to show through the example of Eden's preface, and more broadly through *Othello*, is how these kinds of cultural constructions (of both pagans and Muslims) call into service certain logics of skin color that render blackness simultaneously conditional and unconditional, environmentally produced and innate, susceptible to Christian faith and resistant to conversion.

Specifically, Eden reconfigures the potential obstacle of the dark skin of the New World natives by drawing an analogy between the effects of the sun and the conversion of a pagan soul to Christianity. In doing so, he inverts the trope of the Ethiopian eunuch by suggesting that the goal of conversion is not whitewashing the subject but writing upon or "coloring" him. He proposes that just as contact with the sun transforms skin color, contact with Christian "conversation" will induce conversion:

> For lyke as they that goo much in the soonne, are coloured therewith although they go not for that purpose, So may the conversation of the Christians with the gentyles induce theym to owre religion, where there is no greater cause of contrarye to resyste as in the Turkes who are alredy drowned in theyr confirmed erroure. But these simple gentiles lyving only after the lawe of nature, may well bee likened to a smoothe and bare table unpainted, or a white paper unwritten, upon the which yow may at first paynte or wryte what yow lyste, as yow can not upon tables alredy paynted, unleese yow rase or blot owt the fyrste formes.[65]

After positing that the pagans' susceptibility to the sun provides evidence that they are like a "bare table unpainted, or a white paper unwritten," Eden draws an explicit contrast with Muslim "Turkes," who are like "tables alredy paynted," and cannot be converted "unleese yow rase or blot owt the fyrste formes." However, if he appears to make a distinction between pagans' susceptibility to the sun and Muslims as "tables alredy paynted," he employs the same metaphor of darkening, or "paynting," to describe both. In effect, the logics of convertibility and inconvertibility rely on the same evidence of blackness. And in the cases of both pagans and Muslims, Eden's reasoning reveals an uneasy slippage between the state of the skin and that of the soul. Ultimately, his effort to differentiate pagans from "Turkes" who are "already paynted" belies an underlying recognition that Muslims and Native Americans could both be externally marked by dark skin. Othello's connections to multiple discursive histories and geographies demonstrate how easily a range of religious and national differences could be collapsed under the sign of blackness. Moreover, this duality, by which dark skin could signify both as an openness to being written upon and as ineligibility for conversion, reveals how environmental and innate explanations for blackness were bound up together.

Skin color was not the only receptacle for anxieties about religious conversion, but it certainly was a powerful one with relevance for pagans and Muslims alike. Of course, it is important to acknowledge that not all Muslims were understood to possess dark skin, and in fact there is ample evidence that most were not, though the question of to what degree the stage represented Muslims as dark skinned remains impossible to answer. Was a light-skinned Muslim understood to be more easily converted to Christianity than a dark-skinned one? Perhaps just as revealing as cultural productions that presume the innate resistance of Muslims to Christian conversion are the few that deem it possible. Meredith Hanmer's sermon delivered on the occasion of the baptism of a Turk in London in 1586 offers an illuminating contrast to Eden's preface. The site of the baptism in the Hospital of St. Katherine, located on the northern bank of the Thames River, seems to highlight London's exposure to foreign penetration. However, the title page to the sermon specifies that the Turk in question, "one Chinano," was "borne at Nigropontus," an island bordering Greece.[66] Thus, it is likely the convert was not distinguished by dark skin. The fact that skin color is not mentioned anywhere in the sermon removes its consideration altogether from the question of convertibility. Further, as Nabil Matar suggests, Hanmer's specification of Chinano's birthplace drew attention to a city that had been lost to the Muslims in 1470, and that Protestants might now reclaim "through the power of their faith."[67] John Foxe refers to "Euboea, or Nigropontus" in his *Actes and Monuments* as an island "bordering about Grecia" that had been "wonne likewise by the Turke, from the Christians."[68] Thus, in a sense, Hanmer posits not the conversion of a Muslim to Christianity, but the long overdue *reconversion* of a subject whose native and natural religion was Christianity. Hanmer clearly acknowledges the disparity between Islam, "in greatnes halfe the world," and Christianity, "now couched in the North partes of the world, and so far that it seemeth . . . all frozen."[69] But he makes a plea to reverse this trend by returning God's "lost and wandering sheepe" to the "sheepefold."[70] He concludes with a prayer to "open the eyes of all Infidels, Iewes, Turkes, and Saracens, bring into the folde all lost and wandering sheepe, make all nations one sheepefolde, vnder the head Shepheard and Bishoppe of our soules."[71] In conceiving of the conversion of Jews, Turks, and Saracens as a continuation of the "Gospell," and expressing a desire to "make all nations one sheepefolde," Hanmer justifies the baptism he is about to perform with the rhetoric of universal fellowship. Part of what enables this conversion, I want to suggest, is the fact that the convert's home was formerly a Christian land, as well as the subject's disassociation from a discourse of skin color.

Predestination and the Terms of Salvation

Although in the years leading up to Othello's production in 1604, Protestant conversions of Muslims and pagans were fairly uncommon, the implication that a universal Christianity could encompass all souls had become a source of controversy in English ecclesiological circles. In 1596 Archbishop John Whitgift responded to pressures to revise the language of Article XVII of the Thirty-Nine Articles of the Church of England so as to more explicitly elucidate the terms of double predestination. Whereas Article XVII implied that all Christians were potentially eligible for salvation, the Lambeth Articles insist that "God from eternity has predestined some men to life, and reprobated some to death," that these numbers "cannot be increased or diminished," and that "it is not in the will or the power of each and every man to be saved."[72] Furthermore, according to these terms, "those not predestined to salvation" would be "inevitably condemned on account of their sins," whereas true faith could never be lost "totally or finally in the elect."[73]

I want to suggest that debates surrounding the terms of predestination were partly informed by questions of conversion raised by intercultural contact with non-Christian others, and that at times Protestants attempted to use the logic of predestination to justify exclusion by narrowing the constrictions of universal faith. The debates were complicated, but in one basic sense, the participants disagreed over whether all humans had the capacity to be saved, or whether some were irretrievably predestined to hell. This question directly involved a consideration of non-Christian souls that, perhaps through no fault of their own, were excluded from salvation. In 1596 – the same year that Whitgift devised the Lambeth Articles – Thomas Goad used the example of Turks to illustrate the limits of Protestant grace:

> quoniam extra ecclesiam Turcae et aliae nationes barbarae quamplurimae, licet habeant externa dona hujus vitae communia a Deo concessa, tamen gratia ad salutem sufficiente omnino destituuntur.[74]

> Since the Turks and other foreign peoples are outside of the church, they may receive the superficial gifts commonly granted by God to all humanity, but they nevertheless lack the grace necessary for salvation.

According to Goad, to argue that grace was available to Turks was intolerable. Others, like Richard Hooker, were more inclined to allow that all human beings might be saved. In January of 1604, the same year that *Othello* was first performed, the Hampton Court Conference brought the predestination debates into the public eye. At the conference, King James refused to endorse a more explicit articulation of predestination than that previously outlined in the Thirty-Nine Articles. In other words, the conference resulted in a minor victory for people like Hooker through its refusal to explicitly narrow the terms of eligibility for redemption. Nonetheless, the surrounding debate constituted clear evidence of the beginnings of a controversy that would resurface with significant consequences in the 1620s. In both the early 1600s and the 1620s, these ecclesiastical controversies were, I suggest, influenced by considerations of conversion introduced by transcultural commerce and conflict.

As *Othello* makes clear, England's growing awareness of and reliance on intercultural contact with non-Christian others also informed popular considerations of who was eligible for salvation and who was inevitably damned. In addition, *Othello* negotiated these considerations by drawing playfully upon contemporary ecclesiastical debates. In presupposing the legitimacy of Othello's baptism and then calling his eligibility for redemption into question by depicting his ultimate damnation, the play engages the topical rhetoric of the predestination debates.[75] While I would resist reading *Othello* as a strict allegory of contemporary religious debates, I suggest that the play references debates about predestination as part of its broader exploration of the relationship between physical embodiment and spiritual faith. On the one hand, Shakespeare's representation of a baptized Moor constitutes a powerful testimony to Pauline universalism and its ability to transcend outward difference. On the other hand, the possibility of Othello's inclusion among the Christian elect and the social transgressions it affords him do not go unquestioned in the play, and he is ultimately consigned to a fate of suicide and eternal damnation. That the spiritual sacraments of Othello's baptism and marriage to Desdemona effect an offensive inversion of social and cultural hierarchies is reflected in Brabantio's objection to the marriage: "For if such actions may have passage free, / Bondslaves and pagans shall our statesmen be" (1.2.98–9).

A brief exchange between Cassio and Iago exemplifies how the logic of predestination could be used to challenge universal Pauline grace and narrow the terms of eligibility for salvation. Soon after landing in Cyprus under Othello's command, Cassio draws attention to the possible confusion between social hierarchies on earth and God's determination of who is elect and who is damned. Spurred on by the effects of alcohol, he conflates the two systems of authority:

> Cassio: . . . Well, God's above all, and there be souls must be saved, and there be souls must not be saved.
> Iago: It's true good lieutenant.
> Cassio: For mine own part – no offense to the general, nor any man of quality – I hope to be saved.
> Iago: And so do I too, lieutenant.
> Cassio: Ay, but, by your leave, not before me. The lieutenant is to be saved before the ancient. (2.3.98–106)

Clearly, we are meant to be laughing at Cassio's drunken reasoning, which oversimplifies the doctrine of predestination and confuses it with the military ranking of lieutenant over ancient. But his difficulty in making sense of things also points up the more serious irony of the fact that a black Moor occupies the highest rank of general, and would by Cassio's logic be the first person to get a place in heaven. In drawing attention to the relationship between social hierarchies and those authorized by divine will, Cassio raises questions about Othello's election. Cassio's confusion of social hierarchy with divine will betokens the play's larger ambivalence and discomfort about Othello's status as a Christian. While in one sense, it lines up with Iago's sinful perception that his own relegation to ensign matters more than the eternal destiny of his soul, in another sense, it accords with the resolution of the play, which reveals through Othello's damnation that he could not have been among the elect. In the end, the play realigns social authority with divine authority when, as per Lodovico's order, Othello's "power and command is taken off" and officially transferred to Cassio (5.2.329). By ultimately aligning black skin with damnation, the play rectifies the social inversions enabled by Pauline universalism.

Faith and Female Chastity

Importantly, *Othello* does not attribute the Moor's exclusion from grace directly to his visible difference, but rather to his ultimate lack of faith in Desdemona's fidelity. Thus, Othello's damnation proceeds from his own inability to sustain faith in something invisible and improbable – his wife's chastity. What Othello cannot get past is the possibility that Desdemona can "turn, and turn" (4.1.253) and still remain in outward appearance as white as "snow" (5.2.4). It is not only fitting but instructive that the leap of faith that Desdemona makes, and that Othello cannot make, is measured through an index of chastity, an entity that is fundamentally intangible and beyond assurance, and yet rife with embodied implications. Ironically, it is Othello's own reliance on tangible evidence, or "ocular proof," that seems to reinvest outward appearances with meaning. Though his first instinct is to reject Iago's insinuations that Desdemona has been unfaithful, Othello insists that the dispensation of his mind shall be staked upon visual proof. Thus, he adopts a position that, while appealing to common sense, contradicts the spiritual basis of faith, which eludes all assurances. His desire for proof, in turn, leads him to accept the handkerchief as a physical manifestation of Desdemona's chastity. In contrast, Desdemona persists in loving Othello even after he has visibly shown her reason to withdraw her love. After being physically struck by Othello and called a "whore," Desdemona "kneels" before him and reiterates her unwavering devotion: "Unkindness may do much, / And his unkindness may defeat my life, / But never taint my love" (4.2.161–3). Whereas Othello's faith in Desdemona's love is contingent upon visual proof, her love persists despite the outward evidence of his "unkindness" and demonstrates a faith in him that eludes visual corollary.

Given that the play embraces Desdemona's way of seeing things, Othello is damned not directly because of his outer blackness but because of his inability to sustain faith in Desdemona's intangible faith, or, in other words, for his reliance on outward markers that would in fact attach significance to his own blackness. Ostensibly, the play disavows the value of such outward signs by unabashedly featuring Othello as the object of Desdemona's love and investing in him the very welfare of the Christian state. Othello himself dismisses his own speculation that his blackness or his old age could account for Desdemona's infidelity, scoffing, "yet that's not much" (3.3.270). In addition, the play more generally refutes the authority of outward appearances by emphasizing Iago's deceptive manipulation of the circumstantial evidence that persuades Othello of Desdemona's guilt. In exposing Othello's misguided demand for proof of something that even Iago acknowledges "cannot be seen," the play insists that the only assurance of faith is faith itself. In effect, it punishes those who would require assurance that a black Moor could become Christian, by asserting that such a need is itself evidence of a lack of faith in faith. And yet, the play simultaneously banks on the power of inference to persuade an audience. Othello's private speculation, "haply for I am black," hangs in the air, and, by virtue of the ever-present reminder of his black body, is finally as insuppressible as the materiality of the spotted handkerchief that circulates too freely from place to place (3.3.267).

If the play ultimately elides outward blackness with a lack of faith that renders one too susceptible to visual signs, it gradually imbues female Christian chastity with an unshakable constancy. Iago's determination to "undo [Desdemona's] credit with the Moor," and "turn her virtue into pitch," conflates the process of conversion or exchange with blackening, but in effect what happens is just the opposite: Desdemona's virtue is progressively whitened by the unjust attack (2.3.354–5). Quite simply, the "tragedy" of Desdemona's death hinges directly on the inconvertibility of her chastity. Othello's mistaken charge that Desdemona "can turn and turn, and yet go on / And turn again" invokes the common trope of female sexuality as commodity, but its very inapplicability to Desdemona exposes the unstable and ironic status of her accuser, a Moor with a pronounced history of conversion (4.1.253–4). Hyper-aware of the susceptibility of female sexuality to an economy of exchange, the play holds in tension an implied parallel between female sexual turning and Othello's convertibility, but staunchly resists an equation of the two. If "Moor" is the sign of convertibility in *Othello*, female sexuality is the sign of Christian resistance.

As the following chapters in this book reveal, other early modern plays set in cross-cultural, contested territories of the eastern Mediterranean offer a broader context for reading the significance of Desdemona's chastity. Patterns of gendered resistance in these plays also suggest possibilities for interpreting Desdemona's persecution and murder as triumphant rather than tragic. For example, in the next chapter I demonstrate how the Catholic template of the virgin martyr offered an empowering model of Christian resistance to Islamic persecution because of the way her death through martyrdom constituted resistance rather than capitulation. The virgin martyr's death also underscored her inviolable chastity by providing eternal assurance of her sexual virtue. Although Desdemona's virtue is tied to her married chastity and not to virginity, her partial resonance with this model of resistance may suggest a new way to interpret what many have read as a passive acceptance of her tragic fate. Attracting scorn from feminist critics for her apparent lack of resistance to Othello's abuse in the second half of the play, Desdemona even accepts blame for her own death. In response to Emilia's question of who has killed her, she replies, "Nobody. I myself" (5.2.122). And yet, this somewhat baffling statement of complicity could suggest her willing preference for death over the blackening of her name and her awareness of what it meant to willfully maintain her faith in the face of such persecution. Though Desdemona denounces the unjustness of Cassio's death – "O, falsely, falsely murdered!" (5.2.115) – her stoic acceptance of her own death – "Commend me to my kind lord. O, farewell! (5.2.123)" – suggests a willful act of martyrdom.

Ironically, Desdemona's dead body ensures the triumph of her chastity by lending her faith and innocence a kind of material weight. Othello ensures the integrity of her corpse by vowing, "I'll not shed her blood / Nor scar that whiter skin of hers than snow / And smooth as monumental alabaster" (5.2.3–5). Just as death ensures the virgin martyr's eternal purity, the permanent fixing of Desdemona's body in "monumental alabaster" seals her innocence in stone.[76] Thus, the distinction between the faithful and the faithless is ultimately given assurance in *Othello* through the tangible spectacle of Desdemona's dead body. Moreover, by offering a material index of female chastity that is otherwise immaterial and imperceptible, Desdemona's flesh – "whiter . . . than snow," "smooth as monumental alabaster," and forever "cold, cold" – assumes a certain racial distinction in relation to Othello's outer blackness, even though, in privileging Desdemona's inner vision, the play ostensibly wants to disavow such a distinction.[77] The physical evidence of Othello's inherent damnation emerges in direct, mutual opposition to that of Desdemona's inherent chastity: the whiter and more chaste Desdemona is, the blacker and more damned Othello becomes, and vice versa. Thus, it is by inadvertently rendering both blackness and female chastity visible in opposition to one another that *Othello* pushes faith into a material register, and demonstrates its misgivings about universal Christian fellowship.

Cyprus, the Miracle of Gentile Conversion, and Othello's Damnation

Given *Othello*'s setting in Cyprus, an Ottoman territory that had historically changed hands between Christians and Muslims multiple times, Desdemona's chastity assumes a particular vulnerability that affiliates her with other dramatic heroines whose chastity was under attack in places like Rhodes, Malta, and Tunis.[78] Moreover, Desdemona's persecution and murder by a Moor take on particular significance in relation to the play's contested setting. As Vitkus observes, Othello loosely adapts the story of the Sultan and the Fair Greek, in which the Ottoman siege of Constantinople is followed by the sultan's murder of a fair Christian captive who establishes too threatening a hold over his heart.[79] The wide range of iterations of this story that appeared in print and on the stage during the late sixteenth and early seventeenth centuries establish a clear pattern of linking military imperialism and interracial sexual violence.[80] Like Constantinople, Cyprus was a Christian stronghold and its fall to the Turks was perceived to have devastating symbolic consequences. Cyprus had been under Venetian rule since 1473, but in 1571 Selimus II recaptured the island for the Turks.[81] Venice signed a peace treaty with the Turks in 1573 in which they formally relinquished Cyprus. Despite the fact that Cyprus remained under Ottoman dominion during the time of *Othello*'s initial performance, the play represents it as a Venetian territory. This may reflect a bald fantasy, or, as Horace Howard Furness suggested in his *New Variorum* edition, it may set the action of the play sometime between Venice's conquest of the island in 1473 and the Turks' recapture of it in 1571.[82] Another possibility, suggested by Emrys Jones, is that the play transposes to Cyrus the 1570 Christian naval victory at Lepanto, which King James commemorated in his heroic poem *Lepanto* (1591).[83] Regardless of what Shakespeare had in mind in terms of the temporal setting for *Othello*, however, he clearly departs from all historical accounts in his depiction of the Turks drowning on their way to Cyprus and thus losing the war by default. In effect, the Moor's murder of his Christian wife takes the place of the military battle between Christians and Muslims. Similarly, Shakespeare departs from historical sources in his appointment of a Moor as the leader of the Christian forces in Cyprus, even though it was common for Moorish mercenaries to fight in Christian armies. The poignant irony of Othello's spearheading of the Christian resistance against Islam is certainly enhanced by the possibility of his Muslim or Turkish origins and lends weight to the arguments of Lupton and Vitkus. His position as the Christian general maximizes the stakes of the play's anxious investment in Pauline universalism – holding the possibility that Othello is a sincere and trustworthy convert in tension with the alternative possibility that he is an illegitimate impostor who has dangerously infiltrated the Christian ranks.

For the English, Cyprus was of interest not just because of its symbolic imperial and religious significance but because of its valuable trade. The busy port at Famagusta constituted a rich market and a convenient resting place for ships sailing east on commercial missions or other journeys. Europeans continued to export coveted Cyprian goods even after the island had been repossessed by the Turks. The 1589 edition of Hakluyt's *Principall Nauigations* lists "sumack," "sebesten," and "coloquintida" among the desirable commodities imported from Cyprus.[84] Hakluyt also provides a "list of Christian slaves in the taking of Famagusta," referencing the captives taken by the Turks during the invasion of 1570.[85] As with Ephesus in *The Comedy of Errors*, Cyprus's multiple signification as a site of East-West trade and a site of Ottoman imperial conquest produced a disturbing analogy between exchangeable commodities and convertible souls.

What is more, Cyprus resembled Ephesus through its particular association in the New Testament with Pauline conversion – an association that distinctly illuminates both the miracle of Othello's Christian conversion and the failure of inner sight that prompts his damnation. It was in Cyprus that St. Paul performed his first prominent conversion of a Gentile. As detailed in Acts 13.5–12, Paul visited Cyprus with Barnabas and John when a Roman proconsul called upon them to "heare the worde of God" (13.7). Paul proceeded to teach the proconsul about

Jesus, when a "Jewish sorcerer" named Elymas intervened and tried to "turne away the Deputie from the faith" (13.8). Paul then blinded the sorcerer, and, in turn, the Gentile proconsul was persuaded to convert to Christianity. Thus, the impossibility of the Jewish sorcerer's conversion was set against the miracle of Gentile conversion. It was at this moment (13.9) that Paul, heretofore referred to as Saul, began to be called Paul. St. Paul's momentous conversion of the Gentile proconsul, who, in being made to see the blindness of the Jewish sorcerer, is himself brought into the light, resonates powerfully with Shakespeare's representation of a tragic protagonist whose demand for ocular proof belies an inner blindness. The resonance between Othello and the Jewish sorcerer is further reinforced through Brabantio's charges of witchcraft (1.3.105–7), as well as by Othello's own association of himself with a handkerchief given to his mother by an Egyptian charmer (3.4.58–9, 72). What Shakespeare exposes through Othello's damnation is the impossible conversion that both undoes and sustains Pauline universalism.

Othello's potential connection to witchcraft and to the Jewish sorcerer in Acts 13 may, as Burton argues, constitute a "sign of his irrevocable non-Christian origins," but in other ways this connection may represent a racist judgment by Brabantio, and an internalized racism by Othello, that the play does not necessarily endorse.[86] The difficulty of settling this question points to a larger ambivalence in the play about whether Othello's mortal sin and ultimate damnation result from his victimization by Iago or whether they confirm his identity as an irredeemable infidel. Upon recognizing his error, Othello states that a "demi-devil" has "ensnared [his] soul and body," but is Iago responsible for Othello's damnation or does he merely help to expose Othello's inherent incapacity for Christian faith (5.2.298–9)? On the one hand, Othello undergoes a conversion (or reconversion) at the hands of Iago, but on the other hand, for English Protestants who accepted predestination, Othello's damnation would have had to have been predetermined, and thus could have only confirmed his unalterable status as an irredeemable infidel. Just as the play equivocates about Othello's capacity for Christian conversion, it is unclear about whether its critique of ocular proof is aimed at Othello or at the logic that consigns him to damnation. Leading up to its tragic conclusion, the play seems caught between endorsing the universal sway of Pauline faith and insisting upon a narrower understanding of faith.

Just before committing suicide, Othello offers as clear an insight as any in describing his own understanding of his fall and exclusion from grace. His allusion to his identity as divided between "Venetian" Christian and "turbanned Turk" (5.2.351–2) offers an analogy to the opposition between the converted Gentile proconsul and the inconvertible Jewish sorcerer of Acts 13. It is not so much the specificity of "Christian" and "Turk," "Gentile" and "Jew," that I am interested in here as the way that these terms function as figures of Pauline faith and its limits – the simultaneity of miraculous conversion and certain damnation. Leading up to this moment, Othello instructs Lodovico in how to relate his "unlucky deeds":

> Speak of me as I am. Nothing extenuate,
> Nor set down aught in malice. Then must you speak
>   . . .
>   of one whose hand,
> Like the base Indian, threw a pearl away
> Richer than all his tribe (5.2.340–6)

Critics have noted the difference between the quarto and folio versions of the play, where "Indian" is replaced by "Iudian," and speculated upon the significance of this distinction.[87] By contrast, I am interested in the act performed by this figure – what it means for Othello to compare himself to one who "threw a pearl away / Richer than all his tribe." The act seems to describe both Othello's murder of Desdemona and his rejection of Christian faith. Indeed, Emilia relates Othello's unworthiness of heaven to his unworthiness of Desdemona when she chastises Othello, "This deed of thine is no more worthy heaven / Than thou wast worthy her" (5.2.157–8). The pearl thus connotes Desdemona's innocence and virtue and also alludes to the purity and perfection of heaven symbolized by the "pearl of great price." In the Gospel of Matthew, the kingdom of heaven is compared "to a merchant man, that seketh good perles, Who hauing founde a perle of great price, went and solde all he had, and boght it" (13.45–6). Earlier in his gospel, Matthew addresses the question of proper and improper recipients of Christian faith. He instructs Christ's disciples, "Giue ye not that which is holie, to dogges, nether cast ye your pearles before swine, lest they treade them vnder their feete, and turning againe, all to rent you" (7.6). In light of this precedent, Othello's reference to throwing away the "pearl," as well as his identification with the "circumcised dog," suggest that he recognizes himself to be an inappropriate recipient of the gospel. Whether because of his susceptibility to reconversion or because of the underlying failure of his initial conversion, Othello is excluded from Christian salvation. By virtue of his inability to sustain the faith of his baptism, Othello marks the bodily limits of Christian universalism.

Conclusion: The Unconverted Remainder

Shakespeare's plays reveal the impracticalities of living out universal fellowship in contemporary contexts of religious and economic
rivalry, but I would resist concluding too simply that Shakespeare fails
Paul. Rather, Shakespeare may be said to represent in terms specific to
his own culture an ambivalence inherent in Paul about the persistence
and significance of physical stigmata, whether innate or assumed, and
of unconverted remainders more generally. As Lupton suggests, "While
the general move of the epistles is to dissolve Israel's covenantal bonds,
they nonetheless find a new place in giving linguistic and social groups
coherence within a larger scheme."[88] According to this view, while
Paul dismisses the theological significance of the law, he sanctions its
ethnic or political function: circumcision is no longer a sign of election, but remains as a sign of Jewishness. Critics such as Lupton have
brought into sharper view the persistence of local systems of difference
under Paul's theological universalism by emphasizing messianic continuities and challenging the exegetical closure of Christian typology. As
Kneidel puts it, "The rhetorical occasion of Paul's epistles was not one
of radical or triumphal transformation but of anticipatory or interim
struggle."[89] In drawing attention to the ways that Pauline universalism
undergoes a new struggle in post-Reformation England, Shakespeare
perhaps calls us to the deeper claims of Pauline universalism. He offers
a vision of Christian universalism in which physical badges persist and
continue to hold sway for specific communities and epochs, and in
which the exclusionary significance of these badges continually butts
up against the theological tenet of universalism. More particularly, he
instills with meaning the specific badge of blackness, a badge that is
ambiguously innate and assumed, occupying a fuzzy ground between
biological inheritance and environmental effect. If universalism's reach
is exemplified by its transgression of the limit of what remains possible
– a boundary that it continues to renegotiate by reaching toward the
next level of impossibility – *Othello* locates that limit in the body of
the black Moor. In effect, Shakespeare shows us how the historically
contingent impossibility that threatens Pauline universalism in his own
time was an embodied distinction caught in the process of becoming
racialized.

In exposing this unconverted remainder produced by Christian
universalism in early modern England, Shakespeare represents Paul's
working out of the relationship between universal faith and physical
stigmata in a state of incompletion. Critics have characterized Paul's
unfinished business and its subsequent manifestations in different

ways. Borrowing from Slavoj Žižek, Kneidel usefully suggests that Renaissance writers reveal a "struggling universalism."[90] By contrast, Lupton understands universalism's embrace of Jews and Gentiles as a "death into citizenship," forcing a relinquishment of individual particularity.[91] Agamben considers Paul's messianic implications in terms of time, characterizing messianic time as a period of deferral "between" Jewish and Christian time, the resurrection and the second coming.[92] By contrast, Badiou interprets Pauline universalism as a radical "rupture."[93] In my reading of Shakespeare, universal fellowship represents an impossible ideal – impossible not only because it cannot live in the real world but also because its miraculous potential is evidenced by its very impossibility. What Shakespeare urges us to perceive anew in Paul's theological design is the impossibility of Christian universalism that underlies its possibility. Desdemona's faith in Othello means something precisely because it defies all probability and because of the fact that Othello inevitably forsakes her.

Moreover, Shakespeare exposes Pauline universalism as a system that, like global capitalism, not only conceals its exclusion of others but depends upon these exclusions. In effect, he forces us to apprehend the Jewish sorcerer whose damnation guides the Gentile proconsul into the light, the Turk whose demise brings the Christian into being, the faithless husband whose doubt reveals his wife's undying faith. But in drawing attention to the dialectical relationship between exclusion and universalism, Shakespeare also forces an awareness of the specific historical contexts that animate this relationship. Thus, his revisiting of Paul around the start of the seventeenth century not only illuminates certain struggles inherent in Paul's theology but shows us how these illuminations are fostered by Shakespeare's particular time and place. Amidst the cross-currents of post-Reformation controversies and emerging global trade, the Christianized Moor tests the limits of Pauline universalism. But if Shakespeare's Moor is trapped within the struggling universalism of his time, his very struggle provides a glimpse of potential triumph. In insisting upon the Moor's damnation, Shakespeare also produces a vision of what might be possible in a better world: a black body whose "perfect soul / Shall manifest [him] rightly" (1.2.31–2).

Recycled Models: Catholic Martyrdom and Embodied Resistance to Conversion in *The Virgin Martyr* and Other Red Bull Plays

> I have such terrible fears of being impaled by a Turk.
> WOMAN, Niccolò Machiavelli, *The Mandrake* (1518)

As my discussions of *The Comedy of Errors* and *Othello* illustrate, in the decades surrounding the start of the seventeenth century the popular stage participated in testing the limits of Pauline universalism. Shakespeare's plays explore the implications of an understanding of conversion that both eludes outward marking and overcomes all previous physical and cultural distinctions. Responding to an unstable contemporary religious climate in which commercial and imperial developments also threatened conversions from Christianity, Shakespeare falls back on bodily distinctions to anchor religious differences and to register conversion's embodied effects. This chapter turns to a slightly later time period – the 1620s – after England had established a relatively stable trading presence in the Mediterranean and the threat of conversion to Islam had become a popular theme on the stage. I consider how several early modern plays by Thomas Dekker, Philip Massinger, and Henry Shirley sought to grapple with this contemporary threat by revisiting ancient histories of Christian persecution at the hands of pagans. In evoking correspondences between ancient pagan and contemporary Turkish persecution, these plays demonstrate how Catholic forms of martyrdom and miraculously preserved virginity offered useful models for confronting the contemporary threat. In turn, the particular models of resistance authorized by these plays tell us something about how conversion to Islam was conceived in the popular imagination as an embodied and sexual transformation.

Roughly around the same time that English playwrights were popularizing the adventures of Christian renegades in contemporary Mediterranean settings, the Red Bull Theatre presented a cluster of martyr plays depicting threats of conversion in ancient Cappadocia,

Antioch, Babylon, and Carthage. Three plays in particular – Thomas Dekker and Philip Massinger's *The Virgin Martyr* (1620), Henry Shirley's *The Martyred Soldier* (1619), and the anonymous *Two Noble Ladies and the Converted Conjurer* (1622) – dramatize strategies of Christian resistance to pagan persecution by championing examples of martyrdom. These plays appear to resurrect the legacies and distinct characteristics of Catholic martyrs, while at the same time resonating with contemporary anxieties about Muslim persecution and forced conversion. In this chapter I explore the temporal resonances evoked by these plays, arguing that the reappearance of Catholic martyrs on the English stage speaks to the particular embodied threats associated with conversion to Islam in contemporary Mediterranean contexts. Foregrounding *The Virgin Martyr* in particular, I explore the cultural significance of a heroine who is not only a Catholic martyr but a *virgin* martyr, linking her sexual vulnerability to the specific threats of penetration and bodily contamination associated with conversion to Islam.

While largely neglected by modern critics, Dekker and Massinger's 1620 tragedy *The Virgin Martyr* enjoyed considerable popular success in its time.[1] According to the first quarto's title page, it was "divers times publickely Acted with great Applause, By the seruants of his Maiesties Reuels" at the Red Bull Theatre, and underwent four printings in the seventeenth century as well as a stage revival in 1660.[2] What is striking about the play's popularity is its adaptation of a medieval virgin martyr legend, a genre ostensibly suppressed by the English Reformation. Following attempts in the 1570s by religious authorities to ban the cycles of mystery plays in English towns and cities, most remnants of hagiographical drama had disappeared from the stage.[3] The record of a fee of 40 shillings paid to the Master of the Revels on October 6, 1620, for "new reforming" of the play may reflect its potentially controversial content and offers a reminder of the formal scrutiny that forced London playwrights to comply with official church doctrine.[4]

The small body of critics who have addressed the play over the past fifty years either focus, like Louise Clubb (1964), on the striking anomaly of its apparent Catholic content or else attempt, like Peter Mullany (1970), Larry Champion (1984), and Jose M. Ruano de la Haza (1991), to explain away this content by emphasizing the play's iconoclastic elements or arguing that its religious categories are mere "pretext" for "a simple and clear struggle between good and evil."[5] But despite these scattered attempts to raise or refute the question of *The Virgin Martyr*'s Catholic affinities, the question remains largely unanswered: what accounts for the dramatic appeal in 1620 of a Catholic virgin martyr? Or more specifically, what is appealing at this time about a martyr whose religious constancy is signified through her bodily resistance to torture and, above all, through the preservation of her virginity? Leaving aside the obvious, though admittedly complex, explanation of persisting Catholic sympathies in Protestant England, this chapter accounts for the significance of *The Virgin Martyr*'s particular representation of martyrdom by taking a broader, more global view of the political and religious threats that surrounded its production.

I want to suggest that the appeal of virgin martyrdom and its emphasis upon physical inviolability can be better appreciated in light of England's increased commercial engagement with the Ottoman empire during the early seventeenth century and the particular anxieties the English stage began to attach to the threat of Islamic conversion. As I discussed in the Introduction, the Ottoman empire's commercial and imperial dominance registered in threatening ways for the English during a period when they began to rely increasingly on eastern Mediterranean trade and to imagine themselves as a tiny player in an international arena of commerce and power. Popular English discourses represented the Turkish threat as a threat of conversion or of "turning Turk" – a phenomenon that constituted both a genuine predicament for Christian seamen who were captured by Turks and an imaginative theme or trope on the London stage. *The Virgin Martyr* is roughly contemporary with several plays that overtly thematize Christian resistance to turning Turk, including Robert Daborne's *A Christian Turned Turke* (c.1610), John Fletcher, Nathan Field, and Philip Massinger's *The Knight of Malta* (c.1618), and Massinger's *The Renegado* (c.1624). As detailed through my analysis of *A Christian Turned Turke* in the Introduction, the sexual act that facilitates conversion to Islam seals its tragic and irreversible stakes. If in each of these plays conversion to Islam carries this sexualized connotation, its resistance is modeled through the constancy of a Christian virgin who remains chaste despite her relentless pursuit by lustful Turks and the doubts of her Christian brothers. These plays' mediation of conversion through a register of sexuality reflects a nexus of cultural and bodily transformation that was bound up with the threat of turning Turk. In positing a direct relationship between sexual intercourse and turning Turk, the Renaissance stage implied a form of conversion that was manifested through the sexualized body and that approximated a threat of reproductive contamination, or what we now refer to as racial miscegenation.[6]

The stage's overdetermination of sexual contact as the conduit for Islamic conversion suggests a convergence of cultural and bodily, and religious and proto-racial, differences that distinguished turning Turk from other threats of religious conversion. In turn, dramatic depictions of Christian-Muslim conflict indicated both the theater's reliance on prior templates for Christian resistance to religious persecution, and its refiguring of these templates to address what was perceived to be a new, embodied and sexualized threat. While *The Virgin Martyr* does not overtly feature Turks or Islamic conversion, its particular representation of Christian resistance in the form of bodily inviolability assumes a new currency in the face of the Ottoman threat, and reveals an implicit correspondence between the medieval tradition of vowed virginity and contemporary strategies for imagining resistance to turning Turk. In effect, *The Virgin Martyr*'s idealization of its heroine's physical, and distinctly sexual, integrity recuperates and makes visible the medieval Catholic models that inform contemporary dramatizations of resistance to Islam.

By depicting the pagan persecution of Christians as an occasionally transparent screen for Turkish persecution, *The Virgin Martyr* effects a layering of different temporal moments. For example, Dekker and Massinger's choice of setting highlights a potential correspondence between the persecution of early Christians in the Roman empire and the contemporary persecution of Christians in the Ottoman empire. Caesarea in Cappadocia, the site of Dorothea the heroine's martyrdom, lay in the heart of what was at the time of the play's production the territory of the Ottoman empire (central Turkey, north and slightly east of Cyprus) (see Figure 2.1).[7]

Of the hundreds of saints' tales that Dekker and Massinger could have chosen to adapt, the majority are set not in the East but in Rome, the imperial capital of the Roman empire.[8] But if Christian persecution in Cappadocia registers the more immediate threat of the Turk, it does so not as a mere displacement but rather as a pointed reminder of a long history of Christian resistance based on martyrdom. Just as John Foxe's *Book of Martyrs* uses the larger context of church history to situate sixteenth-century Protestant martyrdom, *The Virgin Martyr* appropriates the history of early Christian persecution so as to construct a viable model of resistance to the contemporary Turkish threat. In addition, the play demonstrates through gender differences how this contemporary model of resistance is both physically and culturally constituted, in that female virginity also serves in the play as a model for the cultivation of voluntary male chastity and civility. After observing Dorothea's example, her pagan suitor Antoninus converts to Christianity and is properly armed to resist the forces of pagan persecution in a Christian manner. By contrasting Antoninus's acquired Christian civility and self-restraint with the ruthless and lustful manners of the pagans, the play

Figure 2.1: A map from the Geneva Bible showing Cappadocia, which can
be located below the number 69 from the top of the map, under Galatia. "The
Description of the Contreis and Places Mencioned in the Actes of the Apostles," from
The Bible and Holy Scriptures . . . [Geneva Bible] (London, 1560). Reproduced by
permission of the Rare Book and Manuscript Library, University of Pennsylvania
Libraries.

draws a distinction between Christian and pagan identity that I will
argue is directly relevant to contemporary English efforts to construct a
self-identity in opposition to the Turk.

The Legend of St. Dorothy

Dekker and Massinger's popular play was based on the medieval
legend of St. Dorothy, which originated around the late seventh
century.[9] Although Dorothy was believed to have suffered martyrdom
during the Diocletian persecutions on February 6, 304, her legend like
that of many other virgin martyrs of the third and early fourth centuries did not emerge until the Middle Ages. By far the most significant
source of the legend's dissemination was the Dominican friar Jacobus

de Voragine's *Legenda aurea*, which appeared in more than 150 editions between 1470 and 1500. Dorothy's legend was not included in Jacobus's original *Legenda aurea*, compiled between 1252 and 1260, but was added by a later author or authors and extensively reproduced in many vernacular renderings. As Karen Winstead has shown, the virgin martyr legend was an enormously popular genre whose readership extended from clerics and anchoresses to lay provincial audiences over the course of the Middle Ages.[10] Dekker and Massinger likely relied on a version of Dorothy's story from one of three prominent English translations available in the early modern period: Osbern Bokenham's *Legendys of Hooly Wummen*, written in 1447; William Caxton's *The Golden Legend*, published in 1483, 1503, and 1527; and Alfonso Villegas's popular *Flos Sanctorvm* (known in England as *The Lives of Saints*), anonymously translated into English and printed at Douai in 1609.[11]

Several defining details continue to be attached to Dorothy's story as it passed through the late Middle Ages. She is born and secretly baptized in Caesarea, Cappadocia, after her parents flee from Rome and the brutal persecution of Christians under the emperors Diocletian and Maximian. As a young woman, her exceptional beauty inflames the love of the prefect of Caesarea, but she staunchly refuses him and publicly maintains that she is the bride of Christ. She spurns the pagan gods and refuses to convert from Christianity. In return, she is repeatedly tortured by hot oil, starvation, iron hooks, beatings, and the merciless burning of her breasts. After emerging from all of these tortures unharmed, Dorothy is sentenced to death by decapitation. Her two sisters, now apostates from Christianity, are sent to plead with her, but she instead reconverts them, and they are ruthlessly executed by the prefect. On the way to her own execution, Dorothy's unwavering faith is mocked by a scribe named Theophilus, who asks her to send some roses and apples from the garden of her spouse, Christ. Shortly after Dorothy's execution, Theophilus is visited by a fair, curly-haired child dressed in a purple garment, from whom he receives the very basket of roses and apples he had requested of Dorothy. Theophilus is immediately converted to Christianity and goes on to help convert most of the city before he too is martyred under the pagan prefect.

Post-Reformation Context

As I have begun to suggest, Dekker and Massinger's dramatic adaptation of this Catholic legend in post-Reformation England is itself a unique and remarkable development. Although hundreds of hagiographical plays were performed on the Spanish stage between 1580 and 1680, *The Virgin Martyr* was quite possibly the last Catholic saint's play performed in England during this period. The play's faithfulness to many elements of the medieval legend of St. Dorothy, including her inviolable virginity, the manner of her torture and execution, and the basket of fruit containing a cross of flowers that she sends to Theophilus, indicate that the play is not wholly evacuated of its original (Catholic) content. Its valorization of female virginity is all the more striking given the strong cultural mandates against vowed celibacy in Protestant England.[12] Despite the cultural valuation of premarital chastity in early modern England, lifelong celibacy (particularly against the pressure to marry) carried negative associations with Catholic religious orders. Of course, Queen Elizabeth's virginity offered a prominent exception, though even her exceptionalism was tainted by a degree of popular controversy and doubt.

The more likely explanation for *The Virgin Martyr*'s popular success is not a sudden, renewed interest in the forced conversion and martyrdom of early virgin saints, but the play's resonance with contemporary concerns about religious conversion in the same geographical territory.[13] As Robert Brenner has argued, English commerce underwent a shift in emphasis from cloth exports to luxury imports in the late sixteenth and early seventeenth centuries due to a new and growing demand for silks, spices, and currants obtained from Mediterranean trade routes.[14] While developments such as the collapse of the Antwerp and Iberian entrepôts opened up English access to the eastern and southern markets, English traders confronted numerous dangers and uncertainties in the largely unpoliced waters of the Mediterranean and its religiously and ethnically mixed trading ports, many of which were under the control of the Ottoman empire. Multiple entries in the *Calendar of State Papers Domestic* in James's reign suggest that acts of piracy committed by Turks and the related capture and conversion of English seamen were of particular and grave concern to the British government around the time of *The Virgin Martyr*'s performance.[15] An entry on May 15, 1622, describes a request made by "Merchants of the several trading companies" in consideration of recent propositions made by Thomas Roe, the English ambassador to Turkey, for the suppression of pirates: "Think the captives taken lately should be redeemed by treaty, but owing to the decay of trade, it is impossible to raise another contribution for suppressing pirates. Think the trade may be better secured if the ships going southward sailed together in fleets."[16] Numerous similar entries attest to the need to negotiate the dual and often conflicting imperatives of maintaining access to the southeastern markets and combating Turkish capture.

Conversion and the "Adventure Play"

As we have seen, the threat of conversion confronted by thousands of English merchants and seamen in the late sixteenth and early seventeenth centuries constituted a complexly imagined theme on the Renaissance stage. In *Turning Turk: English Theater and the Multicultural Mediterranean, 1570–1630*, Daniel Vitkus analyzes some of the ways that anxieties associated with England's expanding Mediterranean commerce informed theatrical representations of Christian adventurers and their particular vulnerabilities to conversion.[17] These dramatic representations emerged, according to Jean Howard, within the context of a new genre of "adventure plays" featuring the travails of European pirates and privateers in southern and eastern Mediterranean port cities like Tunis, Fez, and Antioch.[18] Plays such as *The Famous History of Sir Thomas Stukeley* (1596), *The Fair Maid of the West, Part I* (c.1604), *Fortune By Land and Sea* (c.1609), and *A Christian Turned Turke* (c.1610) celebrate the exploits of swashbuckling renegade heroes, while also setting them in implicit opposition to a recuperative model of gentility, distinguished not by wealth or title but by English civility and self-control. While the renegade hero manifested the excitement of English privateering and imperial fantasies, he also evoked anxieties about cross-cultural commerce and the unstable identity of the English privateer. For example, as Barbara Fuchs has argued, the renegade hero revealed the fuzzy distinction between "categories of licit and illicit commerce" through his resemblance to Turkish and Spanish pirates and his susceptibility to material and bodily temptations that made him a prime candidate for conversion.[19]

Plays like John Day, William Rowley, and George Wilkins's *The Travails of the Three English Brothers* (c.1607) offer a corrective alternative to the swashbuckling renegade by characterizing the Shirley brothers as gentleman adventurers – perfect English models of moral and physical restraint. The female protagonist of Heywood's earlier *The Fair Maid of the West, Part I* suggests a way in which the English adventure hero might be cultivated according to a model of feminine virtue and chastity.[20] Thus, in various ways the early seventeenth-century adventure drama forged a recuperative link between English gentility and physical self-control that protected the adventuring hero against moral deterioration and conversion. This link between cultural and bodily control prefigures the sexual terms through which conversion is conceived in later dramas of the 1610s and 1620s, such as *A Christian Turned Turke* and *The Renegado*, in which sexual and spiritual transgressions are explicitly conflated. Dekker and Massinger's *The Virgin Martyr* resonates with this evolving generic tradition, and demonstrates through Dorothea's spiritually and bodily constituted chastity an empowering model of resistance to the contemporary Ottoman threat.

While foregrounding an earlier history of religious persecution set within the territory of the Roman empire, *The Virgin Martyr* exhibits numerous trappings of the adventure play. Whereas, for example, the Cappadocian geography of Dorothy's legend is located inland from the Mediterranean by about 150 miles and is completely landlocked, it is represented in the play as an active port city. The Caesarean governor invokes the vulnerability of port cities to invasion or escape when he rallies his captain of the guards in anticipation of the Roman emperor Diocletian's visit: "Keepe the ports close, and let the guards be doubl'd, / Disarme the Christians, call it death in any / To weare a sword, or in his house to haue one" (1.1.75–7). In this way, the play characterizes Caesarea in ways that liken it to the Mediterranean port cities of Tunis and Algiers, which dominated the adventure drama and functioned as centers of intercultural trade between Christians and Turks (as well as Jews and Moors). These port cities along the Barbary coast were liminal and unstable places where Christian capture and enslavement were always possibilities. As discussed in the Introduction, the plight of early modern Christians captured by Turks became known to the English not only through popular drama but also through news pamphlets and travel narratives, as well as through prayers and collections directed toward the rescue of enslaved Christians.[21]

In *The Virgin Martyr*, the presence of a slave from Brittaine – summoned by his pagan captors to rape Dorothea – resonates with the contemporary captivity of British subjects in the Ottoman empire, while simultaneously recalling Britain's past colonization by ancient Rome. The chief pagan persecutor's subsequent instructions to release the Christian prisoners invoke the "trauaile" associated with Mediterranean travel and captivity:

> Haste then to the port,
> You shall there finde two tall ships ready rig'd,
> In which embarke the poore distressed soules
> And beare them from the reach of tyranny,
> Enquire not whither you are bound, the deitie
> That they adore will giue you prosperous winds,

And make your voyage such, and largely pay for
Your hazard, and your trauaile. (5.2.74–81)

Theophilus's direct reference to "the port" and "two tall ships" again suggests Caesarea's conflation with the port cities popularized through the adventure drama. The Christian prisoners' escape from "the reach of tyranny" also invokes the contemporary plight of Christian captives enslaved by the tyrannical Turk. And Theophilus's reference to "hazard" and "trauaile" in the last line employs terminology commonly used to describe the danger and toil associated with sailing along the Barbary coast. The early modern interchangeability of "trauaile" (carrying the sense of "toil or labor") and "travel" (referring to "journeying or a journey") reflects the personal dangers that early modern English seamen confronted in the unpoliced, intercultural spaces of the Mediterranean.

At times, *The Virgin Martyr*'s subtle conflations of pagan conversion and the contemporary threat of turning Turk virtually efface the ancient context. For example, Hircius and Spungius, Dorothea's two disloyal servants, bear a striking resemblance to the clownish renegades of the adventure drama who display a propensity for turning motivated not by faith or persecution, but by carnal appetites and material greed. While obedience to parents and the law are offered as the chief motivations for pagan conversion in the tradition of the virgin martyr legend, carnal temptations and material incentives prompt the conversion of early modern renegades in the adventure drama. Hircius and Spungius, who are not present in any of the play's medieval sources, invert the notion of a spiritually and bodily constituted chastity, in that they are spiritually and bodily debased. Their physical lust and lack of restraint is advertised through their very names: Hircius is a "whoremaster" and Spungius a "drunkard." Spungius reveals his shallow allegiances when he says, "I am resolued to haue an Infidels heart, though in shew I carry a Christians face" (2.1.47–8). This disjunction between inner faith and outer show reappears as a persistent theme and source of anxiety in plays about Christians turning Turk.

We encounter another temporal slippage in *The Virgin Martyr*'s frequent allusions to circumcision and castration in relation to conversion – an association absent in medieval narratives of pagan conversion, but often played to comic effect in the turning Turk dramas.[22] That Islamic conversion was inextricably linked with the permanent mark of circumcision – and conflated with castration – in the English imagination underscores its conception as a bodily conversion. In *The Virgin Martyr*, Spungius and Hircius's dialogue is peppered with references to the status of the foreskin as an indicator of religious faith, such as the one contained in Spungius's oath: "As I am a Pagan, from my cod-peece downward" (2.1.75). The following exchange in which Spungius and Hircius are first introduced to the audience bears no affinity to the medieval virgin martyr legend but could easily be lifted from an adventure play set in a contemporary Mediterranean port:

> Spung. Turne Christian, wud he that first tempted mee
>   to haue my shooes walk vpon Christian
>   soles, had turn'd me into a Capon, for I am sure now the
>   stones of all my pleasure in this fleshly life are cut off.
>
> Hirc.   So then, if any Coxecombe has a galloping de-
>   sire to ride, heres a Gelding, if he can but sit him. (2.1.1–6)

Spungius and Hircius's frequent allusions to circumcision and castration in *The Virgin Martyr* frame the story of Dorothy's martyrdom – or her refusal to convert – with the contemporary threat of conversion associated with Muslims and Jews. Their comical collapsing of the distinction between circumcision and castration draws upon an established trope of the Mediterranean adventure drama. In addition, they capitalize upon the adventure drama's frequent association of Islamic conversion with buggery, an association informed by stereotypes about Muslim sexual perversity as well as by the assumption that circumcision, and its slippery relationship to castration, opened one up to anal penetration. By conflating religious circumcision with the eunuchs known to serve in Turkish palaces, the trope also offered a way of emasculating non-Christian men as well as the Christian renegades who converted to Islam. *The Renegado*'s Carazie, for instance, is revealed to be a former Englishman who was captured by Turks and castrated in order to serve as a eunuch in the royal palace. His role as the Muslim princess's bedfellow convinces the foolish Christian servant Gazet to volunteer to become a eunuch as well. Similarly, the clownish Clem of Thomas Heywood's *The Fair Maid of the West, Part I* becomes the butt of jokes when he undergoes conversion and castration to improve his social status, whereas John Ward's implied circumcision in *A Christian Turned Turke* helps to convey the gravity and irredeemability of his transgression. In *The Virgin Martyr*, references to castration are relegated to the comic realm, far removed from the grave repercussions of Ward's conversion or the ancient significance of circumcision associated with Christianized Jews. But in other ways, the play confuses its contexts. Spungius's comparison of being "turn'd into a Capon" and "walk[ing] vpon Christian soles" seems to associate circumcision with Christianity, which in the context of first-century Christianized Jews (predating the fourth-century setting of the play) might have made sense; yet the fact that such a prospect represents something highly unappealing to Spungius aligns it with the contemporary threat of turning Turk and the compulsory circumcision/castration undergone by Christian characters in other Mediterranean adventure plays.

As is also the case with the renegade clowns of the adventure drama, the comic vacillations of Spungius and Hircius point up the difference between the tangible mark of circumcision/castration and the always unverifiable nature of sincere religious conversion. Bemoaning the fact that becoming a Christian has meant relinquishing pleasures of the flesh, Spungius exclaims that he might as well have been castrated. Hircius then suggests that he's ready for action if any man happens to want "to ride . . . a gelding." His easy transposition of Spungius's figurative reference into a literal understanding of castration points to the comical problems created by the serial backsliding of these clown figures and the contrasting permanence of circumcision or castration. As Holly Crawford Pickett has insightfully argued, the play's mockery of Spungius and Hircius offers a commentary on "the [domestic] crisis instigated by multiple apostasy and the attendant questions of the proper roles of reason and theatricality within conversion"; as she observes, "Dorothea's low-life servants . . . convert, unconvert, reconvert, and half-convert a dizzying eight times between them in the course of the play."[23] In a sense, these characters' crude opposing of sexual pleasure to castration, mediated across a boundary of religious conversion, exposes the logic that motivates their repeated confessional shifts. Similarly, in the turning Turk dramas, clown figures are drawn to Islamic conversion because they overvalue and misread the meaning of castration, interpreting the prospect of becoming a eunuch as a promotion in social status or an easy way of gaining sexual access to the Sultan's harem. Like Spungius and Hircius they invert the significance of religious conversion by reducing it to the cut of castration, which they understand in purely sexual terms. And in similar ways, the adventure plays depict castration as a permanent punishment for submitting to conversion for the wrong reasons, branding the serial convert with a mark that cannot be undone.

On another level *The Virgin Martyr*'s setting in Cappadocia invoked a biblical association with circumcision because of its proximity to Galatia, where Paul wrote his letter to the Galatians. As I discussed in Chapter 1, Paul chastises the Galatians for their strict adherence to Jewish laws and in particular for their undue emphasis on circumcision, arguing that these outward rituals created a false distinction between Jewish followers of Christ and converted Gentiles who were not circumcised. Alternately, the possibility that Dekker and Massinger were confusing Caesarea, Cappadocia, where Dorothea's medieval legend is set, with another Caesarea – on the coast of Palestine – links the play to another biblical site where circumcision was fiercely debated. Peter's conversion of a Roman centurion named Cornelius in the Acts of the Apostles leads to a heated controversy about the eligibility of uncircumcised Gentiles for Christian conversion (Acts 10–11). Whether consciously enacted or not, Dekker and Massinger's possible conflation of the two Caesareas in *The Virgin Martyr* reinforces the biblical significance of the setting as a place where questions about the nature of faith, bodily difference, and conversion were of particular concern.

Protestant Valences, Catholic Embodiment

Given the multilayered geographical and religious context I have been discussing for *The Virgin Martyr*, critical interpretations that stress only the play's relationship to a Catholic-Protestant binary opposition seem inadequate. And yet it is important to recognize the extent to which the play engages Reformation polemic by refiguring its Catholic source materials to ally Dorothea with Protestantism and her pagan persecutors with Catholicism. Susannah Brietz Monta demonstrates the presence of "competing martyrdoms" generated by Catholic-Protestant competition, and, echoing Julia Gasper, argues that the play should be read as Protestant propaganda aimed at critiquing England's abandonment of Continental Protestants at the outbreak of the Thirty Years War.[24] In several crucial ways, the play refigures its Catholic source to align Dorothea with Protestantism and her pagan prosecutors with Catholicism. For example, the pagans are repeatedly demonized for their tendency to worship images and statues of false gods, whereas Dorothea consistently repudiates this practice like a good Protestant iconoclast. A particularly transparent example of how the Christian-pagan opposition maps onto the debate around idolatry occurs when Caliste and Christeta, two pagan maidens, are sent to sway Dorothea from her Christian faith. In response to their testimony to the "pleasure" and "prosperity" promised by their pagan gods, whom they "worship . . . in their images," Dorothea offers a parable that exposes the folly of worshipping material forms (3.1.162). She narrates a trajectory by which the "richest Iewels and purest gold" taken from matrons' necks are reformed into a religious "Idoll" and then into a "basing" for washing a concubine's feet, before being transformed again into the form of the god (3.1.167–82). In demonstrating the fungibility of materials used to make religious idols, Dorothea exposes the folly of equating material substances with anything bearing godly powers.

The Virgin Martyr evokes an additional Protestant valence through its immediate resonance with the powerful martyrological tradition established through John Foxe's *Book of Martyrs*. First published in 1563 and available in six editions by 1610, Foxe's compilation provided a contextual framework for reading Christian martyrdom in Reformation terms. Significantly, the first book of the *Book of Martyrs*, entitled in the 1570 edition "The state of the primitive churche compared with this latter church of Rome," is devoted to the ten persecutions of the "primitive" church, including the final persecution of Christians under Diocletian and Maximian.[25] Toward the end of this section, St. Dorothy's name is briefly included in a long list of other martyrs; she appears in the same manner in all editions of Foxe, and this is the extent of her inclusion in the text. As Foxe explains, the abbreviated treatment of Dorothy and other early Christian martyrs (who were so celebrated by the medieval virgin martyr legends) reflects his disdain for the supposed "fabulous inventions" and "superstitious deuotion" of Catholic saints' lives.[26] Nevertheless, in presenting "the state of the primitive church" as a precursor or model for understanding the subsequent persecutions enacted by the "latter church of Rome," Foxe proposes the same link between early Christian persecution and the Catholic persecution of Protestants implicitly presented in *The Virgin Martyr*. In other words, the use of early Christian persecution to frame contemporary religious threats was already familiar to early modern audiences through the wide circulation of the *Book of Martyrs*.[27]

But if *The Virgin Martyr*'s Protestant coherences help to mollify potential objections to the post-Reformation dramatization of a Catholic saint's legend, they do not fully characterize the play's content. Rather, Dekker and Massinger's adaptation of Dorothy's martyrdom insists upon retaining the bodily emphasis of its medieval sources - exemplified through Dorothea's physical virginity and her miraculous imperviousness - suggesting that her Protestant disdain for material forms and matters of the flesh may be literally less than skin deep. The play's insistence on Dorothea's inviolable body, I argue, prevails in the face of the spiritualizing, or dematerializing, influences of Protestant reform and constitutes a form of resistance warranted by the bodily threat of conversion associated with turning Turk. Identifying *The Virgin Martyr*'s complex negotiation of both Catholic and Protestant templates reveals the significance of its distinct strategy of bodily resistance. As both Monta and Huston Diehl have observed, narratives of Protestant martyrdom, themselves, do not emerge in a vacuum but were self-consciously linked to the earlier genre of the medieval saint's tale.[28] Diehl argues that Foxe "appropriates the images and forms of the medieval past only to subvert and reinterpret them" and suggests that his strategy of differentiating Protestantism from Catholicism is dialectic, rather than oppositional.[29] This process of dialectical appropriation and refiguration, which I uncover in the early seventeenth-century invention of a sexually chaste and physically inviolable heroine, is useful for understanding how the relationship between constancy of spirit and physical torture in Foxe differs from its representation in the medieval Catholic tradition.

Torture in Protestant and Catholic Martyrological Traditions

In Foxe, the martyr's resistance to torture is meant to show how the physical and spiritual are distinct: the inner, spiritual self remains untouched regardless of what happens to the body. For example, after Anne Askew is tortured on the rack, she describes herself as "nigh dead" and must be "laid in a bed with as weary and painfull bones as ever had pacient Job"; but despite her physical suffering and the threat of being sent to Newgate, she tells the Lord Chancellor, "I wold rather die, than to breake my faith."[30] In contrast to Foxe's martyrs, the medieval virgin's resistance to physical torture conveys the inviolable nature of her body itself. The miraculous restoration of her physical perfection, rather than the endurance of a separate spiritual self, is the point. In other words, the physical itself constitutes the sign of constancy, rather than being evidence that spiritual constancy endures even when the physical is violated.[31] John Bale's introduction to his edition of *The first examinacyon* of Anne Askew (1546) exemplifies this distinction by paralleling Askew's constancy with a "lyke faythfull" woman named Blandina, who was martyred at Lyons in the year 177.[32] The comparison is intended to illuminate Askew's ties to an older tradition of martyrdom; however, the subtle differences between Askew and Blandina are just as revealing. In response to torture from their persecutors, "Blandina never fainted in torment. No more ded Anne Askewe in sprete."[33] Whereas Blandina exemplifies her faith and virtue through bodily resilience, Askew does so through strength of spirit.

A striking difference exists between the primary methods of torture depicted in Foxe and in the virgin martyr legends. By far the most common method of torture and execution described in the *Book of Martyrs* is burning, an act given iconic emphasis through numerous woodcut illustrations of martyrs engulfed in flames. According to Diehl,

Figure 2.2: "The burning of Rawlins White, Martyr," from John Foxe, *Acts and monuments* (London, 1610). Reproduced by permission of the Massachusetts Center for Interdisciplinary Renaissance Studies.

Figure 2.3: Torture of St. Lucy, from Jacobus de Voragine, *Legenda aurea* (France, s. XIII^ex), MS HM 3027, f. 4v. Reproduced by permission of the Huntington Library, San Marino, California.

the repetition of enflamed bodies in Foxe's commissioned illustrations discourages idolatry and disrupts the devotional gaze by encouraging readers to apprehend martyrdom through the interplay of text and image. In addition, as James Knapp has argued, the iconic repetition in Foxe of the immolation of martyred bodies pointedly diverges from the "universal or typological illustrations" associated with Catholic martyrologies, and emphasizes "not their suffering" or the distinct manner of their deaths, but the Protestant martyrs' "commitment to Christian practice."[34] According to the *OED*, "martyr" became specifically associated with "death by fire" only after the Reformation (and probably as a consequence of Foxe).[35]

By contrast, the bodies of Catholic virgin martyrs are rarely ignited by fire but frequently pierced, penetrated, and dismembered, as well as threatened with rape. The tortures of St. Lucy and St. Euphemia from Jacobus's *Legenda aurea* (Figures 2.3 and 2.4) depict the saints being penetrated through the midsection by a long sword.

Similarly, Antonio Gallonio's *Trattato de gli instrumenti di martyrio*, a post-Reformation Catholic martyrology published in Rome for a Continental audience in 1591, features forty engravings of Catholic martyrs being penetrated by sharp instruments, beaten with cudgels, subjected to the amputation of tongues, breasts, and limbs, stripped and affixed to crosses and wheels, and dragged through the streets by horses

Figure 2.4: Torture of St. Euphemia, from Jacobus de Voragine, *Legenda aurea* (France, s. XIII[ex]), MS HM 3027, f. 128r. Reproduced by permission of the Huntington Library, San Marino, California.

(see Figures 2.5 and 2.6).[36] Though the martyrs' bodies are pierced, penetrated, dismembered, strung up, beaten, broiled, stretched, and dragged, their faces betray a peaceful countenance.[37] In the Catholic tradition, the only thing that bears a permanent physical effect on the martyrs is the final death blow, and even in the moment of death, their bodies often remain unscarred.

The Spectacle of Violence

Revealing her ties to the Catholic martyrological tradition, Dorothea in *The Virgin Martyr* is constantly threatened with physical torture, as well as dragged by her hair, tied to a pillar and beaten, and finally beheaded. A distinctive element of this violence is its enactment upon a body that is completely inert, vulnerable, often restrained by cords or other contraptions, and yet of a physical materiality and integrity that persist beyond all efforts to undo them. Despite their increasing exertions, Dorothea's persecutors find that torture has no effect on her body. They marvel that with every blow, "her face / Has more bewitching beauty than before" (4.2.94–5), and question whether the "bridge of her nose" is "full of iron worke" (4.2.98) or the cudgels being used against her are "counterfeit" (4.2.99). Rather than beg for mercy,

Figure 2.5: Christian Martyrs, from Antonio Gallonio, *Trattato de gli instrumenti di martyrio* (Rome, 1591), sig. H2r. Reproduced by permission of the Henry Charles Lea Library, University of Pennsylvania Libraries.

Figure 2.6: Christian Martyrs, from Antonio Gallonio, *Trattato de gli instrumenti di martyrio* (Rome, 1591), 119. Reproduced by permission of the Henry Charles Lea Library, University of Pennsylvania Libraries.

Dorothea patiently endures and even welcomes the torture inflicted upon her. After receiving a sentence of death, she remarks,

> The visage of a hangman frights not me;
> The sight of whips, rackes, gibbets, axes, fires

Are scaffoldings, by which my soule climbes vp
To an Eternall habitation. (2.3.166–9)

The metaphor of her soul climbing up to heaven via "scaffoldings" composed of torture devices figures the soul as a physical entity and reinforces an affinity between body and spirit. Indeed it is quite likely that the ladder used for Dorothea's execution was the same stage prop used to represent her physical ascent into heaven. Thus, *The Virgin Martyr* sets up an understanding of spiritual faith and salvation that is inseparable from the physical: the soul depends on the physical violence inflicted on the body in order to make its way to heaven. Even the word "habitation," used to describe the soul's final destination, suggests a physical space.[38] Furthermore, the various torture devices that Dorothea lists – "whips, rackes, gibbets, axes, fires" – conjure images of violence that have a strong visceral connotation, recalling the Catholic instruments of the passion. In this way, they are quite unlike the almost exclusive use of fire that obliterates Protestant bodies in Foxe. The play references such instruments of torture a second time when, following Theophilus's conversion, he requests that the "thousand engines / Of studied crueltie" that he has been storing in his own house be seized and used against him (5.2.182–3). He even begs to be allowed to "feele / As the Sicilian did his brazen bull," referencing one of the same cruel devices pictured in Gallonio's Counter-Reformation martyrology (5.2.184–5).[39]

The bodily emphasis of Catholic martyrdom resonates with the performance of Christ's passion in the medieval mystery plays and with narratives of host desecration.[40] The inviolable virgin's body, the crucifixion of Christ, and the bleeding host are deeply powerful precisely because they epitomize presence and wholeness – a melding of body and spirit that bespeaks holiness – while perhaps simultaneously concealing an anxiety about physical absence or lack. The broader Christian resonance of Dorothea's torture is reinforced in *The Virgin Martyr* by the fact that it is carried out by her former servants, Hircius and Spungius, who have turned apostate against her. Upon being confronted with her tormenters, Dorothea exclaims,

You two! whom I like fosterd children fed,
And lengthen'd out your starued life with bread:
You be my hangmen! whom when vp the ladder
Death hald you to be strangled, I fetcht downe,
Clothd you, and warmed you, you two my tormenters. (4.2.79–83)

Just as the conventional stripping and torturing of the virgin martyr recalls the mutilation of Christ's naked body, this scene evokes Christ's crucifixion, wherein Christ sacrifices his flesh to save the souls of those who have sinned against him. Dorothea's identification of her crucifiers as "foster children" suggests a number of possible connotations, including Christ's betrayal by Judas and by Peter, his betrayal by the Jews and converted Gentiles of Israel, and perhaps most tantalizingly, the Christian view of Islam as an illegitimate offspring of Christianity. The comedic status of Dorothea's tormenters complicates these connotations, in one sense mocking the serious portrayal of Christ's passion in the medieval Catholic tradition, but in other ways replicating equivocations inherent to the Corpus Christi plays about the presence or absence of Christ's body.[41] In addition, the potential comedy of the scene mitigates the violence done to Dorothea's body, while at the same time underscoring the play's investment in her embodied virtue by refusing to subject her to more efficacious blows.

What is more, the play preserves Dorothea's bodily integrity by suggesting that she is protected from harm by "divine powers" (4.2.85). Though she welcomes the tortures, saying, "tyrants strike home / And feast your fury full" (4.2.92–3), her tormentors' blows are miraculously deprived of any effects. As Nova Myhill argues, Dorothea's imperviousness to the torture calls attention to the "counterfeit" theatrical nature of the spectacle, which the play pits against the generic conventions of martyrdom that insist upon the true miracle of her physical resilience.[42] I would argue that the combined effects of the comedic tormentors, the scene's self-reflexive theatricality, and the representation of an authentic miracle also serve to sustain a tension between the threat of bodily penetration and the comforting assurance that Christian resistance will prevail. In a sense, the high stakes associated with preserving this delicate balance compel the play's authorization of supernatural forces generated through miracle – phenomena largely associated with Catholicism. These stakes, though ostensibly associated with ancient pagan conversion, are partly informed by contemporary anxieties about Turkish persecution, forced conversion to Islam, and, in particular, the ways that these threats became centered on the penetration of Christian bodies. For English audiences, Dorothea's impervious physical body renders visible proof of Christian triumph even in the face of seemingly insurmountable odds.

Certainly, another part of what made this material good theater was its sadistic and titillating nature. Despite the divine intervention that renders Dorothea's tortures ineffectual, the scene nonetheless produces a spectacle of her body being tied to a pillar and beaten by two men. As Mel Gibson's *The Passion of the Christ* (2004) seems to bear out for modern audiences, this spectacle of violence was potentially erotic and thrilling in the way that pornography might be considered thrilling. Importantly for the stage, what signifies as martyrdom in one register signifies as visual sadism in another – a duality that applied not only to early modern theater but to medieval saints' plays and virgin martyr legends as well.[43] In addition to its reputation for old-fashioned plays, the capacious Red Bull amphitheater, where *The Virgin Martyr* was performed, had a particular penchant for drawing large crowds to witness shocking scenes and violence.[44] To some degree *The Virgin Martyr*'s predilection for Catholic torture was also more practical for the theater, in that it could be simulated more easily and more convincingly than the Protestant igniting of bodies. But I would suggest that the specific spectacle of sadistic torture inflicted upon an inviolable body held a particular appeal of its own in the early seventeenth century.

It was this particular aspect of martyrdom that resurfaced in plays dramatizing the threat of Islam to contemporary Christendom. The thrusting of Oriana's virginal body onto the scaffolding in *The Knight of Malta*, the binding of Vitelli "in heavy chains / That eat into his flesh" in *The Renegado*, and the hoisting of Sir Thomas Sherley's body onto the rack in *The Travails of the Three English Brothers* attested to the physical pressures of religious conversion in places like Malta, Tunis, and Constantinople.[45] The threat of sadistic Turkish violence against Christians was enhanced by its correlation with a real-life danger (Christians *were* being captured and tortured in the Ottoman empire), and in this sense its resonance with a history of Catholic torture and martyrdom offered a particularly empowering model of resistance. Early seventeenth-century sermons preached by Edward Kellet, Henry Byam, Charles Fitzgeoffrey, and William Gouge for the Christian recovery of Islamic converts emphasize the superiority of choosing martyrdom over conversion; Byam specifically holds up the example of early Christian "Women-Martyrs . . . Witnesse S. Agnes at 12. yeeres old; Cecilia, Agatha, & a world besides."[46] As I will continue to argue, the mercilessly penetrated but ultimately impermeable Catholic body retained in the face of Islam an appeal that superseded both the material and commercial concerns of the stage, as well as the spiritualizing influence of the Reformation.

Turkish Torture of Christian Captives

The visual tradition of Catholic martyrdom bears some striking resemblances to seventeenth-century representations of Christian torture at the hands of Turks. A pamphlet printed at Oxford in 1617, entitled

Figure 2.7: A scene of Turkish torture from *Christopher Angell, A Grecian, who tasted of many stripes inflicted by the Turkes* (Oxford, 1617), sig. A4r. Reproduced by permission of the Folger Shakespeare Library.

Christopher Angell, a Grecian, who tasted of many stripes inflicted by the Turkes, features a crude woodcut of two Turks beating a martyr whose arms and legs are bound to a rectangular frame (Figure 2.7).[47] In his narrative, Angell explains that he was "bound hand, and foot in maner of a crosse vpon the earth" while "two men dipping their rods in salt water began to scourge me, and when the one was lifting vp his hand, the other was ready to strike, so that I could take no rest, and my paine was most grievous: and so they continued beating me, saying, turne Turke, and we will free thee."[48] Angell endures this painful torment by meditating on Christ's passion and especially on the torture of former Christian martyrs, who "were fleshly men, and sinners, yet by the grace of God were strengthened to die."[49] Subsequently, he is able to withstand the physical pressure to convert and even attests to a miraculous revival after being beaten, he claims, to death: "I was perfectly dead, and so remained for the space of an houre, and againe after an houre, by the grace of God I revived."[50] In emphasizing tremendous resistance and the miraculous revival of his dead body by God, Angell's narrative resonates with a template of Catholic martyrdom.

Similarly, Francis Knight's *A relation of seaven yeares slaverie under the Turkes of Argeire, suffered by an English captive merchant*, printed at London in 1640, draws an implicit parallel between Catholic martyrdom and Turkish persecution by detailing tortures similar to those depicted in Counter-Reformation martyrologies like those of Antonio Gallonio and Richard Verstegan.[51] This pamphlet contains a woodcut of a Christian being scourged by a Turk (Figure 2.8), and painstakingly describes the sadistic tortures that the author witnessed against Christians in Algiers: "Some were crucified, others having their bones broken, were drawled along the streets at horse tailes, others had their shoulders stab'd with knives, and burning Torches set in them dropping downe into their wounds; the Turkes biting of their flesh alive, so dyed, and foure of them being walled in were starved to death."[52]

In a similar vein, the frontispiece to William Okeley's *Eben-ezer; or, a small monument of great mercy, appearing in the miraculous deliverance of William Okeley* (Figure 2.9) features images of a Christian strung upside down by his feet on a rod and beaten with a baton; a Christian being dragged across the ground by a horse while another Christian has his hair set on fire; and a Christian affixed to a wheel and being beaten with a sharp instrument. Like the visual tradition of Catholic martyrdom, these images of Turkish persecution all emphasize gruesome and painful bodily torment, as well as the merciless sadism of the torturers.[53] Similar accounts of graphic bodily tortures perpetrated by Muslim Turks are featured in John Rawlins's *The famous and wonderful recovery of a ship of Bristoll* (1622), Henry Blount's *A voyage into the Levant* (1636), and even the travel manuscript of East India Company merchant Peter Mundy.[54]

Importantly, Dorothea's martyrdom in *The Virgin Martyr* highlights the spiritual benefits of enduring torture over the easier path of Muslim conversion. In addition, her reminder of the rewards of a Christian afterlife allay fears about the prospect of death. In resignifying death as triumphant resistance, Dorothea's martyrdom subverts the play's classification as a "tragedy" on its first edition title page (1622) and transforms it into a comedy of salvation. Convinced of the heavenly bliss that follows a death by martyrdom, Dorothea models for the male protagonist the eternal advantages that may be achieved through a comparatively brief period of suffering. Prior to his conversion, Antoninus

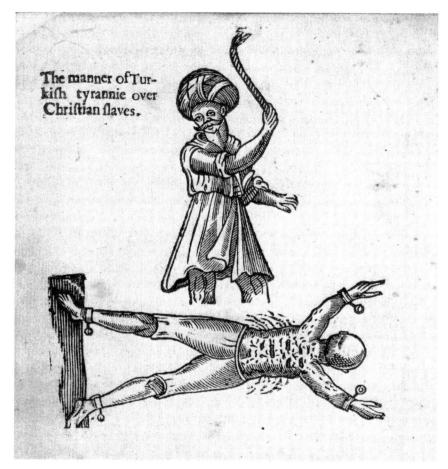

The manner of Tur-
kifh tyrannie over
Chriftian flaves.

Figure 2.8: "The manner of Turkish tyrannie over Christian slaves," from Francis Knight, *A relation of seaven yeares slaverie under the Turkes of Argeire, suffered by an English captive merchant* (London: 1640), frontispiece. Reproduced by permission of the Folger Shakespeare Library.

views Dorothea's impending execution as an irrevocable tragedy and begs Artemia to allow him to be sacrificed in her place: "Preserue this temple (builded faire as yours is) / And Caesar neuer went in greater triumph / Than I shall to the scaffold" (2.3.157–9). By contrast, death is not tragic at all for Dorothea; rather, it represents a hastening to her reward in heaven, the longed-for union with her true bridegroom, and a means to the eternal preservation of her perfect chastity. She counsels Antoninus that his fear of death is misguided: "you onely dread / The stroke, and not what followes when you are dead" (2.3.130–1). In this way, the play offers an empowering model for reconceptualizing

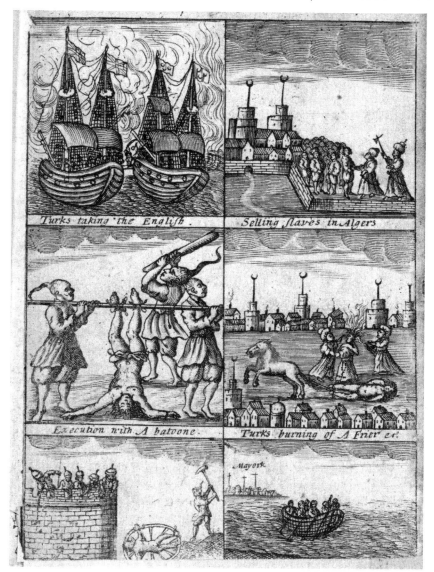

Figure 2.9: Frontispiece, from William Okeley, *Eben-ezer; or, A small monument of great mercy, appearing in the miraculous deliverance of William Okeley* (London, 1684). Reproduced by permission of the Folger Shakespeare Library.

options even in the face of overwhelming persecution. In other words, far better to embrace martyrdom – and reap the infinite rewards of heaven – than to permanently damn one's soul by capitulating to the pressure to convert.

Rape and Virginity

Like the threat of sadistic physical torture, the threat of rape – a threat generally absent from Protestant martyrologies – unites the tradition of Catholic saints' tales and the cultural construction of Christian vulnerability to Turks. In medieval virgin martyr legends the threat of rape plays a distinct and crucial role. Unlike other forms of torture, the implied irreversibility of rape suggests that it eradicates the very thing constitutive of female sainthood. As Caroline Walker Bynum writes of *The Golden Legend*, "the major achievement of holy women is dying in defense of their virginity."[55] In effect, the saint's final martyrdom helps to ensure the perpetual preservation of her virginity. In contrast to medieval martyrs, Foxe's Protestant martyrs are not *virgins*, though they may well be models of Christian *virtue*. Unlike virgin martyrs, whose miraculously preserved virginity reveals their innate virtue, Protestant martyrs are not distinguished by their sexual or physical constancy. Whereas the spiritual endurance of the Protestant martyr is meant to de-emphasize his or her physical body, the Catholic tradition of martyrdom revolves around the resilient physicality of the virgin's body – its deliberate gendering, its intactness, its oneness with the soul, and its physical materialization of sexual and spiritual chastity.

At the same time, the threat of rape and its physical implications take on a new significance in *The Virgin Martyr*, and in early modern England, that I want to argue registers the culture's anxieties surrounding Islamic conversion. Dekker and Massinger's representation of Dorothea's virginity and threatened rape are striking in that they are emphasized far more in the play than in medieval versions of her legend. Whereas in Bokenham, Caxton, and Villegas's versions of Dorothea's legend, the threat of rape is largely implicit, in the play, Antoninus is directly commanded to rape Dorothea. Affronted by the emasculation of his lovesick son, whose advances Dorothea repeatedly rejects, the pagan governor of Caesarea orders Antoninus to

> Breake that enchanted Caue, enter, and rifle
> The spoyles thy lust hunts after; I descend
> To a base office, and become thy Pandar
> In bringing thee this proud Thing, make her thy Whore,
> Thy health lies here, if she deny to giue it,
> Force it, imagine thou assaulst a towne,
> Weake wall, too't, tis thine owne, beat but this downe. (4.1.72–8)

The violence conveyed through Sapritius's instructions to "breake," "enter," "rifle," "force," "assaul[t]," and "beat . . . downe" Dorothea's chastity is striking in its bluntness. In addition, whereas medieval virgin martyr legends tend to emphasize the pagan persecutor's recourse to other forms of torture or a sentence of death in response to the virgin's sexual rejection, the play subjects Dorothea to a threat of rape that is pointed and persistent. Sapritius construes the rape of Dorothea's body as necessary to restoring Antoninus's male body to health, but he also perceives the value of her rape in and of itself. When Antoninus fails to execute his father's command, Sapritius demands that the "slave from Brittaine" be fetched from the galleys to carry out the deed. He then orders that slave to "drag that Thing [Dorothea] aside / And rauish her" (4.1.149–50). When the slave refuses, Sapritius bellows, "Call in ten slaues, let euery one discouer / What lust desires, and surfet here his fill, / Call in ten slaues" (4.1.167–8).

While it would be inaccurate to say that the medieval martyr's physical virginity was less essential or central than it is in Dekker and Massinger's play, Dorothea's virginity seems to assume a different function in the later context. [56] Certainly, as Monta points out, the fact of Dorothea's vowed virginity, coupled with the presumably greater vulnerability of her female body, works to underscore both the excessive cruelty of her persecutors and the remarkable power of God that renders her impervious to physical suffering.[57] But I want to suggest that the play's heightening of emphasis around Dorothea's vowed virginity and threatened rape also betrays a deepening investment in the significance of sexual penetration with respect to religious conversion. Whereas Monta urges an allegorical reading of Dorothea's virginity, suggesting that it "has as much to do with her unwillingness to be dominated by a pagan husband as with her desire to maintain her virginity *per se*," I contend that Dorothea's vow of virginity signifies in a way that is literal and embodied.[58] Indeed, Dorothea continues to cite her vowed virginity as the reason for rejecting Antoninus's marriage proposal even after he converts from paganism to Christianity; she then goes on to convince him of the virtues of assuming a life of celibacy as well. The spectacle of Dorothea's execution, which consists of an onstage beheading, functions on some level as physical proof that her virginity remains intact, that she has not been raped and is now eternally protected from this threat. Her final words, just before "her head is struck off," attest to this, her most fervent hope for her own legacy: "Say this of Dorothea, with wet eyes, / She lived a virgin and a virgin dies" (4.3.178–9). This reconfirmation of her intact virginity serves as the essential sign that she remains a Christian, that she has not been converted, and that her spiritual purity is necessarily expressed through the physical status of her untarnished sexual body.

Part of what informs this emphasis on physical virginity with respect to conversion, I want to argue, are the embodied and proto-racialized ramifications that attended contemporary threats of Christian-Muslim conversion. In popular plays and other narratives about Turkish persecution, the sexual threat of Muslims is played up through characterizations of the excessive sexual libido of Muslim men, the seductive charms of Muslim women, and Islam's general permissiveness toward sexual promiscuity. As reflected in the epigraph for this chapter – a Christian woman's exclamation in Machiavelli's *The Mandrake* that she has "such terrible fears of being impaled by a Turk" – Christian fears about Muslims center on penetration, carrying a connotation that is distinctly sexualized. The idea of "being impaled by a Turk" references the aggressive lust associated with Turkish men and hints at the equally threatening possibility that Christian women might find such a prospect appealing. Plays such as John Mason's *The Turke* (*c.*1607) and Thomas Dekker's *Lust's Dominion; or, The Lascivious Queen* (*c.*1600) seem to pick up on the latter possibility, presenting Christian mistresses as willing accomplices to their Muslim love-interests. The Renaissance stage's conflation of sexual intercourse and conversion draws upon a longstanding cultural tradition of associating Turks with lust, and Muslim conversion with heterosexual seduction, which had roots in Continental romance and other medieval genres. However, I want to suggest that interfaith sexual penetration assumed an immediate, bodily significance on the early modern stage.

The rape of a Christian virgin by a Turk was understood not only to physically destroy her maidenhead but also contaminate her bloodline if she should become impregnated. While the boundary of difference between Christian and Muslim was ostensibly figured through religion, the rather crude causal correlation between sexual intercourse and conversion on the stage demonstrates the intertwinement of religious and proto-racial categories. As Ania Loomba explains, "Sexuality is central to the idea of 'race' understood as lineage, or as bloodline, because the idea of racial purity depends upon the strict control of lineage."[59] The idea that sexual behavior controlled bloodlines created anxieties about female sexuality that were exacerbated by the role Christian women were perceived to play in sustaining Turkish dynasties. Both Foxe's *Book of Martyrs* and Hakluyt's *Principall Nauigations* (1589, 1598, 1600) allude to the particular vulnerability of Christian women to Turkish abduction, conversion, and sexual enslavement in Islamic harems. Similarly, John Barclay in *The mirrour of mindes, or, Barclays icon animorum* claims that the Turkish emperor preferred to beget royal heirs on captured Christian women: "From hence [Christian captives] are his wiues and concubines, and always the mother of that heire that must succeede in so great an Empire."[60] The integration of Christian women into royal Turkish families (like Safiye, concubine and Sultana Valide of Murad III, and mother of Mehmed III) demonstrated Christian women's direct, reproductive roles in the perpetuation of Turkish dynasties. The pervasive threat of rape in the turning Turk dramas and its consistent, miraculous evasion speak to the emerging racial threat bound up in this notion of conversion.

However, unlike accounts of real-life Turkish concubines, the dramatic stage never represented the successful sexual violation of a Christian woman by a Turk. Whereas Christian men frequently conquered the bodies of (conveniently fair-skinned) eastern women on the stage, reinforcing what Lynda Boose has called a "fantasy of male parthenogenesis," which posited the unequivocal genetic dominance of the male's racial features, Christian women were never conquered by Turkish men.[61] But just as the absence of such a union preserved the fantasy that race could be controlled through a logic of male dominance, it also betrayed the anxious knowledge that the physical traits of the Turk would be passed to the offspring regardless of who the father was. While Protestant investments in a Christian universalism based on a "circumcision of the heart" suggested that religious affiliation was in itself intangible, religious difference became distinctly embodied in conjunction with the figure of the Turk. Though in *The Virgin Martyr*, the pagans are not explicitly associated with racialized features, the overdetermined threat of rape in this play is inflected by fears about the forced sexual penetration and conversion of Christians by Turks, a resonance that could not have eluded its seventeenth-century audience.

Other Red Bull Martyr Plays

The production of similar plays performed at the Red Bull Theatre around the same time period suggests that the outdated models and tropes exemplified in *The Virgin Martyr* were not unique to this play, and that they assumed a broader cultural significance around 1620 that made them popular with English audiences. Both Henry Shirley's *The Martryed Soldier* (1619) and the anonymous *Two Ladies of London and the Converted Conjuror* (1623) center on the pagan persecution of Christians under the Roman empire, and in both plays martyrdom serves as an exemplary strategy of Christian resistance and conversion. Like *The Virgin Martyr*, they draw upon and refigure Catholic models of vowed virginity, miraculously avoided rape, and supernatural incidents of divine intervention. Moreover, their renderings of these models within eastern Mediterranean settings of early Christian persecution implicitly evoke correspondences with contemporary Islamic persecutions of Christians in the same territories.

Rape and Supernatural Interventions in *The Martyred Soldier*

Most likely based on the 1605 English translation of St. Victor of Vita's *The memorable and tragical history of the persecution in Africke*, Shirley's *The Martyred Soldier* dramatizes the fifth-century Vandal persecutions that took place in North Africa. The play opens with the Vandals returning from battle with 700 Christian captives in their possession. Celebrating their victory, they boast of the many vile tortures they have inflicted on the Christians: "Foure hundred virgins ravisht / . . . their trembling bodies tost on the pikes / Of those that spoyl'd em / . . . [Others] pauncht, some starv'd, some eyes and braines bor'd out, / Some whipt to death, some torne by Lyons" (1.1; B2r). The captives are ordered by the newly enthroned king of the Vandals, Henrick, to be stripped and abandoned to "the midst of the vast Wildernesse / That stands 'twixt [Africa] and wealthy Persia," there to fall prey to "famine, or the fury of the Beasts" (1.1; B4v). The only prisoner spared is the Christian bishop Eugenius, whom the king detains in the hope of converting him through torture and then using his influence to convert others. Instead, King Henrick's own general, Bellizarius, unexpectedly converts to Christianity after being visited by an angel and witnessing the marvelous example of the Christian captives who somehow interpret torture and death as forms of triumph. After persuading both his wife and daughter, Victoria and Bellina, also to convert to Christianity, Bellizarius is sentenced to death by King Henrick. Bellina goes on to convert the Vandal commander Hubert and vows to either marry him or live a life of perpetual chastity. When Victoria pleads for her husband's life, King Hubert orders that she be raped. However, through acts of divine intervention she is miraculously spared. In a similar manner, the king decrees that Eugenius be stoned to death and all the Christians massacred, but these actions are miraculously diverted and the king himself is ultimately struck dead by a thunderbolt. At the conclusion of the play, the newly Christianized Hubert assumes the throne with Bellina as his wife, and together they vow to convert the empire and "from [their] loynes produce a race of . . . Christians unborne" (5.1; K2r).

Like *The Virgin Martyr*, *The Martyred Soldier* models the Christian
martyr's inviting of torture and death as an exemplary strategy
of resistance to religious persecution, and also demonstrates how
this course of martyrdom elicits God's protection, inspires others to
convert, and effectively transforms the tragedy of death into a form of
Christian triumph. Set in North Africa, where a contemporary scene of
Islamic persecution overlays this ancient history of Vandal persecution,
these examples take on a heightened relevancy in relation to contemporary threats of Islamic conversion. The play's depictions of Christian
captivity, sadistic bodily torture, and the presumed dominance of the
Vandals over the Christians resonate with specific cultural anxieties
about the Ottoman Turks. Most tellingly, the sexual violence threatened against Victoria reflects some of the ways that religious conversion
becomes intertwined with embodied, gendered, and emerging racial
implications under the early modern threat of the Turk. Paralleling the
pagan governor's command that his son and then a Christian slave rape
Dorothea in *The Virgin Martyr*, King Henrick orders a camel driver to
rape Victoria. This scene, which is an invention of Shirley's not present
in his source, explicitly cites a contemporary context through the Camel
Driver's understanding of his task:

> Camel Driver 1
> . . . Is't the King's pleasure I should mouse her, and before all these people?
>
> King
> No, tis considered better; unbind the fury. And dragge her to some corner,
> tis our pleasure, Fall to thy business freely.
>
> Camel Driver 1
> Not too freely neither; I fare hard; and drinke water, so doe the Indians, yet
> who fuller of Bastards? So do the Turkes, yet who gets greater Logger-
> heads? Come wench, I'll teach thee how to cut up wild fowle.
>
> Victoria
> Guard me yon heavens. (4.3; H1r–1v)

The Camel Driver's references to "far[ing] hard" and "drink[ing]
water" seem to acknowledge his lack of physical strength, while his
self-comparison to "Indians" and "Turkes" boosts his confidence by
reminding him that these people share his weakness and are yet are
so fertile as to produce more "bastards" and "logger-heads" than
anyone. His anachronistic reference to "Indians" and "Turks" not
only reveals the ways in which Shirley's fifth-century Vandals are conceived partly in the image of more contemporary non-Christian people,
but also capitalizes on the sexual and reproductive threats that non-
Christian men were thought to pose to Christian women. Importantly,

Muslim Turks and pagan Indians were not always conflated in the English imagination as they are here. However, as I discuss in Chapter 1, both Muslims and pagans began to take on a new sense of difference in the period that went beyond religion to encompass embodied and proto-racial implications. The Camel Driver's allusions to sexual and reproductive consequences speak to this evolving sense of difference.

Victoria's miraculous avoidance of rape demonstrates how the stage resorts to the Catholic trope of divine intervention to prevent her rape in ways that offer tangible proof of God's protection and her uncompromised chastity. Although, unlike Dorothea, Victoria is married and thus not a virgin, the lengths to which the play goes to demonstrate the protection of her chastity against pagan contamination, and in particular its reliance on miraculous interventions, reveal the high stakes associated with interfaith sexual penetration. The first camel driver summoned for the task begins to drag Victoria away, when he is instantaneously "struck mad" and "beate[s] out his owne braines" (4.1; Hv). The king then calls in a second camel driver, who no sooner initiates the task than he is "struck blind" and then, when ordered to continue or else face certain death, is rendered deaf as well (4.1; H2r). After the failure of the two camel drivers, the king calls for two slaves and commands them along with his lord Epidorus to "seize her all three, / And ravish her by turnes," but these would-be rapists immediately lose control of their faculties and, according to the stage direction, "*dance Antiquely, and Exeunt*" (4.1; H2r). While the Christian bishop Eugenius cautions the onlookers to "impute not / This most miraculous delivery / To witch-craft," the miracles certainly demonstrate a kind of magic that might have made them subject to Protestant charges of Catholic superstition (4.1; H2r).

The play suggests connections to Catholic traditions and medieval religious theater in other ways as well, presenting a spectacular resurrection, supernatural effects, and the regular appearance of singing angels. After apparently succumbing to death when her prison guard pours a scalding bowl of porridge over her head, Victoria is miraculously resurrected in a scene that self-consciously borrows from the medieval miracle play tradition. According to the stage direction, "Victoria rises out of the cave [where she has been imprisoned] white," and her clothing is miraculously transformed from prisoner's rags to a beautiful white "habite" (5.1; Ir-v). Rather than suggest the possibility of mocking or discounting Victoria's resurrection, the onstage witnesses to the scene, including the pagan king, are awed and enchanted by it. In addition, the play invests with supernatural power the body of Eugenius, identified as the historical St. Eugenius of Carthage in the play's source, in ways that evoke the idolatry of Catholic relics. After being stung by a scorpion, King Henrick is cured by drinking and bathing in Eugenius's blood; when the king then betrays Eugenius by having him stoned, the stones miraculously turn as "soft as spunges" (3.4; F4v). The play's testimony to the efficacy of such miracles is partly justified by its distant historical setting, but I would argue that it is also called for by its geographical setting in a territory largely conquered by Turks at the time of the play's performance. In positing the healing effects of Eugenius's blood and the inefficacy of his torture, the play illustrates comforting proof of how when faced with overwhelming per-secution, as Christians enslaved in the Ottoman empire also were, mar-tyrdom constitutes a form of resistance that is protected and rewarded by God. This message is reinforced through the songs of the angels, who, for example, celebrate Bellizarius's martyrdom with the words "Victory, victory, hell is beaten downe, / The Martyr has put on a golden crowne; / Ring Bels of Heaven, him welcome hither" (5.1; I3r).

Moreover, the play models the importance of sexual resistance through its example of divine protection against rape. Perversely aroused by the spectacle of Victoria's resurrection, King Henrick assumes the role of lustful persecutor, but Victoria is spared by protec-tive angels who descend around her body and shepherd her to her final death. At the same time, a lightning bolt instantaneously strikes down the king and kills him. It seems that such intercessions by supernatu-ral forces, and the play's authorization of the efficacy of miracles, are not only justified but also necessitated by the greater cultural taboo of engaging the consequences of Victoria's rape. In addition, the martyr-dom of Victoria and Bellizarius clears the stage of pagans, inspiring willing souls to convert and engendering God's punishment of those who remain recalcitrant. This allows Victoria's daughter, Bellina, and Hubert to assume the throne and propagate a new Christian empire in North Africa. Hubert's concluding suggestion that he and Bellina "shall from [their] loynes produce a race of Kings" gestures to the crucial role of reproduction in sustaining Christian identity and empire (5.1; K2r).

If the correspondences between the Vandal persecutions of Shirley's play and the contemporary persecution of Christians in North Africa are largely implicit, Shirley's personal life gave him explicit reason to take an interest in the plight of contemporary Christian captives. His father, Thomas Shirley (*c.*1564–1633), was an English privateer and adventurer made famous by his travels throughout the Ottoman empire and Persia. In 1603 (when Henry was twelve), Thomas Shirley was captured by Turks; abandoned by his crew, he was held prisoner in Constantinople for two years. He and his two adventuring brothers,

Anthony and Robert, were the subject of John Day, George Wilkins, and William Rowley's 1607 stage play, *The Travails of the Three English Brothers* – also performed in the Red Bull Theatre – as well as several pamphlets. Thomas's captivity at the hands of Turks is dramatized in that play, which features him tortured on the rack, pressured to convert to Islam, and nearly martyred. He is eventually rewarded for his steadfast resistance through release and a safe return to Christian territory. At the same time, the play shames Thomas's crew for abandoning him to the Turks and thereby choosing the path of least resistance. As I have been suggesting, the fact that both ancient martyr plays like *The Martyred Soldier* and Mediterranean adventure plays like *The Travails of the Three English Brothers* endorse a common strategy of resistance through martyrdom is not merely coincidental.

That these kinds of plays met a similar demand from English audiences is evidenced not only by their performance in the same playhouse, but by certain aspects of their printing history. For example, John Oakes's publication of *The Martyred Soldier* was entered into the Stationers' Register on February 15, 1638, as "a play called The Martyred Soldior, with the life and death of Purser Clinton." This reference to "Purser Clinton" actually refers to two separate English adventurers who were executed by Queen Elizabeth for piracy and treason. Unlike the martyrs of Shirley's play, Clinton and Purser were construed as renegades who valued self-interest over the more difficult path of virtuous resistance, and thus met with the shameful death of execution, rather than the triumphant death of martyrdom. Their exploits and punishments were popularized for English audiences through Thomas Heywood's adventure play *Fortune By Land and Sea* (*c.*1609) – also performed at the Red Bull – which represented their cowardice and ultimate repentance in contrasting ways to the heroism of the Shirley brothers. It is unlikely that the reference to "Purser Clinton" in the entry for *The Martyred Soldier* reflects a confusion of the two plays, since *Fortune By Land and Sea* was published by a different publisher and not until 1655. More likely, the reference relates to a news pamphlet entitled *A true relation, of the lives and deaths of two most famous English pyrats, Purser, and Clinton*, which was published by John Oakes in 1639, and later attributed to Thomas Heywood. The fact that the stationer acquired the publishing rights to both texts at the same time and published them in close conjunction with one another suggests that he was thinking about their mutual marketability. For one thing, they were both old stories – Shirley's play was first performed in 1618, and Clinton and Purser came to public attention through Heywood's 1607 play and an earlier pamphlet printed in 1583 – that the stationer decided would appeal to a late 1630s audience. The two texts differed, however, in that whereas Shirley's play dramatizes events from deep in the past, Heywood's pamphlet narrates events from the much more recent, Elizabethan past. Thus, if *The Martyred Soldier* shared something with Clinton and Purser, it was not related to their specific temporal contexts, but rather to their mutual interest in conditions of cross-cultural, interreligious contact that emphasized the virtues of Christian resistance and martyrdom.

Female Chastity as Converting Agent in *The Two Noble Ladies*

The anonymous *Two Noble Ladies and the Converted Conjurer*, "a Tragecomicall Historie often tymes acted with approbation at the Red Bull in St. Johns Street by the Company of the Reuells," evokes even clearer correspondences between its ancient conflict and contemporary Christian-Muslim relations.[62] It opens with the pagan Egyptian sack of Christian Antioch during a time when both countries were subject to Roman rule but differentiated by their religions. Suggesting a parallel to the Ottoman sultan, the tyrannical Egyptian Souldan espouses aspirations to rule the world. In plundering Antioch, he kills the Christian king and leaves only the king's virginal niece, Justina, as the last of that royal race. Justina flees to Babylon to hide. Further extending his affinities with the Ottoman sultan, the Souldan makes incestuous advances on his own daughter, Miranda, who in turn also flees to Babylon and assumes a male disguise. Justina is captured by pagan Babylonian soldiers and threatened with rape, but is rescued at the last minute by the cross-dressed Miranda. Justina inspires the love of Clitophon, son to the Califfe of Babylon, who expresses a desire to convert to Christianity. Meanwhile, the Egyptian Souldan learns that Babylon is harboring his daughter Miranda and declares war. Miranda's beloved, Lysander, who is also one of the Soudan's chief commanders, worries over Miranda's fate. The conjuror of the play's title, Cyprian, informs Lysander that his real name is Eugenius (the same as the Carthaginian Christian saint and saintly character in *The Martyred Soldier*), and that he is actually the son of the Christian king of Antioch but was kidnapped as a youth by the Souldan's father and raised as an Egyptian pagan. Though Lysander later professes his loyalty to the Souldan (perhaps disingenuously) in a dumbshow, his sympathetic identification with Christian Antioch has been awakened.

In the second half of the play, the Babylonians capture the Souldan, but Clitophon strikes an alliance with him after learning that his father ordered Justina to be drowned (she is rescued by the conjuror). The cross-dressed Miranda proposes to the Babylonian Califfe that he settle the conflict with Egypt by sponsoring a personal combat between herself and Lysander, fighting on behalf of Babylon and Egypt respectively. The conjuror Cyprian, after applying his magical arts to advance a series of Christian causes, suddenly turns on Justina when she rejects his sexual advances. She vows to remain a virgin or die, and Cyprian attempts to rape her before being converted by an angel. The angel also counsels Cyprian and Justina to return to Antioch and be martyred. When Miranda and Lysander face off in combat, Miranda unveils herself and the two yield to one another, proposing a peace between Egypt and Babylon. The Califfe and Souldan are outraged and plan to kill them, but the Roman emperor enters and enforces the peace by reminding them of their mutual subjugation to Rome. The Souldan then gives Antioch to Lysander, who will marry Miranda and convert to Christianity. Though Justina refuses to marry Clitophon because of her vowed virginity, she inspires him to convert to Christianity as well. Together, both Miranda and Justina, the "two noble ladies" of the play's title, effectively extend Christianity through conversion from the sacked Antioch to both Egypt and Babylon.

Importantly, Miranda and Justina extend conversion to pagan men not through sexual congress but through their steadfast chastity. Though pagan by birth, Miranda reveals her innate difference from her father, the Egyptian Souldan, and her predisposition to Christian conversion, through her natural aversion to her father's incestuous advances. The Souldan's characterization in the image of the lustful Turk is reinforced through his merciless sadism, which takes the form of delight in planning gruesome physical tortures. When he learns that Miranda has escaped the watch of his eunuchs who have been charged with guarding her, he orders that their tongues and eyes be cut out and that their bodies be hewed "in peeces," their "dismembered limbs" displayed "on poles / in eu'ry quarter of the camp" (2.1.399–401). Later, enraged by the news that Miranda has taken refuge in Babylon, the Souldan orders his soldiers to capture her and

> Mangle her enticing face,
> seare vp her tempting breasts, teare wide her mouth,
> and slit her nose, that thus defac'd, my hate
> neither by loue nor pitty may abate. (2.1.553–6)

His desire to see her "enticing face" mangled and to "seare vp her tempting breasts" has a sexually sadistic edge that conveys the depths of his perversity and his tyranny, as well as his reduction of her to a physical spectacle oriented entirely around its effects on him. By contrast, Miranda's aversion to him and her decision to remove herself from his domain by cross-dressing and escaping to Babylon are absolute and unwavering. In turn, her uncompromising separation from her father sets off a chain of events that leads to her own and Lysander's conversions to Christianity as well as their possession of the throne of Christian Antioch. When the Souldan attempts to convince Miranda that marrying him would not be shameful because it would make her the queen of Egypt, adding, "Thou shalt agree Miranda, we must wed," she replies, "Agree with death, not with a fathers bed" (1.2.182–3). Her willingness to face death rather than fulfill her father's incestuous desires allies her with the virgin martyr tradition, underscoring her resolute chastity and her innate distinction from her non-Christian father.

Similarly, Justina is repeatedly threatened by pagan sexual violence and repeatedly prizes her virginity over her life. When Babylonian soldiers capture and attempt to rape her, she begs, "Let your relentless swords enter this breast / and giue my life like happie liberty" (1.4.266–7). Making explicit their intentions of rape and reinforcing the play's association between male paganism and sexual sadism, one of the soldiers responds, "No pretty one, the weapon thou shalt feele / shall be of milder temper then rough steele" (1.4.268–9). Later, she endures repeated sexual advances from the black conjuror Cyprian, to which she remains steadfast in her resistance and committed to a vow of lifelong virginity even at the cost of her life: "Heau'n has my vow, my life shall neuer bee / elder then my vnstain'd virginitie" (4.5; 1.1621–2). When Cyprian's attempts to couch his desires in enticing rhetoric fail, he resolves to use his magical powers to instill a sexual desire in Justina:

>   my blacke art,
> shall make your white thoughts like it.
> [. . .]
> hell shall force her
> to offer vp that Iewell of delight
> which miserlike she yet locks vp in coynesse.
> With greater heat she shall desire her rape
> Then I haue done. These Hells hookes she cannot scape. (4.5;
> 1.1635–41)

Cyprian pits his "blacke art" against Justina's "white thoughts," suggesting a clear contrast between paganism and Christianity, one aligned with the powers of hell and the other with those of heaven. This direct opposition underscores the miracle by which Justina, through her virtue and faith alone, is able to resist Cyprian's powers and convert him to Christianity. Despite Cyprian's attempts to conjure sexual desire in Justina, no such desire materializes, and instead, he senses a transformation in himself. Ultimately, he is moved to regard her as a "Christian Saint which I (in spite of hell) / am forc'd to worship" (5.2; 1.1751–2). Indeed, Justina's character is based upon the virgin martyr St. Justina, who was born in Damascus and, like Dorothy, martyred under Diocletian in 304. According to her legend, Justina converts a pagan magician from Antioch named Cyprian, who is hired by another pagan man to convince her to love him. However, whereas in medieval versions of Justina's legend, Cyprian does not become infatuated with Justina and attempt to rape her, and even the pagan suitor is motivated not by lust but by a desire to win Justina's love, *The Two Noble Ladies* orients all of the pagan attacks on Justina around her sexual vulnerability, and similarly figures her resolute chastity as the agent that converts both Cyprian and the pagan suitor Clitophon.

The play's characterization of the conjuror and the status of his magic warrant closer examination, particularly in light of *The Virgin Martyr*'s and *The Martyred Soldier*'s explicit but in some ways anxious authorization of supernatural forces. Prior to his sexual infatuation with Justina in Act Four, Cyprian uses his magical powers to help Lysander and Justina. For example, when Lysander crosses the Souldan on Miranda's behalf, Cyprian casts a spell that instantaneously freezes the Souldan and his guards in place, potentially to comical effect. Later, he rescues Justina from being drowned by conjuring trumpeting Tritons who seize her captors and force them into the water. In addition, he appears to work in concert with a Christian angel when he shepherds Lysander to the banks of the Euphrates and reveals to him the truth of his birth; immediately following this revelation, an angel appears "shaped like a patriarch, vpon his breast a red table full of silver letters, in his right hand a red crossier staffe, on his shoulders large wings" (stage direction 3.3). Cyprian then reads his own fate imprinted in the table: "it is the gracious heauens will, / that now ere long, this learned heathen man / shall renounce Magicke, and turne Christian" (3.3.1112–14). Though the angel proclaims that he "come[s] not by the call of magicke spells," his supernatural presence and abilities are difficult to distinguish from those of Cyprian (3.3.1117). Similarly, Cyprian's magic is not consistently contrasted with that of angels: the play condones his powers and renders them efficacious when they are directed toward Christian causes, but compares them disparagingly to angelic powers when they work against Christian causes.

This double standard seems to describe more generally the ambivalent authorization of supernatural effects to protect Christian virtue and female chastity in all three of these Red Bull martyr plays. The very act of Cyprian's conversion – a conversion from paganism to Christianity, but also from the use of black magic to that of Christian miracle – illustrates through analogy a distinction whereby Christian "magic" is condoned, despite its associations with Catholicism and the medieval stage, when directed at certain causes. Specifically, these plays legitimize miraculous or supernatural effects when they are aimed at the intertwined imperatives of protecting the female body and resisting Christian persecution. As I have been arguing, the compulsion to rely on miracles in these cases reflects the high stakes associated with the sexual penetration and conversion of the female Christian body at a time of heightened cultural anxiety over Muslim-Christian encounter. Like *The Virgin Martyr* and the *Martyred Soldier*, *The Two Noble Ladies* invites contemporary application through anachronistic slips, as when Cyprian attempts to woo Justina by promising her "Indian mines," "sweet gums and spices of Arabia," and other commodities of the "worlds rich merchants" (4.5; 1.1585–8). However, the play's resonances with the conditions of Mediterranean trade and Ottoman imperialism are most meaningfully revealed through its sexualized interpretation of religious conversion and its anxious refusal to confront the implications of a penetrated female Christian body.

The scene depicting Justina's averted rape by Cyprian and his subsequent conversion to Christianity is highly revealing of the play's complex negotiation of the supernatural and how it seems almost despite itself to authorize supernatural effects while at the same time orienting Christian faith against them. On the one hand, the force of Justina's faith is shown to overpower Cyprian's magical arts, implying the superior efficacy of Christian faith over magic. Discovering Justina asleep in a chair with a prayer book in her hands, Cyprian decides to take advantage of her vulnerability by raping her while she sleeps. The stage direction calls for "divells about her," suggesting that Cyprian's black helpers hover menacingly around the chair (5.2; 1.1753). But when Cyprian attempts to kiss Justina, she wakes and "falls on her knees," then "looks in her booke, and the Spirits fly from her" (stage direction 5.2; 1.1796–7), prompting Cyprian's appropriately named friend Cantharides to remark, "Her prayers haue prevailed against our spells / . . . / Her faith beats downe our incantations" (5.2; 1.1799; 1802). Cyprian too confirms the disarming powers of Justina's faith, which have already begun to turn him to Christianity: "ffaire Christian

/ teach mee the sense and vse of this strong spell / call'd ffaith, that conquers all the pow'rs of hell" (5.2; 1.1816–19).

But on the other hand, the very use of the prayer book as a counter to Cyprian's books of magic locates the powers of Justina's faith in a sacred material object. As both Elizabeth Williamson and James Kearney have recently argued, Protestantism's embrace of the book, and in particular the Bible, was fraught with ambivalence.[63] In Kearney's terms, the Reformation occasioned "a crisis of the book": on the one hand the book "became an emblem of the desire to transcend the merely material and irredeemable fallen world of objects," but on the other hand reformers "distrusted the material dimension of text, of all that might be associated with the letter rather than the spirit."[64] In *The Two Noble Ladies*, the materiality of the book and the magical efficacy of reading and speaking its prayers are precisely what the stage emphasizes. Justina counsels Cyprian, "Doe not feare. / take here this booke; call on that pow'rfull name / those pray'rs so oft repeat, and I'll assist you" while at that moment the stage direction dictates, "The feinds roare and fly back" (5.2; 1.1844–6; 1847). As Cyprian continues to read in the prayer book, soft music begins to play and the "patriarch-like Angell" enters with "his crosier staffe in one hand, and a book in the other" (5.2; 1.1856–7). In turn, "the Devills sinck roaring; a flame of fier riseth after them," and the Angell "toucheth his breast with his crosse," saying "with this touch, let thy carnall lust convert / to loue of heau'n" (5.2; 1.1860; 1869–70). In this way, the angel's book and cross are invested with the power of conversion, contributing to an elaborate visual spectacle that clearly cites the morality play tradition through its inclusion of devils and a winged angel. The angel-as-converting-agent was also a common convention of medieval miracle plays such as the Digby manuscript's *Conversion of Saint Paul* and the Mary Magdalene plays. Although the book and perhaps even the cross (as distinct from a crucifix) ostensibly constitute Protestant symbols, their use as objects that are themselves invested with powers to convert evokes Catholic devotional practices, as do the interventions of angels and devils through the play. Thus, even though the preservation of Justina's virginity and Cyprian's miraculous conversion are partly facilitated through faith and chastity, they are also aided by sacred objects and supernatural forces.

The scene's reliance on an angel and devils to reflect visually the contest between Justina's Christian faith and Cyprian's pagan lust engages figures with explicit confessional implications. Intercessory angels who personally protected or assisted Christians on earth retained a Catholic valence in the early seventeenth century that sparked controversy and objections from the reformed church.[65] Whereas for Catholics, intercessory agency was widely distributed among those with supernatural powers (including angels, saints, relics, priests, the pope, the Virgin Mary, and Christ himself), mainstream Protestants held that intercessory power came from Christ alone. The powerful roles of intercessory angels in all three of the plays I discuss in this chapter have led Holly Crawford Pickett to argue that the "dazzling" effects of angels in the Red Bull plays are not deceptive and corruptive, as Protestant reformers claimed of Catholic idols, but rather redemptive and instrumental of positive conversions.[66] However, whereas Pickett argues against reading these effects as a coded endorsement of Catholicism, interpreting them instead as evidence of a purely secular indulgence of theatrical spectacle, I see no reason why Catholic valences and theatrical spectacle should be mutually exclusive. Rather, the secular stage drew upon Catholic models and effects because, unlike the relative material sparseness of Protestantism, they were so tangibly powerful. While these reappropriated models did not necessarily signal an endorsement of Catholicism for its own sake, I argue that the stage was compelled to reauthorize them despite their controversial associations because they provided effective countermeasures to the particular embodied and sexualized threats associated with Islamic conversion.

Female Virginity and Male Restraint

Although *The Two Noble Ladies* incorporates supernatural forces in order to supplement Christian faith and resistance to rape, it also hints at ways in which these roles can be taken up by human subjects. It does so by offering exemplary patterns of female heroism, virtue, and constancy that serve as models for male protagonists, instructing them how to perform the role of the deus ex machina. For example, when Justina is captured and nearly raped by the Babylonian soldiers, she calls on angels for help, but is rescued not through supernatural interventions but by the cross-dressed Miranda. In this way, the female heroine Miranda models male heroism by risking her life to defend Justina against so many opponents. Justina also serves as a model for men through the example of her unwavering constancy. Despite Clitophon's many romantic overtures, Justina insists upon her vowed virginity and, like Dorothea, expresses a willingness to die for it. Ultimately, it is her unwavering commitment to this vow that convinces Clitophon to convert to Christianity. When, at the conclusion of the play, the Califfe decrees that his son shall marry Justina, she does not hesitate to defy his authority: "No mightie Sir, / my virgin life is vow'd to heauen now / which hath so oft preserved it" (5.2; 1.2081–3). In response, Clitophon reveals not disappointment or anger, but his inspiration to follow her lead by converting: "Happy maide, / Thy vow displeases not, and thy strange story / hath wonne my heart to lay hould on thy faith" (2084–6). Thus, Christian female constancy serves as an agent for male redemption, a pattern that inverts constructions of the sexualized female body as an agent of male contamination.

Ultimately, the idealization of female chastity in the Red Bull martyr plays functions not only as a bar against interfaith sexual intercourse and as a broader symbol of Christian resistance to conversion, but also as a didactic model for masculine civility and sexual restraint. Whereas in *The Two Noble Ladies*, the translation of female chastity into a prescriptive for masculine behavior is mainly suggestive, *The Virgin Martyr* demonstrates Dorothea's fostering of Antoninus's gradual conversion over the course of the play. While Antoninus is initially drawn to Dorothea because of sexual desire, he learns to harness this desire and to direct his energies toward the higher cause of Christianity. His conversion from paganism to Christianity is manifested through his eventual departure from an economy of heterosexual desire and acceptance of a life of celibacy. The terms of this conversion may be understood through the contrasting agendas of Dorothea and Artemia, the marriageable daughter of Diocletian. Whereas Dorothea persuades Antoninus to eschew marriage and bodily pleasures in exchange for heavenly bliss, Artemia attempts to win him over to the role of husband and, eventually, leader of Rome. Dorothea's conversion of Antoninus from dynastic marriage partner to celibate martyr is paralleled by the conversion of Antoninus's attitude toward death. Addressing Antoninus from the place of her execution, Dorothea instructs him to "trace my steps" (4.3.94). In following her lead, Antoninus also helps to inspire the conversion and martyrdom of the chief pagan persecutor, Theophilus. Together, these conversions facilitate a generic conversion, in that the play initially sets up and then subverts the expectations of tragedy by reinterpreting the deaths of Dorothea, Antoninus, and Theophilus as blissful triumphs.

Perhaps most pointedly, Dorothea's conversion of Antoninus's sexual behavior cultivates a code of masculine conduct that marks a distinction between Christian and non-Christian behavior, suggesting clear applications in contemporary intercultural contexts. The specific manner in which Dorothea's rape by Antoninus is diverted in effect displaces the role of divine intervention in the other two plays with masculine restraint, and offers a prescription for Christian chastity that is both physically and culturally constituted. The scene opens with the stage direction, "A bed thrust out, Antoninus vpon it sicke, with Physitions about him, Sapritius and Macrinus, guards" (4.1). As Antoninus's attendants discuss his condition, which apparently stems from a broken heart, his friend Macrinus announces that "a Midwife" is needed to "deliuer him" from his ailment: "[He] will I feare lose life if by a woman / He is not brought to bed" (4.1.22–3). Macrinus continues, "stand by his Pillow / Some little while, and in his broken slumbers / Him shall you heare cry out on Dorothea" (4.1.24–6). In this way, the stage is (literally) set for a recuperative sexual union to take place between Dorothea and Antoninus. However, when Antoninus's father commands him to take Dorothea by "force," Antoninus assures her,

> I would not wound thine honour, pleasure forc'd
> Are vnripe Apples, sowre, not worth the plucking,
> Yet let me tell you, tis my father's will
> That I should seize vpon you as my prey.
> Which I abhorre as much as the blackest sinne
> The villany of man did euer act. (4.1.103–8)

Antoninus's aversion to seeking "pleasure forc'd" stands in stark contrast to the characterization of St. Dorothy's suitor in the play's medieval source materials. The three most prominent English translations of her legend represent her suitor to be the prefect himself, rather than his son. In these sources, Dorothy's rejection of the prefect's marriage proposal fuels his anger to begin with and prompts him to command that she be tortured and ultimately killed. The play's innovation in making Dorothea's chief persecutor the father of her suitor, rather than the suitor himself, produces a tension between persecutor and suitor whereby the suitor's restraint actually facilitates Dorothea's evasion of rape. In direct opposition to the mounting fury of the suitor of the medieval legend, the play's suitor restrains his desires and redirects them toward a different course. Similarly, Antoninus's sexual restraint offers a redemptive contrast to the camel drivers, slaves, pagan soldiers, and other would-be rapists in *The Martyred Soldier* and *The Two Noble Ladies*, eliminating the need for supernatural interventions.

In this way Antoninus exemplifies a new model of male heroism that also emerges in adventure plays set in the contemporary Mediterranean.[67] Cultivated by the female heroine's example of sexual virtue and resistance, he is a gentleman rather than a renegade. Though distinguished in battle and other physical contests, he learns to restrain his sexual appetite and ultimately channels his bodily desires into a love for Christ. His affinities to the chivalric knights of medieval romance illuminate the medieval underpinnings of Christian brotherhood in contemporary seventeenth-century plays like *The Travails of the Three English Brothers* and *The Knight of Malta*, which dramatize pan-Christian opposition to the Ottoman empire. In Chapter 4, I further examine the stage's idealization of restrained masculinity in the face of Muslim adversaries by foregrounding five plays that resurrect the crusading Knights of Malta and seek to reinforce their Order's vow of celibacy. *The Virgin Martyr* brings into view the often indiscernible or otherwise inexplicable ways in which the Renaissance stage imports medieval models of Christian crusaders and virgin martyrs in order to imagine effective forms of resistance to the contemporary Muslim threat.

In addition, in contrast to the frequent gendering of virginity as female in the Middle Ages, the importance of male sexual restraint in *The Virgin Martyr* demonstrates an emerging fluidity between "natural" and "cultural" constructions of racial difference – a connection that becomes increasingly solidified by the eighteenth century. While on the one hand, the preservation of Dorothea's female chastity guards against the literal contamination of her bloodline through sexual generation, on the other hand, the exercise of male sexual restraint suggests a social or behavioral component to racial identity. Thus, racial identity is conceived both as a product of sexual generation and as something that can be controlled through cultural behavior – defined through sexual restraint, self-discipline, and civility. This model of resistance would have been particularly appealing to early modern audiences, given their association of Christian vulnerability to conversion with the male traders and adventurers who were conducting trade in the Mediterranean.

Along these lines, the British slave who refuses to carry out orders to rape Dorothea easily evokes the condition of contemporary British captives in the Ottoman empire. Importantly for this context, the slave demonstrates how resistance guided by Christian principle can offer a sense of empowerment to even the most disempowered of men. His insistence that in refusing to obey such an order, he is merely "halfe a slaue" rather than "a damned whole one, a blacke vgly slaue," suggests a way of retaining one's Christian integrity even under the conditions of enslavement (4.1.154–5). In addition to the contemporary applications of this message, the play's depiction of a fourth-century British slave serves as a reminder of Britain's history of imperial subjugation under Rome, offering an analogy by which England's smallness in relation to the Ottoman empire might be perceived as somehow noble or empowering.

But if *The Virgin Martyr* ultimately produces a model of masculine behavior that is suited to a contemporary context of trade, Ottoman imperialism, and Muslim-Christian persecution, it does so by refiguring tropes and conventions that are rooted in medieval Catholic traditions. Its cultivation of a masculine code of conduct characterized by sexual restraint and civility is only reducible to the tangible vow of virginity that molds and enforces it. This vow is literally and uncompromisingly sustained by the play's saintly heroine. Antoninus's reference to wearing Dorothea's "figure" into battle as a source of protection offers a fitting metaphor for the way his Christian heroism is fostered through her embodied example:

> To Dorothea, tell her I haue worn,
> In all the battailes I haue fought her figure,
> Her figure in my heart, which like a deity
> Hath still protected me. (1.1.461–3)

Reminiscent of the female images imprinted on the insides of medieval shields, the "figure" of Dorothea that Antoninus wears into battle emblematizes an emerging model of male heroism that, like medieval knighthood, is cultivated through the example of female chastity. Though immaterial in nature, this figure, which Antoninus describes as "like a deity," evokes the talismanic qualities associated with Catholic relics. As I explore in the next chapter, it bears a resemblance to the holy relic worn by the Christian heroine in Massinger's *The Renegado* as a protective shield against her Turkish persecutor. The necessity of a supplement, or prophylactic, to counteract conversion assumes particular significance in the context of early seventeenth-century English contact with the Ottoman empire and the proto-racial anxieties it produced.

As I demonstrate in the following chapter, the protective strategy that for a male Christian can exist as a spiritual "figure in [the] heart" requires more tangible physical supplementation for a Christian woman. In *The Renegado*, the Christian virgin has been taken prisoner by a Turkish basha in Tunis and receives the relic from a Jesuit priest. Wearing it, she is immune to her Turkish suitor's predatory desire, which threatens every moment to violate her chastity and convert her to Islam. Like the virgin's intact maidenhead, it offers a physical manifestation of her virtue – her inconvertible Christian essence. The Christian heroine's need for a physical prophylactic is revealing of the deep anxieties surrounding her sexual contamination and its potential to undo the categorical differences between "Christian" and "Turk." Identifying the resonance between *The Virgin Martyr* and contemporary plays like *The Renegado* affords not only a broader interpretation of the former play but also a recognition of the medieval models that inform Christian resistance to Islam in the latter. Moreover, these particular strategies of resistance help us to understand the ways that the threat of conversion has evolved in the English imagination as the result of contemporary Christian-Muslim relations. To contain the contemporary threat associated with turning Turk and its proto-racial valences, the dramatic stage must reach back into the Catholic past for a template of chastity that is both spiritually and physically constituted.

Chapter 3

Engendering Faith: Sexual Defilement and Spiritual Redemption in *The Renegado*

If the plays discussed in the previous chapter suggest certain strategies for resisting conversion to Islam through their depictions of martyrdom in ancient pagan settings, then Philip Massinger's *The Renegado* (*c*.1624) imports these models of resistance into its contemporary North African setting. What may at first appear a disjunctive authorization of seemingly Catholic objects, ceremonies, and figures in a play about Christian-Muslim encounter makes more sense when one considers the empowering template of resistance established by contemporary martyr plays. In the face of Islam – a threat of conversion understood to involve embodied, sexual, and reproductive consequences – Catholicism's material, ritualistic, and embodied forms provided compelling sources of resistance to Turkish torture and sexual violation. While in some ways *The Renegado* seems to celebrate the saving powers of Pauline faith and spiritual redemption to convert a Muslim princess to Christianity and to redeem Christian men temporarily seduced by Islam, it also inadvertently dramatizes the limitations of Christian spiritual faith and redemption. What is more, *The Renegado* reveals the gendered implications of Islamic conversion by foregrounding the question of whether male and female Christians are equally eligible for spiritual redemption if contaminated by Muslim sexual contact. Testing the faith of Pauline universalism through differences of gender, the play reveals the female limits of St. Paul's spiritual universalism through a heroine who is evocatively named Paulina.

As part of the recent wave of interest in early modern encounters with Ottoman "Turks" and the religion of Islam, *The Renegado* has attracted a burst of critical attention. Following the publication of Daniel Vitkus's modern edition (2000), critics including Bindu Malieckal, Barbara Fuchs, Jonathan Gil Harris, Jonathan Burton, Valerie Forman, and Vitkus himself have explored the play's dramatization of contemporary anxieties about Mediterranean commerce and

English contact with the Ottoman empire.[1] Earlier critical interest in the play was sparse and tended to address the Catholic elements of the play, generally understood to be a function of Massinger's (possible) crypto-Catholicism or, at least, his religious tolerance.[2] Although this former interest in the play's Catholic leanings may seem worlds apart from the present critical interest in "Turk" plays, my intention here is to show how the subjects of these two disparate critical approaches are in fact directly interrelated. Specifically, I argue that the play's unlikely investment in Catholic rituals, objects, and bodily practices is directly related to its central concern with the threat of Islamic conversion. Registering an anxiety about the dematerialized, spiritual emphasis of Protestant faith, *The Renegado* turns to more tangible and embodied models of Catholic resistance in order to imagine a viable Christian defense against the particular threat of turning Turk. In addition, the play relies upon the outward, ceremonial emphasis of the sacraments in order to negotiate a means of redemption for select individuals who have previously fallen under the sway of Islam.

Set in the cross-cultural port city of Tunis, a tributary of the Ottoman empire, the play presents two central Christian protagonists, a brother and sister, who both risk sexual defilement and subsequent conversion as the result of threatened unions with Muslim characters. It also dramatizes the plight of a renegade pirate who has previously denounced Christianity and now seeks repentance. While in this play conversion to Islam is mediated across a slippery threshold, both physical and spiritual, it implies a transgression from which there seems to be no return. And yet, despite the tragic repercussions linked with Islamic conversion – its association with permanent and irreversible consequences – *The Renegado* produces a comic ending for each of its Christian protagonists. These comic resolutions, however, turn out to be contingent upon the efficacy of a surprising model of Christian faith and resistance, and reveal a logic of redemption that differs for men and women. Although *The Renegado* overtly posits the triumph of Christian spirituality over Islamic carnality, it anchors Christian resistance in Catholic objects, ceremonies, and bodily practices, and repeatedly marks spiritual redemption in outward, visible, and material ways. For example, a "relic" purported to have magical qualities successfully protects the Christian heroine's virginity from her Turkish captor's carnal designs (1.1.147; 2.5.162).[3] Similarly, the renegade pirate assures his readmission to the church by making his confession to a Jesuit priest – a most unlikely hero on the English Renaissance stage – who is dressed "in a cope, like a bishop" (4.1.72).[4] Enacting the ritual stages of confession and penance, the renegade reverses his former act of apostasy, which was carried out through his disruption of a Catholic mass and desecration of the Eucharistic host. And the play extends Christian conversion to the Muslim princess by requiring her participation in an elaborate baptism ceremony that is performed by a layman, her husband-to-be.

These details position the play explicitly against the practices and beliefs of English Protestantism, and yet the play was given official license for public performance and appears to have been popular and uncontroversial in its time. I want to suggest that *The Renegado*'s depiction of Christian triumph over Muslim conversion involves a complex negotiation of spiritual and material models of faith that suggests a merging of Protestant and Catholic models. In turn, these tensions between spirituality and materiality reveal the ways in which Islam's threat to early modern England was perceived to be not just "religious" in nature, but bodily as well. More specifically, the play's recourse to material, Catholic practices to resist or undo Islamic conversion reveals how Islam was perceived to be a sexual threat, how it was understood to involve a bodily conversion, and how this conversion suggested potential racial implications. It is partly because of Islam's perceived sexual and bodily threat to Christians, I argue, that the stage resurrected older, Catholic models of Christian resistance that were distinctly tangible and embodied.

Importantly, in mounting a Christian defense against turning Turk, *The Renegado* does not merely replace spiritualized understandings of faith with material forms, but rather presents an active tension between the two that is mediated through gender. More specifically, while spiritual fortitude might be enough to ward off the conversion of the Christian hero of the play, the Christian heroine relies for her protection on the outward, material aid of a relic, which in turn safeguards her bodily chastity from the sexual persecutions of a lustful Turk. And while the sexual seduction of the Christian hero by a Turkish woman is reversible, the same is not true for the Christian heroine. Her spiritual status, unlike the Christian hero's, is indivisible from that of her body, and the threatened destruction of her chastity by the Turkish viceroy suggests a permanent and complete undoing of her Christian identity. Thus, the play's insistence upon the need for outward objects and bodily practices to supplement spiritual faith is partly dependent upon the reinforcement of certain gender stereotypes. What is more, these gendered distinctions are bound up with anxieties about embodied and reproductive contamination. Fair skin underscores the Christian heroine's vulnerability to Islamic conversion, as well as the Muslim heroine's eligibility for Christianity. Thus, as Mary Janell Metzger observed of the distinctions between Jessica and Shylock in *The Merchant of Venice*, the intersecting logics of gender, religious difference, and whiteness help dictate the terms of conversion.[5] As I have suggested in previous chapters, the stage's propensity to represent the threat of Islam as a threat of conversion facilitated through sexual intercourse suggests its translation of the religious, commercial, and imperial threat of the Ottoman empire into a personal, bodily threat with proto-racial implications.[6] Within this framework, the Christian heroine's pronounced vulnerability to irrevocable sexual contamination reflects a patriarchal logic that reinscribes her under her male sexual partner and highlights her reproductive role in perpetuating his seed.

Domestic Religious Context

Given the April 1624 licensing of *The Renegado* in the wake of a fierce resurgence of anti-Catholic polemic prompted by royal negotiations for a Spanish match the previous year, and just four months prior to Thomas Middleton's blatantly anti-Catholic *A Game at Chess*, it is certainly remarkable that *The Renegado* should not only escape censure but enjoy considerable popularity and success. It is just this degree of unlikelihood that I want to capture and emphasize, however. *The Renegado* continued to be performed throughout the 1620s until its publication in 1630, and its debut at the Cockpit associated it with one of the most prestigious and lucrative playhouses in London. Such popular success suggests a softening of Protestant attitudes toward Catholicism that has not typically been associated with the early-to-mid-1620s. Critics dating back to William Gifford in 1805 have attempted to explain the play's Catholic elements by speculating that Massinger was himself a crypto-Catholic or by attributing them to Spanish sources.[7] Rather, I suggest that what appear to us as the play's clear Catholic affinities point to a broader, popular sensibility that still relied on Catholic models for conceiving of faith and resistance to persecution. Moreover, *The Renegado* reveals ways in which popular English attitudes toward Catholic and Protestant religious practices were influenced by the seemingly unrelated activity of commercial intercourse with the Ottoman empire. By adopting Catholic models to confront the threat of Islamic conversion, Massinger refunctions these models as acceptable forms of Christian resistance in a culture transformed not only by the Reformation but by increased commercial contact with Muslims.

The real and imagined fear of turning Turk may not only have pressured a return to Catholic models, but also helped to lay the cultural groundwork for the Church of England's gradual shift away from Calvinism in favor of the more sensuous, ceremonial forms of worship associated with William Laud and Arminianism. In carrying out the conversion of the Muslim princess and the redemption of the renegade pirate, *The Renegado* exaggerates the ceremonial elements involved in the sacraments of baptism and reconciliation. As Michael Neill has recently argued, these doctrinal shifts associated with the Arminian ascendancy lent themselves to the "conventional 'turn and counterturn' of tragicomic design."[8] In this way, he links *The Renegado*'s doctrinal stance to the rise of the tragicomic form. By contrast, Benedict Robinson has sought to explain the play's apparent Arminian sympathies by privileging its publication date of 1630 over its earlier performance date of 1624 and placing it in the context of Laudian politics and Caroline drama.[9] I share Neill's sense that the redemptive arc of the play relies on a doctrinal logic that seems sympathetic to both Catholicism and Arminianism, and I am in accord with Robinson's impulse to consider the play's Christian-Muslim opposition in relation to domestic religious factions. In contrast to these critics, however, I link the play's Catholic and proto-Arminian sympathies in 1624 to the embodied and sexualized threat of turning Turk. Because this threat of conversion exceeded the realm of spiritual faith, it demanded physical and material countermeasures in order to believably enact its resistance or reversal. In crucial ways, both the embodied emphasis of Islam and its tangible Christian countermeasures are also encouraged by the visual and theatrical orientation of the public stage.

The Renegado's hypothesis that a male Christian might be able to reverse the contaminating effects of sexual intercourse with a Muslim woman through spiritual fortitude marks a sharp departure from previous dramas in which any contact with a Turk was potentially a prelude to permanent conversion. As recent critics have shown, *The Renegado* is one of numerous plays performed in London between 1580 and 1630 that stage cross-cultural encounters between Christians and Muslims set in the unstable trading territories of the southeastern Mediterranean. As Jean Howard has noted, these adventure dramas typically feature swashbuckling Christian heroes who, through contact with foreign cultures and people, undergo an "actual or threatened transformation . . . into something alien."[10] Most notably, Robert Daborne's *A Christian Turned Turke* (*c*.1610) provides an important precedent for Massinger's play. As detailed in my Introduction, in Daborne's play the sexual seduction of a Christian hero by a Muslim woman leads to immediate Islamic conversion and irrevocable damnation.[11] Daborne's particular yoking of conversion and sexual seduction implied a transformation that was generated through the body and permanent. Further, in interpreting the hero's sexual transgression and subsequent conversion as signs of his unalterable path to damnation, the play follows a tragic arc that is consistent with Calvinist predestination.[12] It is this precedent that *The Renegado* clearly sets out to revise. As Vitkus points out, *The Renegado* seems to "consciously" rewrite the plot of *A Christian Turned Turke*, transforming a tragic ending into a comic one.[13] More specifically, whereas *A Christian Turned Turke* cannot imagine a way to resolve Ward's sexual defilement other than through permanent conversion and damnation, *The Renegado* disrupts the immediate equation by positing that the sins of the body do not necessarily have to damn the soul. Thus, if in Daborne's play the sexual union between Christian protagonist and Muslim woman leads inevitably to the Christian man's religious conversion, suicide, and damnation, in *The Renegado* the Christian-Muslim union can lead to repentance, baptism, and marriage. The earlier play's representation of its Christian hero's irreversible conversion helps us to appreciate the stakes of the intervention that *The Renegado* seeks to make and why it must rely on visual, material indexes of faith in order to mark Christian redemption.

Commerce, Sex, and Fungibility

It is fitting that the Christian hero's seduction by the Muslim princess begins in the Tunisian marketplace, where the purchase and sale of commodities constitutes an analogy for religious and bodily conversion. The play's alignment of commodity exchange and religious conversion emphasizes both the fungibility of human bodies and souls and their potential resistance to fungible or anonymous exchange. As Nabil Matar and others have shown, the historical conditions of Mediterranean trade provided an important context for early seventeenth-century dramas of cross-cultural contact and conversion.[14] The Ottoman empire's control over the majority of southeastern Mediterranean ports and trade routes meant that the English were completely at its mercy for obtaining the luxury goods that their re-export economy increasingly depended upon. While piracy and the captivity of English seamen had also been problems during Queen Elizabeth's reign, they became especially pressing concerns under King James.[15] English seamen operating in the Mediterranean were perceived to be constantly vulnerable to piracy, enslavement, and religious conversion, especially along the Barbary Coast, where privateers of many different nationalities competed for commodities – both nonhuman and human. Like Daborne's play before it, *The Renegado* translates this real-life threat of captivity and conversion into a drama of sexual seduction.

Disguised as a merchant, Vitelli, a Venetian gentleman, has set up shop in the Tunisian marketplace in order to attempt to rescue his sister, Paulina, who has been sold into Turkish captivity by the eponymous "renegade" pirate, Grimaldi. While Paulina is imprisoned in the Ottoman palace and struggles daily to protect her virtue from the Turkish viceroy, Vitelli is diverted by his own seduction by the Turkish princess Donusa. When, in the third scene of the play, Donusa pays a visit to Vitelli's shop in the market, she peruses his wares as he in turn examines her. Though she poses as a buyer and he as a seller, it is not at all clear what or who is being bought or sold. When Donusa asks to be shown "the chiefest of [Vitelli's] wares" (1.3.105), Vitelli hands her a looking glass "steeled so exactly, neither taking from / Nor flattering the object it returns / To the beholder, that Narcissus might / . . . view his fair feature in it" (1.3.109–13). In this way, Vitelli succeeds in "steeling" Donusa's reflection, converting her image into a saleable commodity in his possession. One might note that the opening scene has previously established Vitelli's large stock of portraits of European princesses, which were actually modeled by "bawds and common courtesans in Venice" (1.1.13). The image of Donusa's face in Vitelli's mirror thus aligns her with these "bawds" and "courtesans" and their commodified sexuality. But Donusa destabilizes Vitelli's implied mastery over his wares and her sexuality when she suddenly "unveils herself" and seizes him with "wonder" (1.3.140–1). Donusa then purposely breaks some of his glass wares; no longer a captive image in his mirror, she takes control of the transaction by bidding him to "bring his bill / Tomorrow to the palace and enquire / For one 'Donusa' . . . / Say there he shall receive / Full satisfaction" (1.3.156–60). Donusa thus succeeds in turning the tables on Vitelli, for in transposing the payment of the debt to her turf, she shifts the power dynamic between buyer and seller, and makes the Christian gentleman's chastity, rather than her own, the one at risk.

The relocation from the marketplace to Donusa's chambers removes the transaction from the site of commercial exchange to a private space, making clear that what is at stake is Vitelli's bodily virtue and not his damaged "wares" (1.3.105). When she returns to the palace, Donusa is teased for her interest in Vitelli by her castrated serving man, Carazie, and her female servant, Manto. The eunuch's astonishment at Donusa's susceptibility to such a meager "haberdasher of small wares" (2.3.4) and Manto's mocking reminder that Carazie himself "hast none" (2.3.5) drive home the message of what Vitelli stands to lose in the transaction. That Carazie, the only English character in the play, is a Muslim convert and a castrated servant in the Ottoman palace makes anxious humor of the common conflation of conversion with circumcision and castration.[16] When Vitelli arrives at the heavily protected palace, he slowly penetrates its outer layers to reach Donusa's inner private chamber. Donusa offers him compensation for the "poor petty trifles" (2.4.81) she has "injured" (2.4.80) in the form of "bags stuffed full of our imperial coin" (2.4.83), "gems for which the slavish Indian dives" (2.4.85), and finally sexual intercourse, which she describes as "the tender of / Myself" (2.4.101–2). Both the overpayment of her debt and the uneasy slippage between objects of exchange and her selfhood (or sexuality) reflect a crisis of value that lies at the heart of the play. While, on one hand, *The Renegado* asserts that human souls and bodies are as fungible as commodities, it simultaneously resists this analogy through its emphasis on the deep and permanent effects of bodily transgressions and their potential to outweigh the power of the spirit.

Although Donusa's trading of "the tender of [her]self" in exchange for "poor petty trifles" implies that she is the loser in the bargain, Vitelli's acceptance of the offer seems to threaten a loss that is even greater. His capitulation to Donusa signals the overpowering of his Christian soul by his bodily desires, a defeat that in turn presumes potential spiritual consequences. Vitelli resists Donusa's offers of money and gems, but finds himself powerless against her sexual charms:

> How I shake
> In my constant resolution! And my flesh,
> Rebellious to my better part, now tells me
> (As if it were a strong defense of frailty)
> A hermit in a desert trenched with prayers
> Could not resist this battery. (2.4.108–13)

Vitelli's sense of his "flesh" outmatching the "constant resolution" of his "better part" illustrates the serious infraction of having sex with a Muslim woman and how it was imagined to conflate a bodily transgression with a spiritual one. Vitelli's sexual union with Donusa results in a superficial transformation of his appearance, including a new set of fine clothing, but it also suggests the potential for deeper and more permanent effects. Led by Donusa to the innermost chamber of the palace, "some private room the sunbeams never enter" (2.4.130), Vitelli agrees to relinquish his virginity, exclaiming, "Though the Devil / Stood by and roared, I follow!" (2.4.134–5). His equation of a Muslim woman with "the Devil" suggests a union that will lead him down the path to conversion and thus eternal damnation, setting him up for a fate matching that of the protagonist from Daborne's *A Christian Turned Turke*.

In drawing a causal link between sexual intercourse between a Christian and a Turk and conversion to Islam, plays such as *The Renegado* and *A Christian Turned Turke* suggest an essential, embodied difference between "Christian" and "Turk" that did not apply in the same way to Catholics and Protestants. While Protestant polemic linked Catholicism to the biblical Whore of Babylon in order to denigrate the practice of idolatry, this sexual allusion was primarily understood as allegorical in nature.[17] By contrast, Muslims were associated with a literal threat of sexual and bodily contamination. John Stradling marks this distinction between Catholics and Muslims in his 1623 poem *Beati Pacifici*.[18] Anticipating an objection to his advocacy of a Protestant–Catholic alliance against the Turk, he imagines that someone will hold up the example of Phineas, who fervently slaughtered an Israelite man and Moabite woman as they engaged in sexual intercourse. Rejecting the possible analogy between Catholic and Moabite, Stradling offered the simple response, "Here be no Moabites."[19] In other words, he implies that whereas Catholics were not comparable to the essential difference of the Moabite woman, the Turks were.

Jesuitical Intercession

Indeed, Vitelli's de-virgination by Donusa seems at first to consign him to the same damning fate as Daborne's hero. Wearing a new set of "fine clothes" offered by Donusa, he is met on the street by Francisco, a Jesuit priest who seems to be stationed in Tunis to provide counsel to the Christians, and by Vitelli's servant, Gazet.[20] Francisco alludes to Vitelli's new clothes by remarking that he is "strangely metamorphosed" (2.6.20), and adds, "You have made, sir, / A prosperous voyage. Heaven grant it be honest: / I shall rejoice it then, too" (2.6.20–2). Vitelli makes overtures toward sharing his gold and attempts to justify his new wealth by suggesting that it can be used to redeem Christian captives from Turkish galleys. But Francisco asserts that the sinful source of Vitelli's wealth invalidates the good it can do and suggests that it may have implications for his soul that exceed the outer transformation of his appearance. He exclaims, "They steer not the right course, nor traffic well, / That seek a passage to reach heaven through hell" (2.6.45–6). Thus, he implies that in accepting

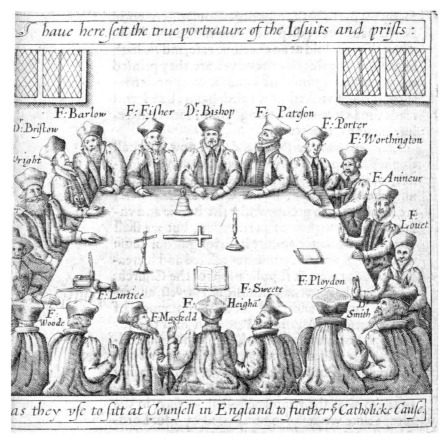

Figure 3.1: Jesuit priests, from Thomas Scott, *The second part of Vox populi* (London, 1624), G4v. Reproduced by permission of the Folger Shakespeare Library.

Donusa's gifts, Vitelli has chosen a sensuous course that cannot lead to salvation.

Importantly, however, *The Renegado* allows for Vitelli to redeem himself and stave off damnation through Francisco's intercession. That Massinger not only portrays this Jesuit priest in a positive light but credits him with the salvation of the Christian characters, their escape from Tunis, and the happy outcome of the play is remarkable given the usual vilification of Jesuits in Protestant England. In fact, there was an outpouring of anti-Jesuit tracts the year after *The Renegado*'s initial performance, associating Jesuit priests with conniving methods of infiltration and conversion, assassination plans, and covert Catholic rebellions.[21] By contrast, *The Renegado* marks Francisco as a hero for advocating equivocation as a means to subvert the Turks (5.2.35–7), and for masterminding a covert plan at the end of the play to facilitate the escape of the Christian characters. The play's happy conclusion depends upon the priest's crafty intercession. In other words, whereas Jesuitical practices were never condoned by the English when used against Protestants, they are condoned in the play for use against Muslims. In addition, the play relies on the Jesuit to counsel and redeem its errant Christian characters, and to lend authority and validation to their inward contrition. After exiting the stage to converse privately with Francisco, Vitelli returns convinced of the error of his ways and resolute in his conviction to redeem himself through future acts.

Notably, the Christian protagonist's sexual transgression has not, as in the case of Daborne's protagonist, occasioned a circumcision. Despite Gazet and Carazie's jokes to this effect, Vitelli emerges from the palace with his foreskin and his testicles intact, and perhaps this helps to account for why his redemption is more easily posited than Ward's. Although the threat of circumcision, and by extension castration, hovers around the edges of this play, its disconnection from the act of sexual intercourse enables Vitelli to emerge from sex unscathed in a way that his sister Paulina might not. Certainly, what Burton characterizes as the play's comedic disavowal of circumcision and castration mask genuine anxieties about these interrelated threats.[22] Their significance in relation to the play's mercantile context has attracted numerous critics. As Fuchs, Harris, and most recently Forman have observed, *The Renegado*'s portrayal of Carazie and the threat of castration expresses fears of English emasculation in the face of Mediterranean piracy, economic loss, and the disruption of trade.[23] In my own reading, the dramatized threats of circumcision and castration function not as allegories for economic anxieties, but as examples of how conversion to Islam assumed an embodied significance in the early modern imagination (though economic and bodily anxieties were also interrelated). As an indelible mark upon the body, circumcision suggested a physical sign of the irreversibility of conversion as well as the convert's relegation to a proto-racial category that distinguished both Muslims and Jews from Christians. Thus on the stage, the significance of circumcision – its theological, covenantal, and communitarian role in the Jewish tradition – was largely recast as a mark of exclusion rather than a signature of covenantal membership that builds communities across time and space. In addition, the stage's comic association of circumcision with the more drastic cut of castration conflated the ritualized ceremony of *brit milah* with the castrated eunuchs identified with the sultan's seraglio. This conflation also projected the threat of circumcision into more extreme and drastic bodily consequences. In Daborne's play, circumcision is closely linked to the sexual transgression that prompts the protagonist's conversion in that it immediately follows his sexual interlude with a Turkish woman. Thus, the fact that Vitelli eludes circumcision is all the more significant. It is precisely by avoiding this consequence that the play seems to acknowledge the role of circumcision in sealing conversion, marking it as a *fait accompli*. By disrupting the association between sexual transgression and circumcision, *The Renegado* sustains the possibility that Vitelli's sexual transgression has not yet converted his body and thus can be reversed through spiritual cleansing.

Male Spiritual Redemption and Female Bodily Resistance

Vitelli's return to the palace enables a palimpsestic rewriting of his previous bodily transgression as a triumph of spiritual resistance. After seeking counsel from Francisco, Vitelli returns to announce his repudiation of Islam and to bear the trial of Donusa's repeated attempts to seduce and convert him. At first he refuses even to look at Donusa because he fears he will be unable to resist her embraces, even if "iron grates were interposed between [them]" (3.5.10). His worry that his "human frailty" might "betray" him "in scorn of reason, and what's more, religion" and his allusion to the "overvalue" at which he has "purchased" Donusa's body suggest a close correspondence between sexual transgression and religious consequences (3.5.12, 16, 15, 41). In fact, Vitelli ultimately decides to look upon Donusa, convinced that "The trial, else, is nothing; nor the conquest . . . / Worthy to be remembered" (3.5.35, 37). Crying, "Up, my virtue! / And holy thoughts and resolutions arm me / Against this fierce temptation!" (3.5.37–9), he enlists his spiritual "resolutions" against Donusa's physical temptations. After avowing his firm allegiance to Christianity, he returns the "casket" of jewels and "cloak and doublet" she has given him (3.5.48, 50). In shedding his rich "livery" (3.5.50), Vitelli draws attention to a distinction between the ease of shedding the external trappings of his corporeal sin and the difficulty of redeeming his inward "innocence" (3.5.45):

> That I could with that ease
> Redeem my forfeit innocence or cast up
> The poison I received into my entrails
> From the alluring cup of your enticements
> As now I do deliver back the price   *Returns the casket*
> And salary of your lust! Or thus unclothe me

Of sin's gay trappings, the proud livery *Throws off his cloak and doublet*
Of wicked pleasure. (3.5.44–51)

Vitelli's manner of comparing the spiritual redemption he desires to "cast[ing] up / The poison I received into my entrails / From the alluring cup of your enticements" seems to reflect a struggle to characterize inner redemption in terms that differ from the outward casting off of Donusa's "livery." Both dialogue and stage directions capture a tension between outward bodily action (Vitelli's "throwing off his cloak and doublet" and "returning the casket of jewels"; the sexual double entendre of Donusa's "alluring cup") and the attainment of inner purification. Although the play resorts to a bodily metaphor, it suggests in the end that Vitelli's desire to "redeem [his] forfeit innocence" has little to do with the body at all, and everything to do with transcendent spiritual redemption.

But if inner contrition can save Vitelli, the same latitude is not extended to his sister, the Christian heroine. Instead, the play vigilantly protects her bodily integrity. Although Paulina is fiercely pursued by the viceroy of Tunis, who holds her captive in the same palace where Vitelli succumbs to Donusa, the play simply will not allow a sexual union to take place between the Christian heroine and a Turkish man. That Paulina's spiritual constancy must be supplemented by her physical virginity reflects the limit of the play's own faith in the efficacy of inner faith as a countermeasure to Islamic conversion. Conjuring St. Paul's spiritualized universalism through her very name, Paulina demonstrates how this notion of faith does not adequately anchor female Christian identity in the contemporary cross-currents of Ottoman North Africa. Rather, the physical body is called into play. Despite Protestant England's general repudiation of vowed female celibacy, it is here construed as a necessary corollary to inner constancy. In this way, the chaste and miraculously inviolable Paulina follows the template of the virgin martyrs of medieval Catholic saints' tales, whose resistance to rape is celebrated in the martyr plays of my previous chapter.

Paulina's Holy Relic

What is more, the play externalizes Paulina's virginity by means of a holy relic that she wears upon her breast, thereby employing a Catholic idol – one of the chief targets of Protestant iconoclasm – as a viable and necessary protector of the Christian faith.[24] Francisco reassures Vitelli that his sister's chastity is protected:

> I oft have told you
> Of a relic that I gave her which has power,
> If we may credit holy men's traditions,
> To keep the owner free from violence.
> This on her breast she wears and does preserve
> The virtue of it by her daily prayers. (1.1.146–51)

Contrary to Francisco's credible association with the relic, publications such as Jean de Chassanion's *The merchandises of popish priests* (1629) perpetuated a demonized association between Jesuit priests and the importation of relics in England. Subtitled "A discouery of the Jesuites trumpery newly packed in England. Laying open to the world, how cunningly they cheat and abuse poore people, with their false, deceitfull, and counterfet wares," De Chassanion's text sought to expose a link between Jesuit priests' use of relics and their deceitful practices (see Figure 3.2).

Nevertheless, *The Renegado* reaffirms Francisco's testimony to the protective "power" of Paulina's relic through its effects on the Turkish viceroy. When confronted with it, Asambeg's predatory lust turns to softness and restraint: "Ravish her, I dare not," he says, "The magic that she wears about her neck, / I think, defends her" (2.5.161–3). Part of the irony of Asambeg's validation of the relic's talismanic qualities lies in the fact that Islam condemned the practice of idolatry just as vehemently as Protestantism did. Although some English Protestants were beginning to re-embrace sacramental and sensuous worship as early as the 1620s, relics were still considered far beyond the pale. Furthermore, the play's association of the relic with a virtuous Catholic virgin goes directly against Protestants' traditional association of idolatry with Catholic whoredom. As Frances Dolan has argued, the tendency for Catholic women to worship false idols, or to assign talismanic powers to "trinkets and toys," was understood to derive from their ignorance, vanity, and superstition.[25] Thus, the play purposefully interferes with Protestant assumptions about women's abuse of relics in order to associate a Catholic woman's use of a relic with the integrity of her virtue.

On some level, the sacred relic that protects Paulina's chastity functions as an outward manifestation of her virginal hymen. Thus, it demonstrates the play's conflation of religious protection against conversion with a sexual chastity that is literally figured through the body. In addition to externalizing religious resistance, the relic's promise of inviolability assuages anxieties about the inherent intangibility of the hymen, which despite its material tangibility is located on the inside of the body and is thus impossible to see from the outside. In fact, as medical discourses from the period point out, verification

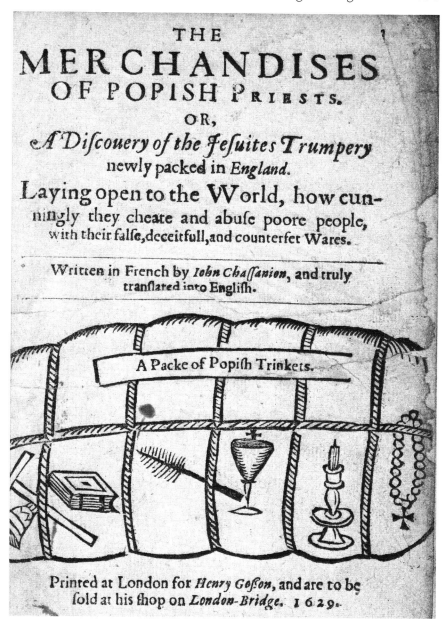

Figure 3.2: Jean de Chassanion, *Merchandises of popish priests* (London: 1629), title page woodcut. Reproduced by permission of the Faculty of Advocates and the Abbotsford Library Project.

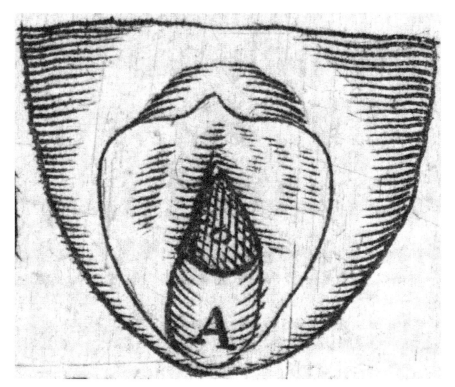

Figure 3.3: Detail of the virginal hymen, from Thomas Bartholin, *Bartholinus anatomy* (London, 1668), 76, plate V. Reproduced by permission of the Folger Shakespeare Library.

of the hymen's status is complicated by the fact that intactness can only be proven through penetration.[26] This problem of verification is directly alluded to in a conversation between the Muslim princess and her servant Manto, when Donusa worries that her loss of virginity to Vitelli might be visible from the outside. After learning that Manto is also no longer a virgin, Donusa asks her, "Could thy friends / Read in thy face, thy maidenhead gone, that thou / Hadst parted with it?" (3.1.12–14). Her use of the term "maidenhead" itself captures a certain slippage between abstraction and materiality, in that the term referred interchangeably in the early seventeenth century to "the state or condition of virginity" as well as the physical "hymen."[27] And indeed, Manto replies that she successfully "passed / for current many years after" without the truth being discovered (3.1.14–15).[28]

The utility of the relic as physical evidence of Paulina's virginity responds to the play's urgency around ensuring her intact hymen. Of course, the use of a relic as sexual prophylactic may not have offered

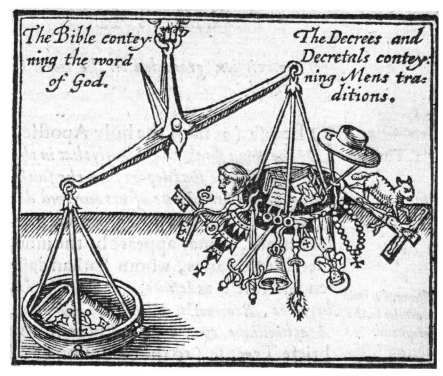

Figure 3.4: Catholic objects weighed against the Protestant Word, from Thomas Williamson, *The sword of the spirit to smite in pieces that antichristian Goliah* (London, 1613), sig. B3r. Reproduced by permission of the Huntington Library, San Marino, California.

complete reassurance. For one thing, English audiences in 1624 could not have viewed the portrayal of an efficacious relic without also remaining aware of Protestant reformers' rejection of the notion that mere objects might possess sacred powers. As critics such as Arjun Appadurai and Harris remind us, material objects cannot be divorced from the meanings they accrue through their social histories and their circulation within systems of economic exchange.[29] Relics represent a particularly interesting kind of materiality in that their value lies in their perceived singularity and sacred presence, and yet they were imminently subject to commodification and forged reproduction. Thus, given their status in post-Reformation England as fakes and commodities, such relics may seem to resemble the unverifiable nature of the hymen and the potential commodification of female sexuality. In that it is nominally sealed off from circulation, Paulina's amulet is at once expressly distinct from the fungible goods of the market scene, as well as the despotic economy of the seraglio, while also suggestive of the potential for commodification. At the same time, I would locate the relic's utility not merely in its "materiality," whose meaning could not be separated from its social history, but in its concrete physicality, which serves to anchor Paulina's uncompromised virginity and to reinforce the audience's faith in its protection. Quite crudely, Paulina's confrontation with a threat of conversion that is specifically sexualized and embodied in nature calls for a physical defense system.

Baptism as Spiritual Re-Virgination

Whereas Paulina's virginity is construed to be completely inflexible and, if compromised, irreparable, the Turkish Donusa's loss of virginity is rendered distinct from her potential to possess inner virtue – a virtue that is instead dependent upon her conversion to Christianity. Clearly, the political advantages of Donusa's marriage to Vitelli play a role in this. However, the play's eagerness to produce some outward assurance of Donusa's Christian conversion, as well as of her repaired virtue, is not without anxiety. Just as Paulina relies on a relic to stabilize her virginity and by extension her Christian identity, Donusa requests an outward assurance of her faith and redemption that will spiritually reseal her hymen and mark her Christian conversion. When asked whether she is "confirmed" (4.3.154) in her Christian faith, she responds, "I would be – but the means / That may assure me?" (4.3.154–5). This prompts Vitelli to seek from the Jesuit priest

> The holy badge that should proclaim her fit
> For these celestial nuptials. Willing she is,
> I know, to wear it as the choicest jewel
> On her fair forehead. (5.1.23–6)

In this way, both Donusa's religious conversion and her spiritual re-virgination are externalized in the form of a "holy badge" worn upon the "forehead." Like Paulina's relic, Donusa's "holy badge" functions on some level as an outer corollary to her hymen – rendering evidence of its spiritual reconstitution. Yet this object also resists materialization in that it does not constitute an actual badge, but is an imagined "jewel," worn as a sign of her mind's purification. And unlike Paulina, Donusa is not an actual virgin, but rather a spiritually born-again virgin. Given the play's unyielding commitment to maintaining Paulina's unbreakable chastity, its willingness to Christianize and render marriageable a de-virginated Muslim woman is certainly remarkable. This willingness seems to suggest that the racial implication of converting a Muslim princess to Christianity by coupling her with a Christian husband was far less threatening than the possibility of a Christian woman's conversion to Islam.[30] Donusa's marriage also serves the purpose of rescuing her from a match with Mustapha, the Muslim basha of Aleppo, who has come to Tunis to woo her – signaling a victory for Christian masculinity.[31]

But in order to carry out the miraculous conversion of Donusa, to redeem her from her sexual transgression and render her marriageable to a Christian man, *The Renegado* must invest tremendous authority in the saving powers of baptism. The "holy badge" that Vitelli requests refers most directly to the sacrament of baptism, a sacrament that was a source of intense debate in the years leading up to Laud's ascendancy. Whereas most Calvinists held baptism to be a symbolic act that could not override predestination, Catholics and later followers of Laud and Jacobus Arminius put real stock in the magic of the ceremony.[32] Vitelli's request to perform a lay baptism of Donusa would have been perceived as validation of baptism's mystical powers and its necessity for salvation – an interpretation that was distinctly anti-Calvinist. Vitelli says of the water he throws on her face, "It hath power / To purge those spots that cleave upon the mind" (5.3.114–15). Similarly, Donusa's reaction to the baptism affirms its transformative powers. After Vitelli "throws [water] on her face" (5.3.116), she responds,

> I am another woman – til this minute
> I never lived, nor durst think how to die.
> How long have I been blind! Yet on the sudden
> By this blest means I feel the films of error
> Ta'en from my soul's eyes. (5.3.121–5)

Donusa's baptism marks a triumph of spirit over body, for the symbolic cleansing of the "spots that cleave upon [her] mind" seems to render the physical defilement of her body inconsequential. Her spontaneous announcement upon having water thrown on her face ("I am another woman"), followed by her Pauline reference to gaining the miracle of sight, characterize her conversion as instantaneous, complete, and miraculous.[33] While, as I briefly consider in the concluding section of this chapter, the self-conscious performativity of this moment reminds us that we are watching a play and not a miracle, the Muslim woman's conversion to Christianity within the fiction of the play not only authorizes but depends upon the ceremonial accoutrements of baptism.

In addition to depicting Donusa's baptism as a magical transformation, *The Renegado* explicitly cites a contemporary debate about lay baptism. Reasoning that it would not be possible for Francisco to gain access to the palace prison in order to perform Donusa's baptism, Vitelli asks, "Whether, in me, a layman, without orders, / It may not be religious and lawful, / As we go to our deaths, to do that office?" (5.1.30–2). Beginning in the later sixteenth century, Presbyterian reformers such as Thomas Cartwright made clear their position that lay baptism was an unequivocally Catholic practice that needed to be abolished.[34] Francisco's reply authorizes Vitelli to perform Donusa's baptism by citing the authority granted to midwives to perform emergency baptisms on dying newborns, as well as that granted to Christian soldiers in the Crusades who performed baptisms on the battlefield:

> A question in itself with much ease answered:
> Midwives, upon necessity, perform it;
> And knights that in the Holy Land fought for
> The freedom of Jerusalem, when full
> Of sweat and enemies' blood, have made their helmets
> The fount out of which with their holy hands
> They drew that heavenly liquor. 'Twas approved then
> By the holy church, nor must I think it now,
> In you, a work less pious. (5.1.33–41)

Francisco's appeal to both "midwives" and crusading "knights" evokes Catholic precedent to justify the performance of lay baptism. While the established church did not forbid midwives from baptizing newborns, radical reformers tended to object to female participation in church rites because they viewed it as a Catholic holdover.[35] In addition, Francisco's allusion to the "knights that in the Holy Land fought for / The freedom of Jerusalem" draws attention to the common Christian history that is shared by Protestants and Catholics alike – a time in the past when the "holy church" denoted a single, unified entity. Drawn from Torquato Tasso's *Jerusalem Delivered* (1581), Francisco's reference to "sweat"- and "blood"-filled "helmets" used as baptismal "founts" links Vitelli's baptism of Donusa to Tancredi's baptism of Clorinda, and to a previous Christian collaboration prompted by the religious and imperial threat of Islam.[36] Specifically, he alludes to the Holy Crusades in which the nations of western Europe united to wrest the Holy Land from Muslim control. Historically, the English fully supported the religious and military crusade that was exemplified by the pan-European Knights Hospitallers of Jerusalem, later called the Knights of Malta, a religious order under the jurisdiction of the pope. In 1540, however, Henry VIII dissolved the English *langue* (or branch) of the Knights of Malta by parliamentary statute, causing many Knights to be executed or forced into exile.[37] *The Renegado*'s valorization of the Knights reinvokes

the Christian Crusades to draw an analogy with the current necessity of converting the Muslim princess. As I explore in the following
chapter, the unlikely reappearance of the Knights of Malta in five post-
Reformation stage plays similarly illustrates the renewed relevance of
medieval Catholic models to help frame the current Christian-Muslim
conflict.

Ecumenical Politics and the Role of the Popular Stage

Indeed, the appeal of a pan-Christian alliance against the Ottoman
empire may provide a partial explanation for the apparent Catholic
sympathies of Massinger's play because it offers a political context
for religious concessions toward Catholicism. At the same time that
Ottoman piracy posed an increasing threat to Christian seamen operating in the Mediterranean, England's attitude toward its traditional
Catholic arch-enemy, Spain, was in a state of transition. England's
relationships to Catholic Spain and the Ottoman empire were in fact
directly interrelated in the period. King James's negotiations for a
Spanish match were ostensibly aimed at securing Spanish assistance in
returning the Palatinate to his son-in-law, Frederick V, but James also
hoped that the match would facilitate general Christian pacification
and a league against the Turk. For example, in 1620 James organized an Anglo-Spanish attack on Algiers, the capital of North Africa's
Ottoman regencies, which, as Malieckal has suggested, may have provided the historical impetus for Massinger's play.[38] Thus, "Protestant,"
"Catholic," and "Turk" were linked together in a triangular relationship
in which two sides were allied against the third.

King James's endorsement of a pan-Christian alliance was shared
by a number of English clergy who operated under his patronage and
espoused the rhetoric of Christian unity against the Turk. For example,
Richard Montagu characterized the Turks as "the grand professed
enemies of CHRISTIANS, Christianity, CHRIST, qua tales," who,
for all their differences, together constitute the universal Christian
church.[39] Montagu's publication of two pamphlets in 1624 and 1625,
titled *A gagg for the new gospell? No. A new gagg for an old goose*
and *Appello Caesarem*, provoked controversy for venturing to narrow
the doctrinal differences between the English and Roman churches
and for accusing the Puritans of threatening the *via media* that James
favored. James's support of pan-Christian unity also paved the way for
the rise of William Laud, who began to gain royal favor in the 1620s
and would attempt to carry out the displacement of English Calvinism

by Arminianism.[40] Laud and other members of the Durham House group began publicizing their views in the 1620s through sermons that countered the central Calvinist doctrine of predestination. His program amounted to a turning away from the iconoclasm and inwardness of the Reformed tradition to a renewed emphasis on ceremonial, sacramental, and sensuous worship. It is important to acknowledge, however, that Laud did not become archbishop of Canterbury until 1633 and his full impact was not felt until Charles's reign.

I want to suggest that *The Renegado* reveals the possibility of a breakdown of the Calvinist consensus prior to and separate from the ecclesiastical ramifications of Laud and the Durham House group. First, the play precedes the formal dissolution of the Calvinist consensus, which Nicholas Tyacke, in his book on the rise of English Arminianism, has influentially argued was accomplished mainly through Bishop Neile and the high church clerical cabal.[41] Second, the play illustrates how challenges to Calvinism may have emerged from the popular domain, anticipating rather than reflecting later ecclesiastical reforms.[42] Thus, it points to a shift that did not emanate exclusively from high culture, but was generated through popular media like the drama.[43] Moreover, the stage shows us that this shift was not just coincident with the competing threat of Islamic conversion, but also powerfully informed by this threat. Specifically, the stage turned to the material trappings of Catholicism, including the miracle of a sacred relic, the bodily practice of chastity, the outward ceremony of the sacraments, and the performance of good works, to provide objective correlatives for Christian resistance, conversion, and redemption in relation to the embodied threat of Islam. Thus, *The Renegado* does not merely reflect evidence of lingering Catholic sympathies or early Laudian influences, but demonstrates how, within the secular domain of the theater, the imagined threat of Islam generated certain kinds of responses that resembled and anticipated later ecclesiastical reforms.

Catholic Prophylactics and the Regulation of Reproduction

In addition, the stage reveals that the forging of a pan-Christian alliance was not just politically strategic and advantageous, but also spoke to a threat of conversion that operated on the level of the body. If the material and ritualistic elements of Catholicism offered a form of resistance to turning Turk that spiritualized faith alone could not provide, then *The Renegado*'s reliance on Catholic models also provides insight into how the threat of the Turk was imaginatively construed as a sexual threat with potential reproductive consequences. In demonstrating the need to fortify Protestant models of spiritual resistance with outward, Catholic prophylactics, the stage conveyed the importance of regulating and controlling religious and proto-racial purity through sexual intervention.

It is no accident that the only characters in the play who are not candidates for Christian conversion or redemption are the Muslim men. In contrast to the Muslim princess, the play renders Asambeg, the Turkish viceroy and would-be suitor to the Christian virgin, inherently unconvertible and ineligible for marriage to a Christian. Deceived and abandoned by the Christians as well as the newly Christianized Donusa at the end of the play, he determines to "hide / This head among the deserts, or some cave / Filled with my shame and me, where I alone / May die without a partner in my moan" (5.8.36–9). That these lines of Asambeg's are also the closing lines of the play signals that his solitary abandonment, stripping him of any sexual partner, is the ultimate factor in *The Renegado*'s comic denouement. Thus, the play renders Asambeg completely impotent and construes his religious difference as permanent and immutable. From the printed text of the play, it is impossible to ascertain whether Asambeg's religious difference was accompanied by specific somatic differences indicated by cosmetics, costume, or other physical markers in the performance. However, the other male Turkish character in the play, Mustapha, is explicitly mocked for his dark skin. Donusa's rejection of Mustapha's courtship links her aversion to his complexion:

> I have considered you from head to foot,
> And can find nothing in that wainscot face
> That can teach me to dote; nor am I taken
> With your grim aspect or tadpole-like complexion. (3.1.47–50)

Her references to his "wainscot [i.e. with hardened and tanned skin, resembling dark oak paneling] face" and "tadpole-like [black] complexion" are further reinforced by her subsequent suggestion that Mustapha should "let [his] barber wash [his] face" since it "look[s] yet like a bugbear to fright children" (3.1.59–60). Quite likely, Mustapha was blacked up with burnt cork or oil, a common theatrical practice by the 1620s.[44] While we cannot know for certain, Asambeg's affiliation with the more overtly darkened Mustapha suggests that he too may have been played in blackface; the play refers to both characters as "Turks" and does not distinguish between them in any categorical manner. At the very least, Mustapha's blackness suggests that at least some "Turks" on the early modern stage were given dark complexions. In addition, the play's anxious avoidance of a sexual union between Asambeg and Paulina suggests that the conversion triggered by such an act would bear not just religious or spiritual consequences, but bodily ones as well. That the miscegenated product of such a union would physically replicate the father reinforces what Lynda Boose has described as "the deepest patriarchal fantasy of male parthenogenesis" in which the woman's body serves solely as the receptacle for male seed.[45] *The Renegado* precludes a conversion of this nature by vigilantly sustaining the Christian heroine's physical virginity.

Ritualizing Grimaldi's Transgression and Redemption

Finally, *The Renegado* posits the redemption of its title character, the renegade pirate Grimaldi, by translating both his denunciation of Christianity and his ultimate return to the Christian fold into visible, material terms. In order to externalize Grimaldi's conversion and reconversion, the play invests with great authority certain elements of Catholic ritual, including the sacramental use of bread and wine, as well as the holy intervention of the priest. We learn from a fellow seaman of Grimaldi's that his initial turn from Christianity was evidenced by his disruption of a Catholic mass held in St. Mark's church. As the captain narrates, Grimaldi seemed to be struck with a "wanton, irreligious madness" (4.1.29) when he suddenly

> ran to the holy man
> As he was doing the work of grace,
> And, snatching from his hands the sanctified means,
> Dashed it upon the pavement. (4.1.30–3)

Thus, the play externalizes Grimaldi's spiritual transgression through his physical desecration of the bread and wine of communion. The particular moment in the mass that Grimaldi chooses to disrupt is the very moment of incarnation, when God is embodied and body and soul are joined. In construing his disruption of transubstantiation as the ultimate form of sacrilege, the play validates the material sanctity of the Eucharist, or the Catholic belief in transubstantiation. I contend that this specific validation of the Catholic Eucharistic ceremony and its investment in the sacred powers of the bread and wine purposefully roots Grimaldi's sin against Christianity in a visible and material act of sacrilege. His outward transgression is necessitated by the larger context of Christian–Muslim conversion that is itself material and bodily.

Similarly, Grimaldi's redemption requires a visual and ceremonial supplement to make the miracle of his Christian regeneration

Figure 3.5: A Eucharistic mass, from Thomas Williamson, *The sword of the spirit to smite in pieces that antichristian Goliah* (London, 1613), sig. C1r. Reproduced by permission of the Huntington Library, San Marino, California.

believable. Although his repentance is sincere, he fears that his act of desecration was so egregious as to bar him from receiving absolution:

> I look on
> A deed of mine so fiend-like that repentance,
> Though with my tears I taught the sea new tides,
> Can never wash off. All my thefts, my rapes,
> Are venial trespasses compared to what
> I offered to that shape, and in a place, too,
> Where I stood bound to kneel to't. (4.1.74–80)

Like the renegade hero of *A Christian Turned Turke*, he presumes that his repudiation of Christianity is irreversible and that his consignment to eternal damnation is irredeemable. But *The Renegado* affords Grimaldi a second chance to save himself, and as with Vitelli, this second chance depends upon the intercession of the Jesuit priest. Francisco enters the stage dressed "in a cope, like a bishop" (4.1.72) to hear Grimaldi's confession, thus enabling Grimaldi to recognize the very priest whom he previously offended at St. Mark's church. The visual materiality of the cope endows Francisco with the authority to perform such a powerful absolution and enhances the ritualized and ceremonial aspect of the sacrament. The exchange between Francisco and Grimaldi that follows Grimaldi's confession further emphasizes the magical nature of his redemption:

> Francisco: 'Tis Forgiven!
> I with his tongue (whom in these sacred vestments
> With impure hands thou didst offend) pronounce it.
> I bring peace to thee: see that thou deserve it
> In thy fair life hereafter.
>
> Grimaldi: Can it be?
> Dare I believe this vision? Or hope
> A pardon e'er may find me?
>
> Francisco: Purchase it
> By zealous undertakings, and no more
> 'Twill it be remembered.
>
> Grimaldi: What celestial balm
> I feel now poured into my wounded conscience! (4.1.80–9)

In instructing Grimaldi that he may "purchase" a pardon for his sins through "zealous undertakings," Francisco invokes a Catholic practice that was condemned by Protestants for its emphasis on outward actions that could be easily simulated without sincere inner contrition. Grimaldi alludes to this controversial debate again when he asks, "Can good deeds redeem me?" (4.1.96). Whereas Calvinists emphasized the notion that faith must precede good works, Catholics believed that faith alone was insufficient to achieve grace. In suggesting that Grimaldi can earn back his place in heaven by performing good works, *The Renegado* again demonstrates how outward acts can anchor and enforce inward convictions, effecting a reversal for the Christian turned Turk, and achieving what faith alone cannot.

In the years between the earliest performance of *The Renegado* and its publication in 1630, the English government and church parishes confronted the problem of what to do with real-life renegades who needed to be reincorporated back into English society. By the 1630s Laud's influence was clearly evident in ceremonies for the reconversion of English seamen who had converted to Islam and undergone circumcision. An official "Form of Penance and Reconciliation of a Renegado or Apostate from the Christian Religion to Turkism," commissioned by Laud in 1637, outlines a series of steps that a penitent could perform over a period of several weeks in order to obtain clemency.[46] Among other things, these steps involved dressing in a white sheet and appearing on the church porch with a white wand. A decade earlier, two sermons preached at Minehead in Somerset on March 16, 1627, by Edward Kellet and Henry Byam (published together under the title *A returne from Argier*) exemplified a similar reliance on tangible steps for reincorporating converts to Islam. The convert in question is said to have been "bound for the streights" when he was "taken by Turkish Pyrats, and made a slaue at Argier [Algiers], and living there in slaverie, by frailty and weaknesse, forsooke the Christian Religion and turned Turke."[47] Kellet's and Byam's sermons may be seen to contradict explicitly the tenets of Calvinist predestination in suggesting that through sincere repentance and good works, the convert could redeem himself and reverse his path to hell.

The sermons preached by Kellet and Byam on the occasion of the convert's "readmission" to the Church of England follow a similar pattern for justifying the convert's regeneration. For example, the various actions that Kellet holds up as countermeasures to the convert's sins emphasize the utility of certain outward and material actions to redeem one from hell. He advocates martyrdom and baptism as effective ways of achieving grace, thereby challenging Calvinism's emphasis on the unalterable will of God. Rather than emphasize God's judgment, Kellet emphasizes God's mercy. Above all, he holds up the power of repentance, betokened by such outward expressions as "tears," the changing of "Habit and Vestmentes," and the performance of good works, to "[open] the Gate of heauen."[48] His insistence that a man's repentance has the power to halt God's punishment and "[purchase] Grace" offers a pointed revision of Calvinist predestination.[49] Moreover, the sermon shows that without such an allowance for free will and repentance, the reconciliation of fallen renegades would not have been possible.

Although *The Renegado* anticipates Laud's theological leanings in many ways, it predates the beginning of his rise to power in the second half of the 1620s. It would be a stretch to argue for the direct influence of Laud's Catholic-leaning practices in 1624, when Massinger's *The Renegado* was first performed on the public stage. The play is therefore striking for its positive portrayal of a Jesuit priest, its investment in a sacred relic and the sacramental powers of the Eucharist, penance, and baptism, and its valorization of female virginity. While as early as the beginning of the nineteenth century, critics began accusing Massinger of Catholic loyalties, such an explanation oversimplifies the theological valences of *The Renegado*. The point is not so much that Massinger was a crypto-Catholic as that England itself was crypto-Catholic, though not just in the sense that Stephen Greenblatt or Eamon Duffy have influentially argued.[50] Rather, factors outside of the Catholic-Protestant conflict compelled a fusing of interests that reauthorized certain Catholic models and anticipated a later high church theology. While I am not claiming a direct causality between Christian engagement with Islam and England's reintegration of Catholic practices or its adoption of Arminianism, I suggest that the stage itself played a role in showing how various sacramental, ceremonial, and material Christian models might offer protection against the threat of Islam and help redeem those who had fallen under its sway. In particular, the stage gives insight into how Islam's conception as both a religious and an embodied threat of conversion pressured a collapsing of Protestant-Catholic differences so as to enable more tangible forms of resistance and redemption.

Secular Performance and Religious Miracles

At the same time, if *The Renegado* may be said to reveal the hidden destinies of Catholicism in Protestant England, it should not be concluded that this is a Catholic play, and nor is it a transparent reflection of religious culture. Rather, the play draws upon the terms of religious culture to refunction Catholic models through performance. The play in fact reminds us of its own performativity at numerous points that come close to parodying the miraculous religious transformations upon which its tragicomic resolution depends. Donusa's instantaneous conversion upon having water literally thrown in her face (5.3.116) and Grimaldi's miraculous redemption, experienced as a "celestial balm . . . poured into [his] wounded conscience," exemplify theatrical moments that call attention to their own performativity (4.1.80–9). Thus, to some extent the play both undermines its miraculous transformations through performance and exposes the performativity at the heart of miracles. And yet such moments of equivocation are countered by certain inflexible "truths" that the play vigilantly maintains: Paulina's intact virginity, her imperviousness to conversion. If in some ways the play equivocates about whether religious moments retain their religious significance by drawing attention to their performativity, in other ways it insists on the efficacy of certain religious miracles that transcend performance. Thus, the play's awareness of its own performativity serves both to undermine the religious significance of its content and to reinforce it.[51]

The extent to which Paulina's constant virtue and Christian faith transcend performance is illustrated through a striking revelation that directly follows Donusa's baptism. Acting on the guidance of the Jesuit

Francisco, who is ironically lauded in the play for his superior skills of equivocation, Paulina feigns conversion to Islam so as to deceive her Turkish captors and facilitate the escape of Donusa and Vitelli. In rapid succession, Donusa declares her miraculous conversion to Christianity, Asambeg sentences Donusa and Vitelli to be separated and executed, and Paulina interrupts their parting with a shocking outburst of laughter: "Ha! Ha! Ha!" (5.3.139). Paulina then says mockingly of Donusa's baptism, "Who can hold her spleen / When such ridiculous follies are presented, / The scene, too, made religion?" (5.3.140–2). Expressly contrasting the performance of the "scene" to true "religion," Paulina calls attention to the very discrepancy between performance and religion that threatens to evacuate drama of its religious significance. Paulina then surprises the Christian and Turkish characters alike by announcing that she "will turn Turk" and partner with Asambeg (5.3.152). It is in this moment that the play demonstrates its commitment to an underlying truth that defies performance, for equivocation in this case serves the purpose of underscoring Paulina's unshakable Christian constancy. We are warned, crucially, from the previous scene to expect and see through Paulina's act because she is operating under the guidance of Francisco, who has relayed to her a set of secret instructions (5.2.92). While the other characters in the play believe Paulina's act of apostasy to be real, the audience knows it to be mere performance. In the previous scene we have heard Paulina confide to Manto and Carazie, whose help she later enlists in executing Francisco's secret plan, that her "chastity is preserved by miracle," so that they should never doubt it. She further explains that though she may "counterfeit" "outward pride," she is "not in [her] disposition altered" (5.2.69, 71, 73). Despite the play's awareness of how performance potentially evacuates religious miracles, the miracle that preserves Paulina's sexual and religious constancy is the one thing we don't doubt. Thus, it is clear that while performance in this play does not offer a transparent window on religion, it inadvertently exposes "truths" that have religious significance.

In other ways as well the secular transformations generated by performance produce something akin to a religious experience. As Anthony Dawson puts it in a recent essay on secular performance, theater itself is a kind of religion defined by moments of "sweaty transcendence."[52] Pressing beyond the question of how the theater directly engages religious themes or redeploys religious language, Dawson importantly draws attention to how the theater's modes of enactment are structured by religion. Alluding to an earlier essay that lays the groundwork for this subsequent meditation on the relationship between religion and drama, Dawson explores how theatrical impersonation effects a "dynamic of presence and absence," which is an "idea derived from the Eucharistic controversy."[53] I would say that this dynamic describes *The Renegado*'s engagement of religion on multiple levels, characterizing its performance of miracles, its renegotiation of religious discourses and ideologies, and its treatment of material props. The penultimate scene in which a secular prop is transformed into a vehicle for Christian escape, and a vehicle for the play's tragicomic resolution, exemplifies the way the theater's secular transformations replicate the dual presence and absence informed by Eucharistic controversy. The scene is taken up with Vitelli's receipt of a baked meat pie, which Francisco has managed to smuggle into his prison cell. Upon "pierc[ing]" its "midst" to discover what "mystery" it conceals, Vitelli turns up "a scroll bound up in a packthread" (5.7.3–5). Following the scroll's instructions, Vitelli uses the packthread to draw up a ladder of ropes from outside the castle window. Thus, the tragicomic resolution of the play is facilitated by the most mundane of objects – a baked meat pie – that conceals in its midst an equally mundane but practical packthread. In effect, the meat pie's successful transformation into a means of Christian escape completes the transubstantiation that Grimaldi interrupts in his initial turn from the Christian church. Religious analogue and parody go hand in hand, as the miracle of turning bread into body is rewritten as a transformation of meat pie into rope ladder. On the one hand, the scene demonstrates how the theater transforms religion into something secular, illustrating Dawson's underlying claim that the stage is "a secular, and secularizing institution."[54] But on the other hand, even the terms of this transformation illustrate the stage's debt to religious culture, its intimate engagement with it. When Vitelli refers to Francisco's intercession as "a pious miracle," he is being completely sincere, even if this sincerity contains multiple layers of irony (5.7.16). If theater has the potential to undermine miracles, it also has the power to create new ones. While I certainly would not argue that the stage is a direct outlet for religious doctrines or discourses, I am convinced that even its transformations of religion into something else are informed by religious structures, and that these transformations sustain both the presence and absence of religion in ways that are simultaneously playful, complex, and sophisticated.

But what ultimately is the status of the Catholic forms that inform the miracle of a meat pie's transformation, and that I have been arguing in this chapter and the previous one signal the gendered and embodied limits of a spiritualized Christian faith? Are these Catholic forms merely a means to an end, a way of apprehending a more important (non-religious) difference between Christian and Muslim, or do they matter in their own right? If critics such as Ken Jackson and Arthur Marotti find fault with some New Historicist critics who treat the representation of religious subject matter as a screen for other power struggles, what I am advocating is not so much a middle ground as a position that encompasses both religion and its role in relation to larger power struggles.[55] What I hope to expose is not simply how religion becomes readable as race in these plays, but rather the process by which religious identities become fused with national, embodied, and proto-racial categories. In confronting the threat of conversion to Islam, the stage draws on the religious forms at its disposal, revealing through its reauthorization of the older, derided forms of Catholicism the inadequacy of Protestantism to imaginatively address this new threat. At the same time, however, the challenge of imagining Christian strategies to resist and redeem conversion to Islam leads the stage to negotiate a Christian practice that, in ways independent of the ecclesiastical domain, suggests an ecumenical position and even anticipates Laudian reforms. Thus, the stage's negotiation of religious models to address the threat of conversion to Islam is both about something that exceeds religious difference and about how that something in turn reshapes popular Christian practice and identity.

Chapter 4

"Reforming" the Knights of Malta: Male Chastity and Temperance in Five Early Modern Plays

While heralded as heroic figures for their crusades against Muslim imperialism during the Middle Ages, the Knights of Malta had fallen into disrepute by the mid-sixteenth century. Up until the Reformation, this pan-European religious and military order had received substantial support from the English crown, but in 1540 King Henry VIII dissolved the Order in England, and outlawed their customary apparel with its distinctive Maltese cross.[1] As a Catholic Order the Knights' allegiance was to the pope, not the king, and in addition to this their increasing association with piracy and other lawless behavior made them identifiable with the loathsome figure of the renegade. Subsequent to their denouncement in England, a variety of English publications condemned the Knights for their Catholic allegiance and their corsair activities, accusing them as well of sexual promiscuity and other forms of overindulgence – of living "betwixt bawds and banquets."[2] Protestant English writers in fact attributed the Knights' degraded morals to their Catholic vows, and in particular to the vow of celibacy, so redolent of the priesthood. Nonetheless, the Knights reappeared on the popular stage in at least five plays between the late 1580s and the early 1620s.[3] In this chapter I explore why English playwrights featured members of this outlawed and denounced Order in roles that often celebrate their heroism against the Turks, and redeem their disgraced reputations not by making them conform to Protestant ideals but by rehabilitating the very vow of celibacy that had come to define them in the popular imagination as incorrigibly Catholic.

In some of these plays, the positive deployment of Catholic Knights on the post-Reformation stage engages with the general ecumenical movement occasioned by the territorial and religious threat of the Ottoman empire. Particularly in the reign of King James, the perception of a shared Muslim enemy generated an official discourse of pan-Christian alliance that reinvigorated the rhetoric of the Crusades.[4] However, I also want to suggest that these dramatic representations of the Knights of Malta all reflect the imaginative capacities of theater to test and redefine cultural boundaries in new ways. The stage simultaneously registered the dishonored status of the Knights and embraced their Catholicism, as well as translating their vow of celibacy into something else entirely. This complex and nuanced recuperation suggests a creative attempt to grapple with the perceived threats of Muslim conquest and conversion, and to envision a model of Christian masculinity that might effectively combat or resist these threats.

In this chapter I analyze the role of the Knights of Malta in five Renaissance stage plays: Thomas Kyd's *Soliman and Perseda* (*c*.1589), Christopher Marlowe's *The Jew of Malta* (*c*.1589), John Fletcher, Nathan Field and Philip Massinger's *The Knight of Malta* (*c*.1618), John Webster's *The Devil's Law-case* (*c*.1619), and Philip Massinger's *The Maid of Honor* (*c*.1621–2). Although all were popular in their time, they have, with the exception of Marlowe's *Jew of Malta*, been largely overlooked by modern critics, and the plays' shared interest in the Knights of Malta has gone unnoticed.[5] Given the thirty-year span of time over which these plays were first performed, it is quite remarkable how consistently they represent the Knights in ways that fly in the face of the Reformed English church. I argue that if these plays "reform" the Knights of Malta, it is by returning them to their most Catholic of vows – the vow of celibacy – and that this reauthorization of Catholicism speaks not simply to desires for ecumenical Christian unity against Islam, but to the particular ways in which Islam's religious and imperial threat legitimated a return to Catholic models of embodied resistance.

All five of these plays focus theatrically on the Knight's body as a site of religio-political conflict and resistance. If, as illustrated through Chapter 3 above, male Christian subjects are eligible for redemption in ways that females are not, the Knights of Malta provided a model through which masculine redemption could be imagined. In recuperating the Order as an exemplary body of genteel, chaste, and honorable Christian men, the plays offer an embodied masculine ideal that serves as a corrective to the denigrated male renegade, a category that collapsed Christian merchants, privateers, and explorers into figures of lawlessness and self-serving godlessness. Furthermore, this ideal addressed fears not only of Islamic conversion and bodily contamination but also of imperial conquest: these plays imply a homology between embodied male chastity and territorial protection.

The settings of these plays on Rhodes, Malta, and Sicily – Mediterranean islands straddling the unstable boundary between western Europe and the Ottoman empire – evoked an extended history of siege, conquest, and reconquest. In addition, these vulnerable island settings invoked fears about England's own vulnerability to invasion. In the late sixteenth century England was still a peripheral island nation with a long history of imperial subjugation by more powerful empires. Just as the Mediterranean islands of Rhodes, Malta, and Sicily had pronounced histories of conquest by Christian and Muslim empires, England regarded its own past in terms of a series of conquests by the Romans, the Saxons, the Danes, and the Normans.[6] Given the Ottoman empire's increasing incursions into eastern Europe and its progress as far as the gates of Vienna, the seat of the Holy Roman Empire, its threat of a possible fifth imperial conquest was not wholly unrealistic. In addition, as a number of critics have recently shown, London's own cultural landscape was changing drastically as the result of its participation in global trade. A growing immigrant population generated fears of change and cultural difference, and locations such as the port and the royal exchange were increasingly regarded as sites susceptible to penetration by foreign visitors and material imports.[7]

But why would the stage foreground male bodies to imagine resistance to territorial and cultural invasion when there existed, even by this time, an established tradition of linking anxieties about invasion to female sexuality? From a practical perspective, the majority of Christians venturing into the Mediterranean and its territories for purposes of commerce, military service, or diplomacy were male, so an interest in vulnerable manhood resonated with this reality. On another level, the Knight's vow of chastity cemented a commitment to pan-Christian brotherhood, which symbolized the strategic alliances between Christian subjects and nations (Catholic and Protestant) against the common Muslim enemy. But these plays also modeled a distinct kind of masculinity that participated in the imaginative work of cultivating a Christian and, perhaps more specifically, English masculinity. This masculine ideal was forged in contradistinction to the fallen renegade or the Muslim tyrant, and provided a model for his redemption. In valorizing a masculine ideal that was temperate, genteel, and committed to regulating reproductive purity through sexual restraint, the stage drew a distinction between Christian and Muslim identity that was increasingly racialized. In addition, these plays focused on masculinity to distinguish between honorable and dishonorable methods of conquest, cultivating Christian conquest in opposition to Ottoman tyranny and providing an early template for imagining English imperialism.

One of the ways that the early modern stage redeemed potential renegades as honorable Knights of Malta was by reimagining the historic Ottoman sieges of Rhodes and Malta. Marlowe's *The Jew of Malta* refigures the Christian victory at Malta as a critique of the commercial greed and moral compromises that belie pan-Christian alliances and their rhetoric of holy war against Muslim infidels. Somewhat similarly, Fletcher, Field, and Massinger's *The Knight of Malta* rewrites the Christian victory at Malta as a cautionary tale in which the Christian brotherhood triumphs by reaffirming its vow of chastity and rooting out a bad seed. By contrast, Kyd's *Soliman and Perseda* retells the Christian *loss* of Rhodes as a triumph of Christian virtue, figured through a narrative of martyrdom. The errant male protagonist, a Knight of Rhodes, learns a lesson in Christian virtue and national allegiance from his female lover, who single-handedly defends Rhodes against Muslim attack and martyrs herself rather than sacrifice her virginity to the sultan.

Other plays, such as Webster's *The Devil's Law-case* and Massinger's *The Maid of Honor*, solidify the bonds of Christian brotherhood by dramatizing the dissolution of rivalries between Christian men and redirecting their aggression against a common Turkish enemy. On the one hand, the Christian brotherhood valorized in these plays is suggestive of the priesthood in that it preserves the vow of celibacy and privileges homosocial relationships over heterosexual ones. But on the other hand, it reappropriates these qualities in order to meet different kinds of objectives that attain relevance in specific cross-cultural contexts. Because the resolutions of these plays involve the resecuring of male bonds against both the Muslim foe and female love-interests, they also reverse the expected outcome of comedy by substituting homosocial brotherhood for heterosexual marriage. In both Massinger's *The Maid of Honor* and Webster's *The Devil's Law-case*, comic resolution is achieved not through heterosexual marriage but through the cementing of male fellowships that redirect masculine energy against the Muslim foe. These plays physically separate their heroes and heroines, even relegating them to nunneries and monasteries, and in effect align the safeguarding of national security with sexual chastity.

In replacing Protestantism's emphasis on marriage with cloistered Catholic alternatives, plays that venerate the Knight of Malta's vow of chastity not only reshape established generic conventions, but reveal how these conventions are informed by particular religious practices, structures, and belief systems. Narratives of interfaith seduction, resistance, and redemption reform generic expectations by refiguring martyrdom as triumphant and Islamic seduction as tragic for Christian women but redeemable and potentially comic for Christian men. Together, gender and genre comprise an interwoven thread that I trace throughout this study to help reveal the complex stakes involved in dramatic

Figure 4.1: A Knight of Malta, from William Segar, *Honor military and ciuill* (London, 1602). Reproduced by permission of the Huntington Library, San Marino, California.

depictions of conversion to Islam. Whereas my second chapter focused primarily on the virgin martyr tradition as a model for female sexual resistance, and my third chapter examined distinctions between male and female, and Christian and Muslim, models of redemption, this chapter focuses on models of male sexual resistance and "gentle" conquest. Of course, none of these models exists in a vacuum, and all of them, I argue, suggest interrelations among the group of plays that I am examining. For example, as I discuss further below, plays about the Knights of Malta often employ chaste heroines, derived from the virgin martyr tradition, to model examples of constancy and self-restraint for the Knights to emulate.

These virginal heroines not only play a didactic role in modeling religious resistance, but also teach the Knights how to conquer women, and by extension territories, in chaste and mutually consenting ways. Thus, the masculine ideal shaped by these plays serves as an early prototype for English imperialism, showing how defenders of Christian territories might also be successful colonizers and missionaries. The brief discussion of John Day, William Rowley, and George Wilkins's *The Travails of the Three English Brothers* (*c*.1607) that concludes this chapter demonstrates how the Knights of Malta supply a model for Christian brotherhood that enables effective resistance and also becomes extended into a missionary agenda. In this way, I reveal how chaste masculine heroism provides a link between plays that dramatize Christian resistance to Islam and those that dramatize incipient forms of Christian imperialism.

Brief History of the Order

The Knights of Malta (also known in earlier periods as the Knights of St. John, the Knights Hospitallers of Jerusalem, and the Knights of Rhodes) were a pan-European religious and military Order that operated under papal jurisdiction.[8] Originally founded in the mid-eleventh century to provide care for pilgrims visiting Jerusalem, the Knights assumed a military role in the First Crusade of 1099. In 1113, they received permission from the pope to become a religious foundation with all members taking vows of chastity, poverty, and obedience. Throughout the Crusades, they devoted themselves to fighting a holy war against Muslim territorial invasion and the spread of Islam.

When they were driven out of Jerusalem in 1291 by the Turks, the Knights first relocated to Cyprus and subsequently, in 1308, took the island of Rhodes from the Byzantines. Although they promoted a rhetoric of Christian defense, they were also aggressors in a violent struggle to accumulate territory and power. Meanwhile the Ottoman Turks had been consolidating their possessions in Asia Minor and southeast Europe, and under Sultan Mehemed II (1451–81) they conquered Constantinople in 1453, Serbia in 1459, and Bosnia in 1464. Venice lost a number of possessions to the Turks and Genoa was forced to give up several trading stations on the Black Sea. In 1480, the Turks laid siege to Rhodes, but were beaten back by the Knights. In 1522 the Ottomans attacked Rhodes again under Sulaiman the Magnificent (1520–66). Despite the fact that the Knights themselves were drawn from a host of noble European families and thus comprised a pan-European organization, the Order struggled to win support during the long siege that followed. As Palmira Brummett has shown, European reluctance to aid the Knights was related to a combination of conflicting truces and tensions (including a tenuous truce between the Ottomans and Venice, and war between France and Spain), which involved competition for foodstuff and other trade.[9] In addition, the Knights had begun to make enemies among other Christians because of their piratical activities, and as Brian Blouet notes, the Order had already "become an anachronism" to certain Christian inter-ests.[10] Under pressure from Rhodian townsfolk, the Knights surren-dered Rhodes to the Ottomans and departed in 1523 for the Venetian island of Crete (or "Candy" as the English called it). They then sailed on to the port of Messina on the northeast tip of Sicily, but were driven out by the outbreak of plague in 1523.

After brief settlements on the island of Sicily, and at Civitavecchia and Viterbo, the Knights finally settled in 1530 on the barren and poorly defended island of Malta, which was given to them in fief by Charles V.[11] Although the Knights retained a degree of neutrality on Malta and were not required to provide the services customarily performed by vassals, they governed under the fiefdom of Spain and were not legally autonomous. On Malta, the Knights confronted hostility from the islanders (whose population at the time was about 20,000), weak mili-tary support, and a shortage of foodstuffs and natural resources, which made them entirely dependent on Sicilian imports. In vain, they agitated for relocation back to Rhodes or to Syracuse. With the Order in a pre-carious state, the Knights devoted themselves to improving Malta's for-tifications. Because of the growing problem of piracy along the Barbary coast, Malta's strategic importance had increased for the Ottomans in that it provided a key fortress for control of the central Mediterranean seaways. The Turks attempted an attack on Malta in 1551, but were driven back. They again laid siege to Malta in 1565 and after a long and

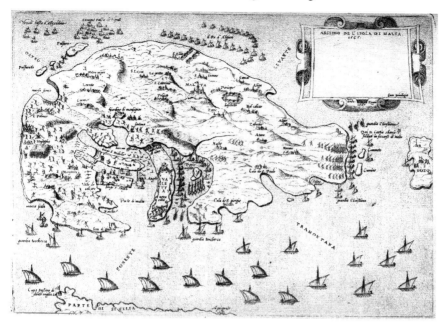

Figure 4.2: Domenico Zenoi, "Assedio de L'Isola di Malta" or "The Siege of Malta" (1565). Reproduced by permission of the Newberry Library, Chicago, IL.

brutal battle were defeated by the Knights under the Grand Master Jean de la Valette. As Aaron Kitch has put it, the Christian defense of Malta during this four-month assault would go down in English history as an "apocalyptic struggle between East and West."[12] Stories of the "miraculous" Christian victory were subsequently told and retold many times, spawning a production of pamphlets across Europe aimed at glorifying the providential triumph of Christian forces against the Muslim enemy and attracting support for future Christian missions.[13] The Knights as a pan-European crusading force were back in business.

Catholic Roots

From the English perspective, the Knights of Malta had become a source of controversy because of their Catholic roots and their continued jurisdiction under the pope.[14] Whereas in 1530 there were eight *langues* in the Order – Aragon, Germany, France, Italy, Castile, Provence, Auvergne, and England – in 1540 the English dissolved their *langue* with the passing of a parliamentary statute. This statute deemed English membership in the Knights of Malta treasonous because of the Order's recognition of the pope's authority. In addition, it outlawed in England, Ireland, and any other English dominion the wearing of any apparel or "sign, mark, or token" associated with the Knights, reclaimed their properties, and rendered their "privileges of Sanctuaries" "utterly void and of none effect."[15] English Knights were forced to choose between their loyalties to the English monarch and the Catholic pope, and a number of them were executed or forced into exile. Though the English *langue* was briefly restored by Queen Mary in 1557, it was again dissolved in 1559 (six years before the Knights' victory on Malta) by Queen Elizabeth.

Of course, despite the Reformation, English intolerance for Catholics was tempered by their shared stake in combating the Ottoman Turks. England's sense of peril associated with events such as the siege of Malta frequently overshadowed the influences of sectarian divisions. Archbishop of Canterbury Matthew Parker decreed that public prayers be said for Malta's deliverance from the Turkish siege. As Bernadette Andrea contends, these prayers "display an uncanny dynamic of identification and disavowal" with regard to the Knights' mission in Malta.[16] An attitude of "identification and disavowal" may be said to characterize English views of the Knights throughout the late sixteenth and early seventeenth centuries, though these views shifted in response to specific political and economic developments. But even during the Laudian reforms of the 1630s, which were perceived as making a number of concessions to Catholicism, the Knights of Malta retained unassimilable Catholic associations.

To offer one example, Thomas Fuller's *The historie of the holy warre*, first published in 1639, repeatedly condemns the Knights of Malta for their licentiousness, corruption, treasonous allegiance to the pope, and superstition. Describing England's eventual break from the Knights, Fuller explains,

> But Barnabe's day itself hath a night, and this long-lived Order, which in England went over the graves of all others, came at last to its own. [The Knights] were suffered to have rope enough, till they had haltered themselves in a Pramunire: for they still continued their obedience to the Pope . . . whose usurped authority was banished out of the land.[17]

Fuller, a respected church cleric and historian, as well as a moderate royalist, clearly viewed the dissolution of the English *langue* of the Knights as a positive conclusion to their treasonous allegiances. He further mocks them for their inadequacy in martial affairs, stating, "Better it had been that Cardinall Columna had been at his beads, or in his bed, or anywhere else, then in the camp in Egypt, where by his indiscreet counsel he brought all the lives of the Christians into danger."[18] The Knights, Fuller in effect argues, were distracted from their important task of combating the Muslims by their adherence to Catholic devotional practices.[19]

Probably the anti-Catholic charge against the Knights most directly relevant to my present discussion is Fuller's accusation of sexual licentiousness, which he links ironically to their vowed celibacy. He explains that the Knights "lived inter scorta & epulas – betwixt bawds and banquets," and goes on to surmise that it is "no wonder if their forced virginity was the mother of much uncleannesse: for commonly those who vow not to go the highway of Gods ordinance, do haunt base and unwarrantable by-paths."[20] Fuller's reference to the Knights' degenerate sexual reputation resonated with a range of earlier English texts. In *A true relation of the travailes* (1614), William Davies explains, "The manner of their Oath of Knighthood is this: that they shall neuer marry, by reason they shall neuer have Children legitimate . . . yet they are suffered to haue as many whores as they will."[21] Davies's distinction between bachelorhood and celibacy illustrates how the Knights' unmarried status might produce the opposite of chaste behavior, explicitly manifested through the production of illegitimate children. Somewhat similarly, George Sandys criticized the Knights for interpreting their vow of chastity as a ban on marriage but not as a ban on unmarried sexual promiscuity.[22] He describes how easily the courtesans in Malta made customers of the Knights of Malta, using "the arte of their eyes" to "inueagle those continent by vow, but contrary in practise, as if chastitie were onely violated by marriage."[23] These condemnations of the Knights' vow of celibacy as a condition that helped facilitate sexual incontinence stand in stark contrast to the popular depiction of the Knights of Malta on the Renaissance stage. As I will demonstrate below, if the English stage faults the Knights of Malta for corrupt or lascivious behavior, it redeems them not by advocating their abandonment of the vow of chastity but rather by reclaiming this vow and enforcing it.

Thomas Kyd, *Soliman and Perseda*: An Object Lesson in Failed Male Heroism

First performed fifty years prior to the publication of Fuller's *Historie of the holy warre*, Thomas Kyd's *Soliman and Perseda* also critiques the Knights for their degraded values; however, it suggests that the Knights can regain their honor not by shedding their Catholic associations but by re-embracing the virtues of chastity. The play takes as its subject the 1522 siege of Rhodes, figuring this historic Christian loss through the individual failures of its flawed hero. Simultaneously, it recasts the Ottoman invasion as a sexual seduction in which the Christian heroine successfully resists the Turkish sultan. Thus, the play models the redemption of a Christian Knight through the exemplary chastity of its heroine, illustrating how masculine reform may be modeled upon an example of feminine resistance and restraint that centers on sexual chastity. By depicting Perseda's willingness to fight to the death as an act of martyrdom, the play reconfigures the political tragedy of Rhodes's conquest as a personal triumph of Christian resistance. Moreover, it explicitly contrasts Perseda's honorable example with the inadequacies of its male protagonist, suggesting that Christian male heroism might be redeemed in accordance with this female model of heroic resistance and restraint.[24]

One way in which *Soliman and Perseda* juxtaposes feminine heroism and masculine failure is through its two protagonists' varied success at interpellating the gendered ideals of medieval romance. The play opens with an international sporting competition that invokes the medieval fantasy of a chivalric code that transcends religious and national differences. We soon learn, however, that the tournament's Turkish representative had been sent only to ascertain "how Rhodes is fenc'd" and how the Turkish sultan "best may lay / [his] neuer failing siege to win" the island (1.5.5–6).[25] Erastus, the Christian hero, wins the tournament, but remains unaware of the sultan's ulterior motives. Soon after, he engages in a duel that further illustrates his blindness to Rhodes's national interests and prevents him from participating in the war against Soliman's army. Having killed a fellow Christian Knight in a misguided attempt to protect his beloved's honor, Erastus flees the island and takes refuge in Soliman's Ottoman court, drawn by the Turkish reputation for "renowned" and "heroyicall" virtues (2.1.270–1). Thus, the interests and values of the courtly lover are set in opposition to those of his country. Once in Turkey, Erastus forges a chivalric bond with the sultan by engaging him in a friendly swordfight. Soliman beseeches Erastus not to hold back, but to "thinke me thine enemie, / [and] euer after thy continuall friend" (3.1.109–10). In turn, Erastus "ouercomes Soliman," and they walk away the best of friends. However, the play's insistence on Soliman's essential Muslim difference problematizes the traditional logic of chivalry in which, as Lisa Celovsky puts it, "competition paradoxically establishes fellowship."[26] The play soon exposes this masculine code of chivalry that proclaims to transcend religious and national differences as a misguided and outdated belief system.

Arthur Ferguson has argued that the decline and transformation of chivalric idealism resulted from an emerging national consciousness in the early modern period that privileged collectivity over the individualistic emphasis of chivalry.[27] In some ways, *Soliman and Perseda* seems to exemplify this argument. However, the play also offers a more complex picture of early modern political nationalism that challenges the neat trajectory outlined by Ferguson and any sense of a clear opposition between chivalry and nationalism. In identifying Rhodian national interests with the more general Christian opposition against the Turk, the play reveals the impossibility of isolating "national interests" from a more universal Christian cause. Further, in conflating military and sexual conquest, it demonstrates how religious and national interests are imaginatively bound up with anxieties about bodily contamination and miscegenation. At the same time, the play represents the Christian cause not in collective but in highly individualistic terms – as a love triangle between three individual characters – thus replicating the supposed individualism of chivalric romance. In this way, *Soliman and Perseda* captures the emergence of national consciousness as an uneven and messy process, rather than a clear-cut or modernizing response to the outmoded ideals of the Middle Ages.

As Erastus progressively pushes the boundaries between male bonding and treasonous behavior, he demonstrates the various points at which they intersect. For example, the playful camaraderie between Soliman and Erastus escalates when Soliman appoints Erastus as captain of the Janissaries, a position that English audiences associated with compulsory conversion to Islam and imperial expeditions against Christian countries. Erastus negotiates this conflict by accepting on condition that he not be forced to convert or to fight against his native Rhodes – an impossible compromise that exposes the inextricability of religious and national allegiances and the lack of middle ground between a Christian and Muslim, or Rhodian and Turkish, identity. While Erastus remains a passive resident of Soliman's court, Soliman sends his henchman Brusor to lead the attack on Rhodes. Thus, the Christian failure to ward off the Turks at the historical battle of Rhodes is presented as an object lesson in failed male heroism.

If Erastus's inadequacy exposes a potential distinction between the rank of Knighthood and honorable behavior befitting such a title, the play offers a more extreme parallel to Erastus through the comic character of Basilisco, an Italian Knight of Rhodes. As Lukas Erne has observed, the character of Basilisco is Kyd's invention, not present in his primary source, Henry Wotton's *A courtlie controuersie of Cupids cautels* (1578), or in Jacques Yver's *Printemps d'Yver* (1572), the

French text upon which Wotton based his translation.[28] Thus, Basilisco underscores the thematic shaming of the Knights of Rhodes that is unique to Kyd's play. Moreover, he demonstrates how the inconstancy exemplified by Erastus can lead not just to conversion, but to an embodied corollary. Given to boastful pronunciations about his military and amorous exploits, Basilisco quickly abandons his bravado the minute he is put to the test by Soliman's invading forces. Confronted with the threat of death, he immediately forsakes his countrywomen, Perseda and Lucina, and opts for conversion, proclaiming, "I turne, I turne; oh, saue my life, I turne" (3.5.11). Then, misreading his subsequent conversion ceremony as a testimony to his self-importance, he brags of being subjected to circumcision: "Amidst their Church they bound me to a pillar, / And to make triall of my valiancie, / They lopt a collop of my tendrest member" (4.2.21–3). As the play makes clear, it is precisely Basilisco's lack of "valiancie" that proves his inadequacy as a Knight and leads to his emasculating conversion and circumcision. In addition to offering an exaggerated and comic version of Erastus's failures as a Knight, Basilisco demonstrates the potential bodily consequences of masculine inconstancy.

Rather than stage the siege of Rhodes as a military operation, the play emphasizes the ramifications of Turkish invasion by depicting the sexual captivity of Erastus's beloved, the Christian virgin Perseda, and her countrywoman Lucina. Presented with these Christian women as "part of the spoile of Rhodes," Soliman delights, "This present pleaseth more then all the rest" (4.1.66, 68). Handing Lucina over to Brusor, Soliman says, "Heere, Brusor, this kinde Turtle shall be thine; / Take her and vse her at thy pleasure" (4.1.73–4). He then stakes his claim on Perseda, saying, "But this kinde Turtle is for Soliman, / That her captiuitie may turne to blisse" (4.1.75–6). In paying homage to her beauties, Soliman's blazon includes a long list of comparisons that draw attention to the unnaturalness of their threatened sexual union, itemizing Perseda's

> Cheekes, where the Rose and Lillie are in combat;
> Necke, whiter then the snowie Apenine;
> Brests, like two ouerflowing Fountaines,
> Twixt which a vale leads to the Elisian shades. (4.1.82–5)[29]

This parody of courtly love conventions is enhanced by the contrast between Soliman's Turkish appearance, likely distinguished by a turban, Turkish robes, and facial makeup, and Perseda's "necke, whiter then the snowie Apenine."[30] His mimicry of the Petrarchan lover only points up his inappropriateness as a sexual partner for Perseda.

In contrast to Erastus, who displays much greater susceptibility to Soliman's courtship, Perseda staunchly resists any personal union with the Turkish emperor: "Solimans thoughts and mine," she proclaims, "resemble / Lines parallel that neuer can be ioyned" (4.1.109–10). This metaphor extends to describe Rhodes's unwillingness to submit to Turkey, but it is significant that it originates at the level of sexual union between two differently gendered and increasingly racialized bodies – a Christian woman and a Turkish man. When Soliman orders Perseda to capitulate to his sexual advances or be put to death, Perseda chooses martyrdom. Ultimately, her resistance models a strategy for territorial resistance to Turkish invasion: the play suggests that rather than submit to a mightier force, a true Christian should go down fighting. When Perseda refuses Soliman, he orders her to kneel, "And at my hands receiue the stroake of death. / Domde to thy selfe by thine owne willfulness" (4.1.112–13). Echoing the constancy of Christian martyrs, Perseda responds by inviting the execution: "Strike, strike; thy words pierce deeper then thy blows" (4.1.114). But as Soliman wields his sword over her head, he is halted by the sight of "her milke white neck, that Alabaster tower" (4.1.122). A prelude to Desdemona's "alabaster" corpse, Perseda's "milke white neck" constitutes both the vulnerable sight that compels Soliman's lust and the tower of virtue that stops him from carrying out his murderous act. Overcome by this spectacle of Christian virtue, Soliman spares Perseda's life and grants her wish to "liue a Christian Virgin still, / Vnlesse my state shall alter by my will" (4.1.142–3). However, his miraculous conversion to Christian mercy proves to be short-lived. He allows Perseda and Erastus to return to Rhodes as his colonial governors, but soon regrets his decision and hatches a plan to eliminate Erastus and obtain Perseda for himself.

In using Erastus's colonial governorship to expose indirectly his treason against Rhodes, the play suggests that Christian sovereignty, even at the expense of annihilation, is the only acceptable outcome. To dispose of Erastus, Soliman summons him back to Constantinople to appear in court on trumped-up charges that he has committed treason against Turkey. In court, false witnesses testify that Erastus secretly vowed that "Rhodes must no longer beare the Turkish yoake" (5.2.59). The irony is that the witnesses accuse Erastus of what would have actually been the honorable action to take – freeing Rhodes from Ottoman rule – whereas Erastus has in fact done no such thing. In *not* committing treason against Soliman, Erastus is guilty of committing treason against Rhodes. The play's dramatization of the treason involved in betraying Christendom for Islam overshadows the less dire charges of treason associated with the Knights of Malta for their dual allegiance to both the pope and the English monarch. Erastus learns that "friendship" with a Turk is an allegiance that cannot be trusted, and he is forced to suffer the consequences of his erroneous judgment. Betrayed by Soliman, he compares his accusers to "Synons," the Greek spy in the *Aeneid*, and himself to "poor Troy" (5.2.79). However, I would argue that the play frames Erastus's subsequent death by execution not as an act of tragic martyrdom, but rather as the consequence of his failure to extricate Rhodes from Soliman's "yoake."

By contrast, Perseda refuses to compromise her loyalties to Rhodes, and it is upon her virtue and vow of protection that the island's future depends. Likely performed by Pembroke's Men before a court audience, the play clearly invokes both England and Queen Elizabeth through its portrayals of Rhodes's vulnerability to enemy attack and Perseda's virtuous defense of the island. Its heroic portrayal of Perseda resonates with Elizabeth's recent triumph against the invasion of the Spanish Armada and her commitment to military resistance. At the same time, the play both raises and assuages contemporary anxieties about Elizabeth's efforts to support commercial intercourse with the Ottoman empire, as well as aid against Spain, by fostering diplomacy with the Sultan.[31] Basilisco, the foolish Italian Knight, draws attention to the fact that with Erastus dead, Rhodes depends for its protection on a woman: "The great Turque, whose seat is Constantinople, / Hath beleagred Rhodes, whose chieftaine is a woman" (5.3.84–5). The final words of the play, spoken by the allegorical character Death, reinforce the correlation between Perseda and Elizabeth by suggesting that although Perseda has died, her honor will live on just like "sacred Cynthia's friend," or Queen Elizabeth, "whom Death did feare before her life began" (5.5.37–8).

Perseda's willingness to die by her own hand rather than "yeeld to" Soliman's "letcher[y]" offers a strategy of martyrdom that applies to the protection of both her body and her country (5.3.60–2). In portraying her death, the play refigures the popular story of the Sultan and the Fair Greek, mentioned above in Chapter 2, in which the Ottoman siege of Constantinople results in the captivity and beheading of a Christian woman. Kyd's take on the story, however, is unique in that it interprets the Christian maiden's death as a triumphant martyrdom rather than as tragedy. Cross-dressing as a male soldier, Perseda implements an ingenious plan to martyr herself by challenging Soliman to a swordfight she knows she cannot win. (Tragically, we know that if Erastus had remained loyal to Rhodes, *he* could have overcome Soliman in such a contest.) In addition to shaming Erastus for his failure to defend Rhodes, Perseda's impersonation of a male soldier both protects her chastity and enables her to flight in Rhodes's self-defense. Coming *"upon the walles in mans apparell"* to confront Soliman, she announces, "Thou are not Lord of all; Rhodes is not thine" (5.4.20). She then spars with Soliman, and, upon receiving the fatal blow, unmasks her true identity. In addition to revising the story of the Sultan and the Fair Greek, Perseda's orchestration of her own death at Soliman's hands departs from Kyd's direct source, as well as from Kyd's earlier *Spanish Tragedy*. In Wotton's *A courtlie controuersie of Cupids cautels*, Perseda is killed accidentally by "two bullets sent from a Musket," and in *The Spanish Tragedy*'s play-within-a-play, Bel-imperia playing Perseda kills herself after stabbing Balthazar playing Soliman.[32] By contrast, Perseda's planning of her own death in *Soliman and Perseda* ensures that it is neither accidental nor shrouded with the shame of weak surrender or suicide.

Whereas Daniel Vitkus reads Perseda's death as a "symbolic rape" that signals her defeat, I read it as a willful act of resistance that is triumphant because she controls it.[33] Indeed, Perseda's refusal to submit lies at the heart of this play, which rewrites the masculine defeat at Rhodes as a triumph of feminine resistance and chastity. In addition, Perseda's martyrdom transforms miscegenation into an act that spontaneously self-destructs. By planting poison on her lips, Perseda ensures that the moment Soliman initiates sexual contract – by kissing her lips – he simultaneously triggers his own death. Thus, Perseda orchestrates Soliman's demise by foreseeing his lustful act and, in doing so, she also hastens their eternal separation. Although Soliman makes a dying request to have his body "interd" together in the same tomb with Perseda and Erastus (5.4.142), we know that Perseda and Soliman will be forever divided in the afterlife by their separate destinies in heaven and hell.

"Will Knights of Malta Be in League with Turks?": Marlowe's *The Jew of Malta*

Contemporary in performance to *Soliman and Perseda*, *The Jew of Malta* similarly revisits an earlier historical conflict between Christian Knights and Ottoman Turks centered on the possession of a Mediterranean island – this time, Malta.[34] However, Marlowe's play diverges substantially from Kyd's in that it critiques the Christian Knights not for their alliance with the Turks, but for their alliance with other Christians. As Emily Bartels has argued, Spain functions in the play as an imperial competitor vying for control over Malta, thus likening Malta's alliance with Spain to a colonial relationship, which Ferneze then reproduces through his own subjugation of Barabas.[35] According to Bartels, while the play is unclear whether Ferneze's misreading of Spain's "domination as alliance" results from "blindness or insight, naivete or cunning," his actions, however motivated, reflect poorly on him.[36] The close proximity between the play's first performances and the 1588 attack of the Spanish Armada heightens the probability that English audiences would have perceived Ferneze's concessions in particularly distasteful terms. In this sense, *The Jew of Malta* may be seen to affirm Elizabeth's resistance to an ecumenical alliance with Spain by exposing how Ferneze's alliance masks an inequitable power structure and selfish economic motives under the rhetoric of Christian fellowship.

At the same time, there is a risk in concluding too easily that the play unconditionally objects to Malta's pan-Christian alliance with Spain. Indeed, the object lesson illustrated through Erastus's failure to oppose the Turks at any cost resonates here. When the Spanish captain Martin del Bosco arrives on Malta early in the second act, he explicitly invokes the Christian loss of Rhodes in order to inspire Ferneze, the Maltese governor, to ally with Spain. Encouraging the Maltese to refuse to pay their tributary debt to the Turks and sever the Maltese-Turkish league that exists at the start of the play, del Bosco reasons,

> Will Knights of Malta be in league with Turks,
> And buy it basely too for sums of gold?
> My lord, remember that, to Europe's shame,
> The Christian isle of Rhodes, from whence you came,
> Was lately lost, and you were stated here
> To be at deadly enmity with Turks. (2.2.28–33)[37]

Of course, del Bosco wants to displace the Maltese-Turkish league so that he can use Malta as a base for trading Turkish slaves: his own economic motives expose his hypocrisy. Nevertheless, his appeal to an inherent "enmity" between Christians and Turks and his characterization of the Knights' loss of Rhodes as "Europe's shame" constituted powerful arguments that could not be entirely dismissed by English audiences. As del Bosco's reference to the Christian loss of Rhodes as "Europe's shame" indicates, many understood the loss to have resulted from the failure of Christian nations to band together and support Rhodes. I would like to argue that as much as *The Jew of Malta* exposes the costs of Christian fellowship and its hypocritical religious rhetoric, it regards a Spanish-Maltese alliance as far preferable to the absolutely untenable alternative of a Turkish-Maltese alliance. In imagining Malta under Turkish subjugation, the play constructs an immediate either/or contrast between Ottoman and Spanish colonization that forces Ferneze, and the play's audience, to make a hard choice. While unwilling to idealize pan-Christian alliances or to depict the Christian-Turkish conflict as a clear-cut binary opposition, *The Jew of Malta* presents the Spanish-Maltese alliance as Ferneze's best available option. In this regard, it may share more with Kyd's *Soliman and Perseda*, as well as the Knight of Malta plays of the Jacobean period, than one might first presume. Furthermore, the play suggests that what makes this alternative untenable is not merely its religious implications but the imperial and embodied repercussions that were becoming inextricable from the religious threat of Islam.

The Jew of Malta explores the conditions that render certain kinds of alliance natural or unnatural, acceptable or unacceptable, by drawing analogies between political alliances and various personal alliances based on such bonds as friendship, romantic union, and enslavement. Along these lines, I want to suggest that the play underscores the unnaturalness of a Maltese-Turkish alliance by re-envisioning it through the perverse sexual relationship between the Turkish Ithamore and the Christian Bellamira. In imagining a sexual relationship between a Muslim slave and a Christian courtesan, *The Jew of Malta* reveals its shared concern with other plays about the bodily consequences of Muslim-Christian contact within an imperial framework. The union between Bellamira and Ithamore presents a Turkish-Christian "league" in the form of miscegenation, revealing its deviant nature through a comic spectacle of sexual and bodily degradation.

I use the term "miscegenation" loosely here to describe an unnatural sexual union, with the understanding that the precise nature of Ithamore's ethnic and physical distinctions is frustratingly difficult to pin down. Marlowe may have intended him to be a Thracian or Greek who was enslaved and converted by the Ottoman empire, judging from Ithamore's self-description as born in "Thrace" and "brought up in Arabia" (2.3.130).[38] At the same time, Ithamore is repeatedly identified by other characters simply as a "Turk," and as critics have pointed out, his name contains a homophone for "Moor," perhaps implying a connection to North Africa. As Julia Reinhard Lupton has observed, his name also "exploits the typological linkages between Islam and Judaism" through its similarity to "Ithamar," Aaron's youngest son.[39] At best, Ithamore represents an amalgamation of subjugated, non-Christian differences. But if modern critics are incapable of knowing exactly what Ithamore looked like, the play repeatedly acknowledges how his appearances signified in negative ways, through jokes that center on his physical debasement. For example, Ithamore comments to himself upon reading an invitation to Bellamira's house, "I wonder what the reason is. It may be she sees more in me than I can find in myself, for she writes further that she loves me ever since she saw me" (4.2.31–3). The less attractive Ithamore is, the funnier his speculation that Bellamira might be swayed by the sight of him.

Ithamore's seduction of Bellamira in 4.2 draws attention to the comic disparity between Bellamira's admiration of her lover's physical appearance and its actual offensiveness. If, as Phyllis Rackin has discussed, Shakespeare's sonnets parody the Petrarchan tradition with the thematic insistence that the young man "copy" himself by having children, Bellamira's courtship revolves around the unspoken assumption that Ithamore's sexual reproduction is precisely to be avoided.[40] Although it is difficult to know whether Ithamore was played in blackface, the humor of the scene and the physical spectacle of the pair's interactions may suggest a debasement and dirtiness manifested in terms of a color distinction. Bellamira and Ithamore kiss and embrace several times, after which Ithamore remarks in an aside, "Now am I clean, or rather foully, out of the way . . . I'll go steal some money from my master, to make me handsome" (4.2.46–8). As Bevington and Rasmussen's gloss suggests, Ithamore "plays with the paradox of clean and foul," simultaneously invoking the use of burnt cork or other substance to blacken the actor's face and the trope of washing the blackamoor white.

Clearly parodying the courtly love conventions of pastoral lyric and romance, Ithamore's protracted declaration of love resembles Soliman's hyperbolic veneration of Perseda in Kyd's play: "we will leave this paltry land," he declares,

> And sail from hence to Greece, to lovely Greece.
> I'll be thy Jason, thou my golden fleece;
> Where painted carpets o'er the meads are hurled,
> And Bacchus' vineyards overspread the world,
> Where woods and forests go in goodly green,
> I'll be Adonis, thou shalt be Love's queen.
> The meads, the orchards, and the primrose lanes,
> Instead of sedge and reed, bear sugar-canes.
> Thou in those groves, by Dis above,
> Shalt live with me and be my love. (4.2.88–98)

As in Kyd's play, the humor of the speech relies on the visual dissonance between what the audience *sees* and what it *hears*. In addition, Ithamore's particular appropriation of classical mythology conveys the dual irony of both the lover's and the beloved's unworthiness. His reference to Bellamira as "the golden fleece," which Jason and the Argonauts retrieved after overcoming many great dangers, is humorous precisely because Bellamira is a prostitute and the "dangers" that Ithamore overcomes to win her consist of extorting money from his

Jewish master. Shakespeare both reinforces and offers a variation on Marlowe's use of this classical allusion in his slightly later *Merchant of Venice*, when Bassanio compares Portia's suitors to "many Jasons [who] come in quest of her" (1.1.172)[41]: Bassanio's own economic incentives to win Portia align him with Ithamore, whereas his and Portia's shared nobility and fairness sharply distinguish their union from that of Ithamore and Bellamira.

In his prayer to "Dis above," Ithamore reveals a worldview characterized by up-is-down reversal that reflects his inversion of social codes and his incongruity as a great epic hero. His prayer suggests a reversed cosmology, possibly reflecting his distorted worldview as a Muslim who worships the devil or anti-Christ in the form of Muhammad. In addition, his description of Bellamira as his "golden fleece" may reference the exclusive knightly Order of the Golden Fleece, suggesting that by wearing Bellamira as his badge of membership, he gains admittance to this prestigious European Order. Ithamore's status as a slave with no core loyalties and Bellamira's as a prostitute who will sell her affections for money also evoke the fungible allegiances of Christian renegades who turn Turk to suit their own interests rather than endure the difficulties of resistance. The play's oblique suggestion that Ithamore may be a native Thracian converted to Islam, rather than a native Muslim, further aligns him with the figure of the spineless renegade whose submission to conversion was often understood as a voluntary form of enslavement.

The sexual relationship between Ithamore and Bellamira reflects the exploitative power dynamics that characterize political alliances in the play. Bellamira seduces Ithamore in order to exploit his relationship to Barabas, her pimp Pilia-Borza exploits her in turn, and Ithamore betrays his alliance with Barabas in order to sleep with Bellamira. These layers of exploitation further reflect upon the perversity of their union, the extent to which it dishonors and disempowers all parties, and its singular orientation around monetary gain. On the one hand, their mutual debasement reduces the stakes of their union by translating their courtship into low comedy. But, on the other hand, the use of comedy to defuse the seriousness of this sexual union also betrays its dangerous and transgressive associations. Ithamore's speech is laden with sexual and reproductive suggestions: his comparison of Bellamira to the fecund and sensual "mead," "orchards," and "primrose lanes," which "instead of sedge and reed, bear sugar-canes," suggests a movement from island to mainland, from the reproduction of marginal plants along the shoreline to that of ripe fruits that grow inland and tropical sugar-canes associated with Africa, China, and the West

Indies. As Stevie Simkin observes, Ithamore's reference to Bacchus "conjures up images of debauchery rather than tender love," and in place of the marbled whiteness of Adonis we are forced to substitute the Turk.[42] The Muslim slave's projection of himself as plunderer and the European Bellamira as ripe colonial fruit conjures a disturbing image of subjugation. What cannot be imagined in serious terms without engendering irrevocable tragic consequences becomes an easily dismissed scene of comic release. And yet as I go on to show, its hints of the taboo function somewhat like the hovering reproductive threats that link all five of the early modern plays I discuss in this chapter. While *The Jew of Malta* does not privilege sexual chastity as the other plays do, it represents Turkish imperialism in not just political but bodily terms. In turn, the debased sexual union between Ithamore and Bellamira throws into relief the strategic alliance between Ferneze and del Bosco that guards against such unnatural alliances.

Placing *The Jew of Malta* in relation to the other Knight of Malta plays enables a broader view of Ferneze and del Bosco's alliance than an isolated reading of the play permits, exposing this alliance both as an object of critique and as something more complicated. The shifting alliances that develop in the final scene reveal the imaginative limits of acceptable and unacceptable Christian alliance. At the outset of the scene, Ferneze feigns alliance with Barabas in order to capture Calymath the Turk, but at the last minute he spares Calymath so as to catch Barabas in his own trap. Thus, Ferneze's defeat of Barabas compels a startling truce between the Maltese and the Turks that replicates the Turkish-Maltese league from the start of the play, but also gives the Maltese the advantage. Extending a proverbial hand to Calymath, Ferneze explains, "Thus [Barabas] determined to have handled thee / But I have rather chose to save thy life" (5.5.92–3). Ferneze has effectively disposed of the Jew and extended Christian mercy to the Turk; however, the play cannot leave things here and still deliver a comic Christian resolution. The alignment between generic form and Christian victory reveals the limits of Christian mercy with respect to the Turks as well as the irrevocably tragic consequences associated with Turkish imperialism.

Of course, as the 1633 title page indicates, *The Jew of Malta* was classified as a tragedy at the time of its first printing, or more specifically as "The famous tragedy of the rich Jew of Malta." By extension, one might see how the "tragedy" of a Jewish protagonist secured a comic triumph for the opposing Christians. But clearly the generic affiliations of this play also exceed the two sides of this binary opposition. As I have shown, the threat of the Turks adds another layer of opposition that frames Christian-Jewish opposition, just as the Maltese-Spanish alliance frames Christian-Turk opposition. The complex ways in which the play interrelates alliances and oppositions, tragedy and comedy, ensures that any resolution is at best equivocal. In this sense, the play is perhaps most accurately understood as an early form of tragicomedy. As Zachary Lesser has recently suggested, plays that endorse a "paradoxical mixture" of political positions so as to support two sides of an argument are particularly suited to the peculiar form of tragicomedy.[43] Although *The Jew of Malta*'s earliest performances predate the more overt and steady production of tragicomedies that began in the 1620s – which included *The Knight of Malta*, *The Devil's Law-case*, and *The Maid of Honor* – it may be seen to presage these tragicomic structures through its startling reversals as well as its political equivocation about Christian alliance.

One way that the final scene illustrates both reversal and equivocation is through its emphasis on securing Malta's "freedom" from the Turk. In this scene, Barabas first tempts Ferneze into an alliance by emphasizing the promise of freedom: "Nay, do thou this, Ferneze, and be free / . . . Here is my hand that I'll set Malta free. / . . . And I will warrant Malta free for ever" (5.2.90, 95, 101). His ironic suggestion that an alliance with the treacherous Jew will set Malta "free" only drives home the point that true freedom constitutes an impossibility for Malta.[44] By depicting Ferneze's options as a choice among two imperial alliances, the play exposes how political sovereignty and autonomy are always compromised within an imperial framework. Thus, when Ferneze stands beside del Bosco after defeating Calymath and announces triumphantly that "Malta shall be freed," he resignifies "freedom" to accommodate a preferable imperial alliance (5.5.112). While certainly this allusion to Malta's freedom is nearly as equivocal as the first, it secures the one thing about which the play will not equivocate. Whereas it is possible to imagine a comic Christian resolution in which Malta allies with Spain, it is simply not possible to do so if the Knights "be in League with Turks."

The Knight of Malta: Pan-Christian Alliance and Sexual Chastity

The Turkish siege of Malta again became a subject for the English stage approximately thirty years later in John Fletcher, Nathan Field, and Philip Massinger's *The Knight of Malta* (c.1618).[45] Performed in the middle of King James's reign, this play's portrayal of the Knights of Malta as a heroic alliance of Christian nations reflects a significant shift from *The Jew of Malta*'s skepticism about pan-Christian alliance. In this, it may be seen to accord with the political policies of King James, discussed in my previous chapter in relation to *The Renegado*, which included an openness to alliance with Catholic Spain in combination with a reinvigorated sense of animosity against the Ottoman Turks.[46] In addition to fostering the possibility of a royal match between England and Spain, as well as that of military alliance against the Ottoman empire, James's position manifested itself in a *via media*, or middle way, between Rome and Geneva, between Catholicism and strict Reform Protestantism.

To some extent all three of the Jacobean plays I discuss in the second half of this chapter may be seen to endorse James's embrace of a *via media*. Performed within five years of one another, these plays effect the theatrical return of the Knights of Malta after nearly thirty years of absence since *The Jew of Malta*. The plays' renewed interest in redeeming the Knights reflects a reanimated cultural desire for a model of pan-Christian alliance against the Turkish threats of imperialism and piracy, as well as a political climate that made it possible to view Protestants and Catholics united in this heroic fellowship. *The Knight of Malta* demonstrates James's *via media* through its wholly positive portrayal of a Spanish protagonist, a candidate for induction into the Order, which is also portrayed as an honorable and sacred institution. In addition, the play's reclamation of the Knight's vow of celibacy arguably reflects Jacobean concessions toward Catholic traditions. However, I want to argue that these apparent concessions are inextricable from the concomitant threat of the Turk, which signified not merely as an imperial and piratical threat but also as an embodied threat with reproductive and proto-racial implications.

Whereas *The Jew of Malta* reimagines the 1564 Turkish siege of Malta to expose the costs of Christian fellowship and its underlying commercial motivations, *The Knight of Malta* appropriates the historical circumstances of the siege to shore up the bonds of the Christian fellowship modeled by the Knights of Malta. The play defines these bonds and the values they represent by staging the exposure and expulsion of a villainous Knight and a contest to select an honorable replacement. Both of these challenges hinge on the necessity of policing male chastity and thus interpret the safeguarding of the fellowship in purely sexual terms. *The Knight of Malta* thus makes explicit what is primarily an implicit connection between the Turkish threat to Malta and the sexual contamination of the Christian body in *The Jew of Malta*. In dramatizing a contest of sexual restraint between two gentlemen for their induction into the Order, the play underscores the vow of chastity as an absolute requirement for joining the Order. Similarly, in expelling a villainous Knight who has broken his vow, the play repairs a vulnerable link in the fellowship that threatens to compromise or contaminate it. In doing so, it refigures the Christian military defense of Malta by displacing the threat of Muslim conquest by that of an internal blight upon the Christian fellowship itself. As with the Turkish threat to Cyprus in *Othello*, the danger of a military attack on Malta is contained by the beginning of Act Two, leaving the rest of the play to deal with a domestic crisis that emerges in its absence. Thus, Christian triumph is not so much a matter of protecting the island from the Turks as of restoring the sanctity of the Order that defends it, by flushing out a polluting force from within its ranks.

The play tests, purges, and refortifies the male fellowship of Knights by employing three different externally marked heroines: a fair Christian virgin, a light-skinned Turkish captive, and a dark-skinned Moorish villain. As I discuss in the Introduction and Chapter 1 of this book, skin color was just one of many potential indications of an emerging sense of racial difference in the early modern period, but it was also unique in that it constituted an outward distinction that was understood in terms of both environmental effects and biological inheritance. *The Knight of Malta* is striking for its direct linking of skin color with biological inheritance managed through sexual reproduction. Its three physically marked protagonists police the sexual behavior of the male fellowship of Knights by modeling lessons about rape, consensual sex, the virtues of celibacy, and the dangers of sleeping with the enemy. Moreover, the play both implicitly and explicitly expresses the consequences of male sexual behavior through a logic and rhetoric of reproduction. In punishing the expelled Knight by forcing him to marry the dark-skinned Moor, the play directly associates the consequences of dishonorable sexual behavior with interracial coupling. Thus, while male chastity functions partly as sign of Christian gentility, temperance, and restraint, it is also associated with the practical regulation of sexual reproduction.

The polluting force within the Order is embodied by an evil French Knight named Mountferrat, whose opening soliloquy reveals his dishonorable intentions toward the Christian heroine, Oriana. Mounteferrat's villainy is suggested not only by his desire to seduce a virtuous woman but by his savage resolution to force her submission:

> Dares she despise me thus? Me that with spoile
> And hazardous exploits, full sixteene yeeres
> Have led (as hand-maides) Fortune, Victory,
> Whom the Maltezi call my servitors?

> . . .
> The wages of scorn'd Love is banefull hate,
> And if I rule not her, I'le rule her fate. (1.1.1–4; 25–6)[47]

His faulty assumption that his "sixteene yeeres" success "with spoile / And hazardous exploits" earn him the right to possess Oriana illustrates the play's insistence that just as honorable crusading goes hand in hand with honorable romantic seduction, so do dishonorable conquest and the forceful subjugation of a woman. In turn, the play associates virtuous masculinity with the ability to win a woman's consent, and distinguishes the best men through their subtle capacity to discern a woman's virtue even after her reputation has been tarnished. After being rejected by Oriana, Mountferrat attempts to frame her for treason by accusing her of a love affair with the basha of Tripoli that will help facilitate an Ottoman invasion. Her exoneration reveals the heroism of a Spaniard named Peter Gomera, as well as aligning Oriana with other Christian women falsely accused of sexual infidelity, including Desdemona in *Othello*, Alizia in *A Christian Turned Turke*, and Paulina in *The Renegado*. Like these other heroines, Oriana clings to a narrative of martyrdom. When charged before her brother, the Maltese Grand Master, and sentenced to death, she responds, "I die a martyr then, and a poor maid, / Almost yfaith as inocent as borne" (1.3.173–4). Although she has no "proof" of her innocence, her transcendent virtue convinces Gomera to rise up in her defense and challenge her accuser to a duel. Thus, her fate differs from that of the other persecuted heroines because she has the right man to defend her. In turn, Gomera's ability to perceive her innocence reveals his inherent honor.

The contest between Gomera and an Italian gentleman named Miranda for induction into the Order consists not of hostile competition but of self-sacrifice and a recognition of their shared alliance against the Turkish enemy. After Gomera challenges Mountferrat to settle the question of Oriana's innocence, Miranda worries that Gomera's advanced age could cause him to lose the duel, and tricks Mountferrat into letting him fight in his place. Concealing his true identity under Mountferrat's armor, Miranda then loses on purpose in order to ensure Gomera's victory and Oriana's release from a sentence of death. This example of vindicating a woman's honor through masculine self-sacrifice stands in stark contrast to Erastus's duel in *Soliman and Perseda*, which leads Erastus to kill his own Christian countryman and seek refuge in the Turkish court. One might note too that Gomera and Miranda's duel refigures the suitors' duel in *The Jew of Malta*, which also leads to tragic consequences for two Christian suitors. Whereas Barabas orchestrates the violent opposition between Mathias and Lodowick, Miranda orchestrates a feigned opposition that uses the pretense of the duel to bolster the suitors' common Christian cause. In addition to modeling a pan-Christian alliance, Miranda and Gomera's duel exemplifies masculine virtue through physical restraint rather than violent conquest.[48]

Above all, the contest between Miranda and Gomera for induction into the Order is determined by their mutual struggle to overcome carnal temptations. Both men are distinguished by the same set of pre-requisite qualities that make them good candidates for Knighthood. As the Maltese Grand Master attests, they are "royally descended," "valiant as war," and for "full ten years . . . have serv'd this Island, [and] perfected exploits / Matchles, and infinite" (1.3.16–20). However, the play suggests that the true test of their fitness for the Order involves not these military and class-related qualifications, but their ability to maintain the vow of chastity. At first both Miranda and Gomera plead general unworthiness for the honor of knighthood, but it soon becomes clear that the real reason for their hesitancy is their mutual love for the same woman Mountferrat desires. In posing the question of their fitness for the Order, the play emphasizes their readiness or not to undertake the vow of celibacy. For example, Gomera initiates a protracted dialogue with the Grand Master that cycles through a sequence of possible reasons for his exclusion before zeroing in on the precise reason: "none but a Gentleman / Can be admitted" (1.3.93–4), "no married man" (1.3.96), "none that hath been contracted" (1.3.97), "none that ever / Hath vowed his love to any woman kinde" (1.3.99), "or finds that secret fire within his thoughts" (1.3.100). Gomera's guilt of the final possibility – harboring "secret fire" or love for Oriana – ultimately excludes him from the Order but wins him a wife, since he lays claim to Oriana before Miranda does.

Determining that Gomera shall marry Oriana while Miranda pursues a path to a higher "Mistreese," the Maltese Grand Master, Valetta, describes service to the Order as a variation on heterosexual marriage and reproduction:

> I have provided
> A better match for you, more full of beauty:
> I'le wed ye to our Order: there's a Mistresse,
> Whose beauty ne're decayes: time stands below her:
> Whose honour Ermin-like, can never suffer
> Spot, or black soyle; whose eternall issue
> Fame brings up at her breasts, and leaves 'em sainted.
> Her you shall marry. (2.5.193–200)

His description of marriage to the Order invokes the metaphor of Christ as bridegroom and the church as bride, which are the terms used to describe a man's entrance into the priesthood. Valetta emphasizes that this bride, a distinctly Catholic Order, will never "decaye" or "suffer / Spot, or black soyle," thus inverting Protestant charges against the Catholic church that emphasize its moral decay. Further, he declares that the offspring, or "issue," from a Knight's marriage to the Order will be nurtured at the "breasts" of "fame" and will gain immortality through sainthood. This non-sexual production of saints stands in contrast to the sexual reproduction of mortal and sinful bodies, even as it evokes the denigrated Catholic practice of reproducing idols and relics. Ironically, it is the Spaniard, from the greater Catholic enemy to England than is Italy, who is destined for the more Protestant path of heterosexual marriage in this play. This flattering portrayal seems possible only in light of James's ecumenical goodwill toward Spain, an alliance pressured by the Muslim enemy and not uncontroversial. Bertha Hensman has argued that the play's depiction of Gomera was intended to flatter the Spanish ambassador, Gondomar, who visited England in September of 1618 and may have attended the first performance.[49] It is also possible that Gomera's marriage to Oriana was intended to convey support for a Spanish match, which James had already begun to consider by 1618.

At the same time, the play reserves the possibility of the more heroic honor of Knighthood for Miranda. It builds suspense around the question of whether he will be inducted by drawing out his struggles to overcome the temptations of women. First, the Turkish captive Lucinda requests to meet Miranda and is initially denied by a friend who attempts to protect Miranda's interests. Angelo, a former Christian slave to the Turks who is rescued along with Lucinda, explains to her,

> You are a woman of a tempting beauty,
> And he, however virtuous, is a man
> Subject to human frailties; and how far
> They may prevaile upon him, should he see you,
> He is not ignorant: and therefore chooses,
> With care t'avoyd the cause that may produce
> Some strange effect, which wil not well keep ranck
> With the rare temperance, which is admired
> In his life hitherto. (3.3.14–22)

Implicit in this explanation is the sense that Lucinda's foreignness makes her a rare temptation who could produce a "strange effect" capable of disturbing Miranda's "rare temperance." The extent of Miranda's "human frailties" and the uncertainty of his chastity are revealed when he later succumbs to his desire to meet Lucinda and is overcome by her beauty. His loss of self-control reveals the delicate line between honorable mastery and dishonorable possession.

The play's interest in testing Miranda's suitability not only as a defender of Malta but as an honorable conqueror is revealed through Lucinda's commendation of her Christian enslavers, whose civil treatment of her bespeaks their potential for honorable conquest. Whereas she expected her loss of liberty to be nothing but a "heavy and sharpe burden," she is pleasantly surprised to be met instead with "all content and goodnesse" (3.4.36, 42). She explains, "Civility and sweetnesse of behavior / Dwell about me; therefore, worthy Master / I cannot say I grieve my liberty" (3.4.43–5). But Miranda finds himself so beguiled by Lucinda that he at first fails to uphold this standard of "civility." He draws near her and whispers into her ear, "I must lie with ye Lady" (3.4.74). He then asserts, "I would get a brave boy on thee, / A warlike boy," and to Lucinda's concern that such an act should result in "ill Christians," Miranda explains, "We'l mend 'em in the breeding" (3.4.90–2). As Ania Loomba notes, Miranda's implication that "the children of Muslim women can be blanched of their inner stain" through the penetrating seed of the Christian male reinforces a colonial paradigm.[50] However, Lucinda's reference to "ill Christians" also refers to the moral taint that would result from such an unchristian act as rape. *The Knight of Malta* relies on male sexual restraint to define a different model of Christian conquest. Rather than endorse a model of colonial penetration, the play points to the benefits of physical restraint, demonstrating a strategy of subjugation and containment that avoids self-contamination.

Ultimately, Lucinda successfully tames Miranda's advances with the aid of a particular material sign that anchors his Christian identity. She directs his attention to the "holy badge" upon his probationer's robe, which contains the cross, warning, "If ye touch me, / Even in the act, ile make that crosse, and curse ye" (3.4.148–9). As we shall also see in *The Maid of Honor*, the Knight's distinctive costume provided a visual cue for the honorable behavior he should uphold. It also signified the collective unity of the original eight nations or *langues* of the Knights of Malta, under their shared Christianity. William Segar in *Honor, military, and ciuill* (1602) describes how the symbolic eight-pointed cross originated with Pope Urban the second, who, during the Knights' siege on Antioch, "sent vnto the Captaines a white Crosse, with commandement that all the soldiers should weare the like."[51] Segar also attributes the tradition to Gerard, often credited with founding the Order, "who commanded that he, with all others of that house, should

Figure 4.3: Caravaggio, *Knight of the Order of Malta* (c.1608). Oil on canvas. 46⅝ × 37⅝ in. (118.5 × 95.5 cm). Galleria Palatina, Palazzo Pitti, Florence, Italy. Photo Credit: Scala/Art Resource, NY.

weare a white Crosse vpon a blacke garment, which was the originall of the Order, and euer since hath bene vsed."[52] Though England outlawed the Knights' apparel because of its Catholic associations in 1540, the costume retained power for a long time. Clearly, the theater company owned and reused – possibly shared? – this costume, exploiting its continued authority and familiarity to English audiences. Lucinda's use of the figure of the cross exemplifies the stage's reliance on material objects and ritual performance to help sustain the immaterial principles of faith and chastity. As Elizabeth Williamson has argued, though crosses, as opposed to crucifixes, were not strictly forbidden by the Reformation, their association with miraculous properties could easily invoke the idolatrous use of Catholic crucifixes.[53] Lucinda reaffirms the magic-like power of the cross on Miranda's badge by professing its ability to "save in dangers," "in troubles, comfort," "in sicknesse, restore health," and "preserve from evils, that afflict our frailties" (3.4.127–31). Thus confronted, Miranda relents: "Forgive me, heaven, she sayes true" (3.4.137).

Later, the Christian Oriana also helps tame Miranda's sexual desires when he continues to pursue her even after his trial with Lucinda and despite Oriana's marriage to Gomera. Oriana uses a rhetoric of reproduction to distinguish the spiritual example generated by a chaste union from the mortal offspring generated through sexual contact. When Miranda begs her for a kiss, Oriana counsels him to "master" his desires as she does her own and "Think on the legend which we two shall breed" (5.1.70, 93). Her reference to the superiority of their chaste connection and the offspring it will "breed" contrasts sharply with the "ill Christians" that would come of Miranda's forced union with Lucinda:

> And in this pure conjunction we enjoy
> A heavenlier pleasure then if bodies met:
> This, this is perfect love: the other short
> . . .
> Nor is our spirituall love, a barren joy
> For mark what blessed issue we'll beget,
> Deerer then children to posterity,
> A great example to mens continence,
> And womens chastity, that is a childe
> More faire, and comfortable, then any heire. (5.1.122–4, 128–33)

By embracing such sentiments, Miranda overcomes the sexual temptations of both a fair Christian and a Muslim captive. In both cases, the cultivation of honorable Christian masculinity relies on the more secure virtue of a woman. Oriana associates celibacy not with "barreness" but with a different kind of reproductive fertility – one that breeds not a human child, but a narrative "example" or "legend" of chastity. In a sense, this play and the next two I discuss in this chapter provide these very "examples," perpetuating with each retelling a reformed and honorable reputation for the Knights of Malta. According to Oriana, the "childe" of a chaste connection is even "more faire" and "comfortable" than a biological "heire." Her reference to the "faire" offspring ensured by chaste behavior seems to refer more directly to general beauty than to skin color; however, the play's sustained interest in reproduction, along with its attention to distinctions of skin color among its female characters, suggests awareness of the reproductive consequences of these distinctions.

In addition to setting the virtue of Gomera and Miranda in contrast to Mountferrat, the play distinguishes Gomera and Miranda from their Danish peer, Norandine, who is lauded for his military heroism but who lacks gentility and chastity. Described in the play's title page (1647) as "a valiant merry Dane" and "Commander in chief of the Gallies of Malta," Norandine belongs in a class of uncouth renegade heroes such as John Ward, Antonio Grimaldi, and Thomas Stukeley. As he himself acknowledges, he has just enough "compunction of conscience . . . to save [him], and that's all" (5.2.65–6). Norandine asserts that making him a Knight would require the Maltese to "make your Captaines capons first," for he professes to "have too much flesh for this spirituall Knighthood" (5.2.68–9). In other words, he would need to be castrated in order to live by the rules of the fellowship. His reference to the implicit contradiction of having "too much flesh" to join a "spirituall" fellowship underscores the interdependency of spirit and flesh that was perceived to characterize the Knights' vows.

Norandine exemplifies his unfitness for honorable conquest through his view that rape is an acceptable practice. After returning from battle with the Turks, he takes inventory of the booty his men have amassed and, after discovering the beautiful Turkish captive, Lucinda, instructs his soldiers to "Share her among ye" (2.1.154). Later, he tells Miranda that he would sleep better if he had "a kind wench / To pull my Boot-hose off, and warm my night-cap" (3.4.12–13). His thoughts immediately spiral back to Lucinda: "now I think on't / Where is your Turkish prisoner?" (3.4.16–17). She is spared from the "Souldiers wildnesse" only by virtue of her eloquent speech, which succeeds in taming Norandine's savagery (2.1.157). Lucinda's patient rebuke counsels Norandine about the difference between honorable conquest and dishonorable theft: "he that can conquer, / Should ever know how to preserve his conquest, / Tis but a base theft else" (2.1.161–3). In drawing an analogy between sexual and military conquest, the Turkish maid coaches her captor and converts his sexual aggression into restraint.

Certainly, *The Knight of Malta*'s sexual rhetoric operates on a metaphoric level, but I also want to suggest that it responds to literal concerns about the reproductive consequences of Christian-Muslim contact. In contrast to the fair Lucinda, whose Muslim difference can be "mended in the breeding," the play presents Zanthia, a "blackamoor" villainess who conspires with Mountferrat. The blackness of her skin would have been visually obvious to audiences, but it is also emphasized through repeated references. Mountferrat refers to her as "my black cloud" (1.1.164), "my black swan" (1.1.190), and "hels perfect character" (4.1.64), and Zanthia assures us that "No bath, no blanching water, smoothing oyles / Doth mend me up" (1.1.179–80). She is also persistently contrasted with the "white innocent sign" of the magically charged Maltese cross, as well as with the "spotless white" attire worn by Oriana, who identifies it as "the emblem of [her] life." Defined against Christian purity, Zanthia's blackness makes her the perfect co-conspirator to Mountferrat's crimes, a physical externalization of his internal blackness. Their conspiracy is also sexual, in that Mountferrat sleeps with her in order to gain her trust and assistance. When Mountferrat's crimes are discovered at the end of the play, the Grand Master punishes him not only by expelling him from the Order, but by ordering him to marry Zanthia – a punishment construed as worse than death. The Danish Norandine draws attention to the reproductive implications of Mountferrat's punishment when he says, "Away French stallion, now you have a Barbary mare of your own, go leap her, and engender young devillings" (5.2.279–80). Again, improper masculine behavior toward a Muslim woman is expressed in terms of undesirable reproductive consequences. Whereas Lucinda helps to cultivate a model of European masculinity that can honorably convert and redeem the colonized subject, Zanthia represents the threat of moral and bodily contamination that results from masculine behavior that is reckless, uncivil, and dishonorable.

In some ways, these two Islamic women serve similar functions in the play, whereas in other ways their functions are oppositional. Both serve in subjugated roles, Zanthia as servant to Oriana and later to Mountferrat, and Lucinda as slave to Miranda. Gomera in fact regrets that he cannot give Lucinda to Oriana "as companion to [her] faithfull Moore" when he returns to Malta with the spoils of war (3.2.80). His comparison of Zanthia and Lucinda obscures the gulf that separates them. Lucinda is fair, whereas Zanthia is black; Lucinda is a chaste virgin, whereas Zanthia is sexually promiscuous; and as Bindu Malieckal has observed, Lucinda is convertible to Christianity, whereas Zanthia is not.[54] With the help of these two female foils, the play fulfills two distinct imaginative agendas: that of gentle conquest and conversion and that of resistance to moral and bodily foreign contamination. In addition, these two Muslim women help to perform a necessary maintenance of the Christian fellowship by facilitating the expulsion of the sexually unrestrained Mountferrat and the induction of the resolutely chaste Miranda. During his expulsion, Mountferrat is condemned as "a rotten, / corrupted, and contagious member," and subjected to an elaborate undressing ceremony that involves the untying of a knot, the removal of his cross, spurs, and sword, and the hanging of a halter around his neck (5.2.214–15). Immediately after, Miranda stands upon the same altar and receives the cross, publicly proclaiming, "I vow henceforth a chaste life" (5.2.242). Importantly, the reformation of Christian fellowship relies not on the cultivation of a disembodied or spiritual faith, but on the enforcement of bodily restraint through the Catholic vow of celibacy.

"Proof" of Noble Bloodlines in Webster's *The Devil's Law-case*

If *The Jew of Malta* implicitly links the stakes of pan-Christian alliance to an embodied threat, and *The Knight of Malta* makes this connection explicit by illustrating the sexual and reproductive consequences of the Knight's broken vow of chastity, Webster's *The Devil's Law-case* reveals the extent to which these embodied consequences were informed by anxieties about bloodlines. As Jean Feerick has argued, the significance of blood as a category proximate to social rank brings into view a crucial discursive phase in the making of modern race.[55] She seeks to distinguish taxonomies of skin color from this more dominant system of blood that anchored race in the early modern period, but in doing so she also reveals how racial distinctions of skin color were "predicated on and entangled with the decline" of blood as a system for marking a heritable social hierarchy.[56] Contemporary in performance to *The Knight of Malta*, Webster's play seems to capture the process of transition between these two systems of race, revealing how social hierarchies determined by bloodline were understood to be regulated through sexual activity. The play problematizes the illegibility of bloodlines and their vulnerability to contamination through two interrelated plotlines. In the first, a greedy merchant who has impregnated a nun convinces his virginal sister to feign pregnancy so that his own illegitimate child will inherit the estates that have been willed to his sister by two suitors. In the second, the merchant's mother brings a lawsuit against her son that accuses him of being the illegitimate product of an affair, thus preventing him from claiming the inheritance left by his actual father, now deceased. The play frames these two interrelated plotlines within a larger context of eastern trade and Ottoman imperialism that inform the anxieties about reproductive contamination and legitimacy. In addition, its depiction of a contest between two Christian suitors, one a Knight of Malta, models a lesson about pan-Christian alliance that substitutes homosocial fellowship for heterosexual marriage.

Though set entirely in Naples and containing only Christian (implicitly Catholic) characters, *The Devil's Law-case* repeatedly invokes a broader context of global trade and Christian-Muslim warfare, involving failed investments in the East Indies, an expedition against the Turks, and the climactic appearance of a blackface disguise. Revealed in disjunctive and disturbing ways, this contextual frame crucially informs the play's thematization of anxieties about reproductive illegitimacy. As Kim Hall has discussed, *The Devil's Law-case* foregrounds concerns over noble descent as a way of dramatizing anxieties about England's growing merchant class and its upward mobility – a development framed by foreign trade and early colonial initiatives.[57] In addition, as I argue, the play registers the vulnerability of noble bloodlines not just to new forms of capital accumulation but to reproductive manipulation and foreign contamination. The play's commitment to shoring up bloodlines against these particular threats starts to become apparent through the complicated and unexpected ways that it contrasts Jolenta's two suitors and resolves the contest between them. In the opening scene Romelio, the greedy merchant – later identified more specifically as an "East Indy Marchant" (4.2.80) – asserts his control over his sister, Jolenta, and her choice of a husband in the absence of their dead father.[58] The two suitors are Ercole, a wealthy Knight of Malta, and Contarino, who descends from a noble family but who has sold most of his land to Romelio in order to generate enough income to live.

Ultimately, the play subverts this economic opposition, replacing the contest between suitors with a Christian homosocial alliance. At first, Romelio's self-serving preference for Ercole's wealth over Contarino's noble descent sets up an expectation that Contarino will triumph. Though Ercole also professes to descend from gentle breeding, his wealth, given his profession as a Knight of Malta, would have been associated with commercial and piratical activities. We also learn that he received his Knighthood from the Spanish king, an association that would have aroused suspicion in an English audience, despite Spain's authority within the play as the imperial ruler of Naples (also a contemporary fact). Ercole is further implicated as the wrong match for Jolenta by the fact that Jolenta herself loves Contarino and suffers under her brother's oppressive preference for Ercole. However, the play proceeds to thwart the expected comic resolution in which inherited nobility and love triumph. For example, it begins to cast doubt on Contarino's motives and to signal Ercole's redemption through his moral integrity. But instead of ultimately matching Jolenta with Ercole, the play displaces the anticipated heterosexual union altogether by a homosocial bond between Contarino and Ercole. In addition, it uses the dissolution of their contest to bring about a kind of redemption for both characters, who ultimately distinguish their shared heroism in opposition to Romelio's villainy. The concluding masculine alliance disrupts the possibility of heterosexual reproduction and demonstrates the advantage of dissolving the class fracture between title and wealth so as to cement a more essential alliance based on national and Christian interests.

The Devil's Law-case deploys a duel – reminiscent of the self-sacrificing duel between Perseda and Soliman, as well as the duel between Miranda and Gomera in *The Knight of Malta* – in order to reveal its protagonists' heroism in unexpected ways. Agreeing to fight for the right to Jolenta, Contarino and Ercole embrace, a gesture that overtly signals their gentlemanly agreement, but covertly allows each to determine whether the other is armed. The disingenuous embrace thus signals their mutual distrust at the start of the play. But the duel ultimately supplies a surprise twist in that both men suffer grave wounds and collapse upon one another as "perfect lovers," leading the others to believe that they are both dead (2.2.41). In actuality, both Ercole and Contarino survive their wounds, but their perceived deaths create an opportunity for them to negotiate a different relationship to one another and to discover a new masculine ideal that supersedes the competition between suitors and transcends the binary opposition between money-less nobility and ignoble wealth. The duel also redirects the energy in the play by turning a contest of self-interest into one of self-sacrifice. When Ercole rouses himself from his injuries to discover that he has miraculously survived, he comes to the realization that he "has fought for one [Jolenta], in whome I have no more right, / Than false executors have in Orphan's goods" (2.4.7–8). He then decides to preserve the rumor of his own death so as to allow Contarino, whom he believes to be alive, "to enjoy what is his owne" (2.4.20). Although the play does not explicitly acknowledge the vow of celibacy that Ercole would have taken as a Knight of Malta, it implicitly realigns him with this vow by redirecting him away from marriage and toward a male alliance with Contarino – a redirection the play presents as the proper course of events. In addition, the false impression of their deaths enables Contarino and Ercole to identify their common adversary as Romelio.

Although, as in *Othello*, the true villain in this play is a domestic figure, in that he is Christian and a native of Naples, his villainy is largely informed by his ties to eastern trade and colonization. When Romelio learns that Jolenta stands to inherit the estates of both Contarino and Ercole, he masterminds a plan to allow both himself and his illegitimate offspring to benefit from the suitors' apparent deaths through a complex set of frauds and manipulations. However, the tragic ending that Romelio threatens in this tragicomedy is ultimately dictated by the fact that all his hopes and money are tied up in eastern trade and investments. Early in the second act, Romelio receives news of his tremendous losses in the East Indies, which motivate him to attempt to capitalize on the deaths of his sister's suitors. In addition, Romelio's refusal to pay a "yearely Custome" to the Spanish king makes him the target of a Spanish spy. His attempts to act as a free agent put him in breach of the imperial alliance between Spain and Naples – an act of selfish independence that the play does not sanction. By associating Romelio's commercial activities with greed, risk, and secrecy, the play disparages commercial intercourse in the East and West Indies and sets it in opposition to anti-imperial warfare against Turkish forces in the Mediterranean. Conversely, it works to redeem Ercole by playing up his crusading role against the Turk and downplaying any association he may have with commerce and colonialism. It is also significant that the presence of the Turkish enemy makes an alliance with Spain acceptable.

The temporary complications and solutions that ensue when Romelio attempts to manipulate his sister into feigning a pregnancy reveal in comic ways just how far appearances can stray from the truth when it comes to forging lines of descent. Jolenta informs Romelio, dishonestly, that she is already pregnant with Contarino's baby, thus adding the specter of one too many babies. Romelio then reasons that they can pretend she's had twins, though, as Jolenta points out, the lie might be exposed if the two children lack sufficient resemblance to one another. Later, Contarino misunderstands Jolenta's revelation that the child is really Romelio's, and assumes that Jolenta has been impregnated by her own brother. Taking pleasure in how vulnerable bloodlines are to manipulation, Romelio reflects with amusement on "how many times ith world Lordships descend / To diverse men . . . for any thing belongs to'th flesh, / As well to the Turkes richest Eunuch" (3.3.168–9, 171–2). Thus, in associating the indiscriminate fungibility of monetary wealth with the universal pull of sexual desire and the impossibility of policing or verifying sexual reproduction, the play suggests that bloodlines can be manipulated and faked to look legitimate. At the same time, it denies this possibility by dramatizing the inevitable revelation of the truth, a revelation that reinforces the association between anxieties about bloodlines and foreign contamination.

If Romelio's attempts to conceal the illegitimacy of his child are ultimately thwarted, then so are his mother's dishonest attempts to dispute his legitimate lineage. Bringing a lawsuit that accuses him of being a bastard, she attempts to deprive him of his name and nobility by revealing that his true father was a Spanish houseguest who stayed with her while her husband was traveling in France. She thus accuses Romelio of possessing an illegitimate social status, "as if he bought his Gentry from the Herauld, / With money got by extortion" (4.2.112–13). Fortunately, the Spanish houseguest, Don Crispiano, turns out to be present in the courtroom, for he is the same Spaniard sent by the Spanish king to spy on Romelio. He proves the truth of Romelio's legitimate descent by repeatedly drawing attention to the year of Romelio's conception – 1571 – which Crispiano identifies as the year of the battle of Lepanto, and recalls that during this momentous Christian victory over the Turks, he was in the Indies and decidedly not in Naples. In thus proving that Romelio is the legitimate heir to the family fortune, the play shores up the integrity of Romelio's noble descent and proves that in fact bloodlines are not as vulnerable to manipulation as they might appear. In the final analysis, lines of descent are rendered visible and subject to proof.

Contemporary non-dramatic discussions of the Knights emphasize how the criteria for joining the Order of the Knights addressed a particular concern for securing the purity of Christian bloodlines. Fuller's *Historie of the holy warre* stresses the restrictions on a Knight's parentage: to join the Order, a man must be "at least 18 years of age; not descended of Jewish or Turkish parents; no bastards unless bastard to a prince, there being honor in that dishonor; and descended of worshipful parents."[59] Similarly, a much earlier text, Richard Jones's *Booke of honor and armes* (1590), lists these prerequisites: "proven gentilitie; no man descended of a Moor, Jew, or Mahometan, even if descended of a Prince"; "Diverse other Articles there bee, but for that they are full of Superstition, I omit them."[60] William Segar's *Honor military, and ciuill* (1602) nearly replicates Jones's language, excluding the descendant of "a Moore, a Iew, or Mahometan" from the fellowship "although he were the sonne of a Prince," and omitting other articles "for that they are full of superstition."[61] While Jones and Segar avoid naming the vow of celibacy by couching it under Catholic "superstition," they insist, like Fuller, on the purity of the Christian bloodline. Edward Grimstone's *The estates, empires, & principallities of the world* (1615) maintains that no bastards could become Knights, unless "descended from some great family," as well as "no man issued from a Iew, a Marran, or a Mahometan, even were he the sonne of a prince," and he also excludes anyone "indebted or married."[62] Taken collectively, these sets of criteria suggest that gentility trumps illegitimate parentage but not religious difference: if gentility is a precondition for becoming a Knight, it is possible to be a gentleman bastard but not a gentleman Turk. Indeed, the overlapping categories that implicitly come to define a "gentleman" in the late sixteenth century – high birth, refined manners, Christian bloodline – are reflected in the etymological links between "gentle," "genteel," and "gentile." Like *The Devil's Law-case*, these non-dramatic texts' concern for controlling reproductive purity betrays the interconnections between class, religious identity, manner, and heritable distinctions.

Significantly, the nature of the proof that legitimizes Romelio depends upon the audience's familiarity with the historical battle of Lepanto to mark the date, as well as an awareness of a larger world into which Christians are displaced from their native lands. It is precisely because Crispiano was engaged in East Indian trade – and thus physically detached from Naples – that he could not have fathered Romelio. In this way, the play assuages anxieties relating to cross-cultural contact and reproductive contamination by using Crispiano's foreign displacement to detach him from the alleged site of sexual contact. The newly forged alliance between Ercole and Contarino also becomes readable in relation to a larger global context. On the one hand, their bond is constructed in opposition to Romelio's villainy, but on the other hand, it is constructed in relation to a larger enemy that Romelio helps to make visible through his attempts to drive a wedge between the two suitors.

When Ercole charges Romelio with Contarino's murder in court and is questioned about the strange reversal of his former enmity toward Contarino, Ercole replies,

> Tis true: but I begun to love him,
> When I had most cause to hate him, when our bloods
> Embrac'd each other, then I pitied,
> That so much valour should be hazarded
> On the fortune of a single Rapier,
> And not spent against the Turke. (4.2.597–602)

Almost as inexplicable as Crispiano's invocation of the battle of Lepanto, Ercole's reference to the "Turke," who dissolves conflicts between Christian enemies, calls attention to the larger context of Christian-Muslim conflict that frames the play. In response, Contarino speaks up in support of Ercole, though he wears the disguise of a "Dane" to conceal his identity. When Ercole responds, "Sir, I doe not know you" (4.2.611), Contarino replies, "Yes, but you have forgot me, you and I have sweat / In the Breach together at Malta" (4.2.612–13). While clearly not literal in nature, this explanation draws attention to the greater "breach" that divides Christian strangers from a common Muslim enemy.

The new lines of alliance that are drawn in this play construct a new standard for "nobility" and complicate assumptions about noble versus non-noble bloodlines. Even as Romelio's nobility is legitimized, his villainy illustrates how a noble bloodline is not necessarily linked to noble conduct. Thus, while the play shores up the readability of bloodlines, it refuses to essentialize them. Instead, it negotiates a new definition of genteel behavior that is not contingent on inherited nobility. For example, Ercole exhibits genteel behavior in a way that transcends the logic of reproductive descent when he learns of Jolenta's pregnancy. Accused of fathering the child (and knowing that he could not have), Ercole surmises that the baby must be Contarino's and resolves to accept it as his own. He reasons, "There never was a way more honourable, / To exercise my vertue, then to father it, / And preserve her credit, and to marry her" (3.3.335–7). Ironically, Romelio's attempt to manipulate lineage through Jolenta's feigned pregnancy creates an opportunity for the Knight of Malta to demonstrate honor through claiming a child who is not his own descendant. At the same time, while this gentility may dissolve distinctions of nobility among Christians, it finds its limits outside of the Christian fold – a point finally driven home by the disturbing specter of Jolenta's transformation into a Moor.

The reconciliation between Ercole and Contarino also posits a relationship that supersedes the bonds of lineage but that is forged in alliance against the Muslim foe. In the final scene, the two men embrace for a second time in the play, this time replacing their former suspicion with a genuine show of affection. Ercole declares, "You were but now my second, now I make you / My selfe forever," thus concluding a play that began as a marriage plot with a homosocial union between two men who were at first differentiated by social status (5.6.27). The judge's final sentence, in which he orders Contarino, Ercole, and Romelio to embark for sea and commit seven years to fighting the Turks, reinforces the larger significance of Ercole's and Contarino's alliance. In addition to forestalling the possibility of heterosexual reproduction, this resolution underscores the importance of dissolving disputes and distinctions among Christian men – their Catholicism and Spanish ties notwithstanding – in order to create a united front against the Turkish enemy. In turn, the three female protagonists (Jolenta, Leonora, and the pregnant nun) are ordered to remain at home to build a monastery. Thus, by relying on Catholic institutions that enforce sexual separation and celibacy, the comic resolution of marriage is postponed in order to attend to the more pressing business of cementing a Christian crusade against the Turks.

The larger context of interreligious and interracial conflict that frames this play is most pointedly revealed through Jolenta's shocking use of a blackface disguise in the final scene to prove her innocence of sexual defilement. According to the stage direction, she enters the courtroom with "her face colour'd like a Moor." Ironically, the outward transformation of her appearance is intended to provide proof that her virtue and bloodline remain untainted, her body devoid of a pregnancy. Though she contends that "the Downe upon the Ravens feather / Is as gentle and as sleeke, / As the Mole on Venus cheeke," her point in putting on blackface is that her whiteness is so secure that it transcends the outward appearance of blackness (5.6.41–3). Gesturing to the pregnant nun, she asks, "Which of us now judge you whiter, / Her whose credit proves the lighter, / Or this blacke, and Ebon hew, / That unstain'd, keeps fresh and true" (5.6.50–3). In demonstrating the potential for appearances to deceive, she proposes the power of her innocence and virtue to transcend legal proofs and appearances. In turn, Ercole immediately recognizes her true identity as Jolenta, exemplifying the Knight's ability to discern a virtuous woman even when outward evidence suggests the contrary.

Although Jolenta's intention is to illustrate her unscathed and virginally intact body, the fact that her "proof" invokes a figure of interracial contact acknowledges a world beyond the domestic sphere of Naples that supplies its worst fear of sexual contamination. In this context, Moorish blackness functions as a figure for sexual sin and reproductive contamination. Given the setting of the play in a Spanish territory, the history of the Moorish invasion of Spain offers a specific resonance of genetic anxiety. As Barbara Fuchs has discussed, the expulsion of the Moriscoes from Spain (1609–14) "attempted nothing less than to cleanse Spain finally and completely of the Moorish taint."[63] Spain's infamous blood purity statutes excluding descendants of Moors and Jews from positions of power within civil and religious institutions also "loomed large in the culture's imagination."[64] Unexpected and yet not quite unimaginable in the Naples courtroom, the Moorish disguise registers the potential for intercultural contamination and miscegenation that hovers around the play. The domestic disputes at the center of *The Devil's Law-case* become fully intelligible only when read within a frame of East Indian trade, the battle of Lepanto, Moorish invasion, and the continuing Christian crusade against the Turks. The fact that Jolenta's particular disguise serves as a visual analogy of the various attempts throughout the play to fake or conceal legitimate bloodlines reveals what is at stake in pinning down the illegibility of bloodlines. Certainly on some level, the play's anxieties about illegitimacy have to do with

the destabilization of class status and the undermining of noble bloodlines such as Contarino's by wealthy corsairs like Ercole. But I also
want to suggest that Jolenta's embodiment of Moorish blackness as a
sign for the reproductive vulnerability of bloodlines is not distinct from
these class anxieties, that in the mercantile and imperial world of this
play, class and racial anxieties constitute two sides of the same coin. In
another sense, the Moorish specter embodies the links between blood
as rank and blood as race, which are fused by commerce and imperialism. The Knight's vow of celibacy, I further argue, presents one way
of addressing the dual anxieties of rank and race. Ercole's vow, which
is implicitly preserved through the disruption of the marriage plot,
thus functions as a corollary to Jolenta's use of a Moorish disguise to
"prove" her virginity, and by extension her nobility, her whiteness, and
her untainted bloodline.

Philip Massinger, *The Maid of Honor*: Masculinity Redeemed

First performed around 1621–2 by Queen Henrietta's Men at the
Phoenix, Massinger's *The Maid of Honor* recenters the question of
the Knight's redemption on the vow of chastity. In doing so, it thwarts
the generic association between comedy and marriage and departs in
pointed ways from its sources. At the same time, it illustrates how the
recuperation of this Catholic vow is shaped by particular historical
circumstances that elevate masculine fellowship over marriage and
resignify the function of chastity as protection against sexual and racial
contamination. In employing a virtuous heroine who supplies a model
for masculine reform and resecuring a pan-Christian alliance between
two Knights, the play clearly cites the earlier plays discussed in this
chapter. In particular, *The Maid of Honor* may be viewed as a rejoinder
to Kyd's *Soliman and Perseda*, illustrating the successful redemption of
an errant Knight of Malta through his recognition of his national obli-
gations and his renewal of his vow of celibacy. However, this play also
extends the function of the Knight's redemption into an imperializing
context by depicting its hero as an invader rather than the subject of a
country being invaded.

Although *The Maid of Honor* is set in Sicily, where the Knights of
Malta briefly settled before taking over Malta in 1530, it dramatizes
a fictional set of historical circumstances. The plot involves a military
effort led by a Sicilian Knight of Malta, named Bertoldo, to aid the
duke of Urbino in an attack against Siena. The king of Sicily, who is
Bertoldo's brother, refuses to support the plan because it endangers a

truce between Sicily and Siena, but he allows Bertoldo to assemble a band of volunteers to supplement Urbino's forces. When Siena prevails and Bertoldo is taken captive, the king refuses to ransom his brother. A virtuous Sicilian maid, Camiola, takes mercy on Bertoldo and offers him a marriage contract, including "two parts of [her] estate," that will supply his ransom (3.3.195).[65] Bertoldo fails to honor the contract when he receives a more advantageous offer to marry Aurelia, the duchess of Siena, who promises to smooth over his rift with his brother Roberto and reseal the alliance between Sicily and Siena. The comic denouement is achieved when Camiola orders Bertoldo to court to make good on his marriage contract and then unexpectedly releases him from the obligation, shaming him into repentance. In doing so, she draws attention to the disjuncture between her expectation of him as a noble and virtuous gentleman and the reality of his ingratitude and lack of honor. In the end, Bertoldo redeems himself by re-embracing his vow of celibacy, and Camiola, having sacrificed herself for his redemption, decides to enter the nunnery.

Aligning comedy with celibacy rather than marriage, the play's peculiar resolution is foreshadowed in the first act when Bertoldo proclaims his love for Camiola and she rebukes him, saying, "Alas Sir, / We are not parallels, but like lines divided / Can nere meete in one Centre" (1.2.120–2). Echoing Perseda's rebuke of Soliman ("Solimans thoughts and mine resemble / Lines parallel that neuer can be ioyned"), as we saw above, Camiola speaks not of an interreligious distinction barring her marriage to Bertoldo, but of a distinction dictated by the laws of their shared religion. Answering Bertoldo's objection that "no disparatie" exists between them, since Camiola is "an heyre / Sprung from a noble familie, faire, rich, young, / And every way my equall" (1.2.137–40), Camiola explains:

> Religion stops our Entrance, you are Sir
> A Knight of Malta, by your Order bound
> To a single life, you cannot marrie me,
> And I assure my selfe you are too noble
> To see me (though my frailtie should consent)
> In a base path. (2.1.146–51)

Camiola thus elevates the Knight's vow of chastity to a position where its transgression would be akin to marrying outside of one's faith, class, or social station. By drawing attention to her own female "frailty," she also appears to lay the onus on Bertoldo to maintain this vow. Thus, in contrast to the earlier *Soliman and Perseda*, the lesson of virtue and chastity that Camiola models is explicitly transferred to the male protagonist.

Although one might presume that the play will find a way around
the religious obstacle that stands between these otherwise well-suited
lovers, Camiola forecloses this possibility by aligning Bertoldo's vow
with God's will, which cannot be transgressed without tragic repercussions. When Bertoldo suggests that a "dispensation" would "easily
absolve" him of his orders, Camiola rebukes him in a way that suggests
the impossibility of absolution and the irreversibility of his Catholic
vow (1.2.151–2):

> Camiola: O take heed Sir,
> When, what is vowed to heaven, is dispens'd with,
> To serve our ends on earth, a curse must follow,
> And not a blessing.
> Bertoldo: Is there no hope left me?
> Camiola: Nor to my selfe, but is a neighbour to
> Impossibility: true love should walke
> On equall feete, in us it does not Sir.
> Bertoldo: And this is your
> Determinate sentence?
> Camiola: Not to be revok'd. (1.2.152–61)

Thus, the play sets out as a challenge the possibility of revoking
Camiola's "determinate sentence," but also stipulates that such a
reversal could only be followed by a "curse." Whereas other comedies
would find a creative way around the curse, this play insists that the
Knight's Catholic vow cannot be compromised without leading to
tragedy. Indeed, as the tragicomic plot unfolds, we see that the tragedy
very narrowly averted is in fact marriage. Ultimately, *The Maid of
Honor* moves beyond the tragic ending of *Soliman and Perseda* precisely because Bertoldo is able to reconcile himself to a life of chastity
in the fifth act: he is successfully redeemed.

If in some ways *The Maid of Honor* brings the tragic lessons of
Soliman and Perseda full circle, it also revises the earlier play's prescription for masculine heroism through its response to a different set
of political conditions. Whereas *Soliman and Perseda* may be seen to
celebrate Elizabeth's militancy (particularly against Spain), *The Maid
of Honor* seems to advocate King James's pacifism and his efforts not
to endanger England's peace treaty with Spain. As Eva Bryne observed
in 1927, the play's 1621 production presents a fairly close allegory of
recent political events.[66] Specifically, the king of Sicily's refusal to aid
Bertoldo's coalition with Urbino against Siena invokes King James's
refusal in 1620 to aid his son-in-law, the elector Palatine, Frederick V,
in war against Ferdinand II, Catholic archduke of Austria. Mirroring
James's reluctance to cross Ferdinand, who was backed by Spain and

the Catholic League of Germany, Roberto shies away from aiding Urbino for fear of endangering his truce with Siena. Bertoldo's critique of the king clearly resonates with critiques of King James's pacifism and his alleged susceptibility to court favorites. Labeling the advisors who praise Roberto's caution "sycophants," Bertoldo contends that "vertue, if not in action, is a vice" and that "peace (the nurse of drones, and cowards)" is indicative not of "health," but of "disease" (1.1.181–9).

Bertoldo's argument is eloquently phrased and not wholly unsympathetic, but ultimately the peace-making Roberto receives the moral sanction of the play. Weighing his concern for his subjects over that for his own fame, Roberto cites as justification for his pacifism a general aversion to violence motivated solely by imperial ambition:

> Let other Monarchs
> Contend to be made glorious by proud warre,
> And with the blood of their poore subjects purchase
> Increase of Empire. (1.1.158–61)
> . . .
> Wee that would be knowne
> The father of our people in our study,
> And vigilance for their safety, must not change
> Their plough-shares into swords, or force them from
> The secure shade of theire owne vines (1.1.164–8)

Here, the critique is not of a soldier who fails to jump into action, as in *Soliman and Perseda*, but of one who fails to recognize the virtues of peace. In expressing solidarity with his peacefully laboring subjects and refusing to sacrifice them to the bloodshed of an "unjust invasion," Roberto simplifies the conflict between Urbino and Siena so as to render it morally clear-cut. In addition, as I discuss further below, he espouses an anti-imperial rhetoric that the play picks up on in other contexts to model a distinction between honorable and dishonorable masculine conquest.

If *The Maid of Honor* shames Bertoldo for leading a rogue army against Siena and advocates the retention of peace between Sicily and Siena, it does so partly in response to the implied but invisible presence of the Ottoman empire. Just as the Ottoman enemy compels a kind of truce between Protestant England and Catholic Spain, it engenders a recognition in the play of the unnaturalness and dishonor of Christian knights who turn their forces against one another. After quelling the attack by Bertoldo's army, the general of Siena, Gonzaga, at first perceives virtue in his opponent's military prowess, but then retracts his approval when he discovers him to be a fellow Knight of Malta:

The brave Bertoldo!
A brother of our Order! By Saint John,
(Our holy patron) I am more amaz'd,
Nay thunderstrooke, with thy Apostacy,
And praecipice from the most solemne vowes
Made unto heaven, when this, the glorious badge
Of our redeemer was conferr'd upon thee,
By the great master, then if I had seene
A reprobate Jew, Atheist, Turke, or Tartar
Baptiz'd in our religion. (2.5.49–58)

Exclaiming that he is more shocked by Bertoldo's attack upon Urbino than if he had seen the baptism of "a reprobate Jew, Atheist, Turke, or Tartar," Gonzaga compares the undoing of a Knight's "solemn vows" to the impossibility of converting non-Christians to Christianity. His explicit references to St. John and the "glorious badge / Of our redeemer," a holy cross worn on the Knight's uniform, invoke the Catholicity of the Order and, in doing so, demonstrate how Catholicism stands in for "Christian" when set in opposition to the unconvertible "Jew, Atheist, Turke, or Tartar." Whereas in other contexts, the Catholic may have joined this list of reviled others, he is here set in opposition to them. As this chapter has argued, English Protestant audiences' identification with the figure of the Knight and his Catholic vows becomes possible because of the need to recognize the more insurmountable difference of those outside the fold of Christianity.

But the play does not merely encourage an identification with Catholicism as a matter of ecumenical practicality, echoing the logic of a Catholic-Protestant alliance against the Turk. It goes further in specifically locating power in the Catholic objects and vows that are particular to the Knight of Malta. When Bertoldo first enters the stage, his costume is remarked upon by a counselor of state: "He in the Malta habit / Is the naturall brother of the King" (1.1.37–8). As we have seen, this distinctive costume, distinguished by long black robes and a characteristically shaped and readily identifiable "Maltese" white cross, was outlawed in England by the parliamentary statute of 1540. Though relegated to the prop bin, the Knight's "Malta habit" produced a visual spectacle on the stage that still retained power. After Gonzaga recognizes Bertoldo as a fellow Knight, he tells his men that Bertoldo was once worthy of wearing the cross because of his "matchless courage" "against the Ottoman race," and then proceeds to rip it from his chest (2.5.69, 71). Bertoldo begs in turn, "Let me dye with it, / Upon my breast" (2.5.76–7). Though a mere object, the cross signifies in the play as an external manifestation of Bertoldo's Catholic vows and his identity as a Knight. Only when he renews his vow of celibacy at the end of the play is the cross restored to him. Thus, the question posed and answered by the play is not whether the Knight of Malta's cross retains any value, but whether Bertoldo is virtuous enough to wear it.

If chastity serves as a barometer for Bertoldo's virtue, it represents a larger set of masculine behaviors that the play defines in relation to imperial activities. The play's interest in reforming masculinity also resonates with contemporary anxieties about the deterioration of English masculinity in the wake of peace, including worries about unemployed English soldiers whose poverty bred discontent and restless renegadism. One of Roberto's advisors reveals the growing number of these men in Sicily when he informs the king that "more [men] than you thinke" have joined Bertoldo's volunteer army: "All ill affected spirites in Palermo / . . . whose poverty forc'd em / To wish a change, are gone along with him" (2.1.11–15). Prior to his redemption, Bertoldo embodies the voice of these soldiers. Reminding King Roberto that his command lies "not in France, Spaine, Germany, or Portugall," but in a small "Island" that lacks "mines of gold," "silver" or worms of "silke," Bertoldo suggests that the solution to Sicily's poverty and overpopulation is overseas plunder (1.1.194–7). Finally, he points to England as both an example of former imperial might and an object lesson in contemporary passivity:

> Let not our armour
> Hung up, or our unrig'd Armada make us
> Ridiculous to the late poore snakes our neighbors
> Warm'd in our bosomes, and to whom againe
> We may be terrible: while wee spend our houres
> Without variety, confined to drinke,
> Dice, Cards, or whores. Rowze us, Sir, from the sleepe
> Of idlenesse, and redeeme our morgag'd honours. (1.1.229–36)

Invoking a contemporary critique of James's court, the play uses Bertoldo to model a misguided solution to the drink, dice, cards, and whores of unemployed soldiers, in the form of imperialism. However, rather than advocate a return to Elizabethan imperialism, the play suggests that national and masculine honor must be restored in another way. Accordingly, it seeks to reform Bertoldo into a gentleman by idealizing chastity as a sign of imperial restraint. His innate potential for such reform is suggested by his patient suffering when divested of all luxuries as a prisoner in Siena; rather than give over to violence or dissolution, he expresses a willingness to "weare / These fetters till [his] flesh, and they are one / Incorporated substance" (3.1.189–91).

Significantly, the transgression that disbars Bertoldo from the knighthood – aiding Urbino in its attack on Siena – is figured not just as a crime against a fellow Knight of Malta but as a crime against a woman, the duchess of Siena. When Aurelia questions Gonzaga about whether the man they hold captive (Bertoldo) is a Knight of Malta, Gonzaga explains, "Hee was, Madam, / Till he against his oath wronged you, a princesse, / Which his religion bound him from" (4.4.35–7). In turn, the play demonstrates the iniquities of offending a woman and models the virtues of consent over force by drawing an analogy between heterosexual relationships and imperial ones. For example, Camiola reprimands Roberto for trying to subjugate her to a suitor she does not love: "Tyrants, not Kings, / By violence, from humble vassals force / The liberty of their souls" (4.5.63–5). She suggests that the honorable course to take both in political and in heterosexual relationships is one based on consent and mercy, rather than tyranny and violence. Similarly, Aurelia rebukes the duke of Urbino by invoking the bad example of "the Lordly Roman," who humiliated "kings and Queenes" by forcing them "to wait by his triumphant chariot wheeles," and thus "depriv'd himself / Of drawing neare the nature of the gods . . . in being mercifull" (4.4.3–8). She concludes, "To seeke by force, what courtship could not win, / Was harsh, and never taught in loves milde school" (4.4.11–12).

This lesson of mercy informs Camiola's attempts to reform Bertoldo, and the resolution of the play needs to be read in this context. In fact, without understanding Camiola's decision to release Bertoldo from his marriage contract as an act of mercy, rather than an act of self-interest, it is difficult to make sense of the ending. The play draws explicit attention to the conflicting motives of self-interest and self-sacrifice by first setting the audience up to believe that Camiola will force Bertoldo to make good on the marriage contract and then showing her do just the opposite. When, in the second-to-last scene, Camiola learns that Bertoldo has betrayed her and is about to marry Aurelia, she responds,

> You perhaps
> Expect I now should seeke recovery
> Of what I have lost by teares, and with bent knees
> Beg his compassion. No; my towring vertue
> From the assurance of my merit scornes
> To stoope so low. I'll take a nobler course,
> And confident in the justice of my cause,
> . . .
> Ravish him from [Aurelia's] armes; you have the contract
> In which he swore to marrie me?
> . . .
> He shal be then against his wil my husband. (5.1.102–12)

We assume that Camiola's alternative to "seek[ing] recovery / Of what [she] has lost by teares, and with bent knees" will be to force Bertoldo "against his wil" to marry her. She removes an expectation of supplication and creates an expectation of force, but then delivers the unexpected by acting in mercy. It is clear that although the audience does not anticipate her decision, she is already planning it in this scene, when she sends for her "confessor" (5.1.128), Father Paulo, and announces that she will "attire [her]selfe / Like a Virgin-bride, and something . . . doe / That shall deserve mens prayse, and wonder too" (5.1.130–2). In the next scene, with the king and Aurelia serving as judges, Camiola releases Bertoldo from the contract and thus brings about his voluntary contrition. She then takes orders to enter the nunnery and "conjure[s]" Bertoldo "to reassume [his] Order; and in fighting / Bravely against the enemies of our faith / Redeeme [his] morgag'd honor" (5.2.286–8). Bertoldo's white cross is then restored by Gonzaga and he replies, "I'll live and die so" (5.2.290). Thus, Camiola's unexpected mercy successfully cultivates virtuous masculinity in Bertoldo, a masculinity anchored in his restored identity as a becrossed Catholic Knight.

The Maid of Honor is striking not only for its equation of vowed celibacy with masculine redemption but for its positioning of this resolution as its celebratory and comic conclusion, openly defying both conventional marriage plots and Protestant culture's emphasis on marriage. It is a conclusion made uniquely possible through tragicomedy – a genre that frequently rendered the impossible possible and at the same time was much beholden to specific historical conditions. Understood in relation to the larger themes of imperial restraint, Christian brotherhood, and the ongoing crusade against the Turks, the Knight's vow of celibacy and the maid's virginity lend special poignancy to their decisions at the end of the play to devote themselves to separate and chaste lives. In Massinger's source, William Painter's *Palace of Pleasure* (1566), as well as Boccaccio's tale of Camiola and Rolande before it, the male protagonist is not a Knight of Malta and his resignation to a chaste life is not depicted as a fructifying or triumphant resolution. Rather, the fact that the lovers remain unmarried in the end signifies as a punishment for the hero and as testimony to the heroine's virtue and refusal to compromise for an unworthy man. Similarly, when Massinger's *The Maid of Honor* was revived in 1785 at the Theatre Royal, it failed dismally because audiences deemed the ending unintelligible – why would the two lovers not end up together? By contrast, in its own time the play enjoyed great popularity and remained in the repertories of the Phoenix and Red Bull for eighteen years. This popularity, I submit, arises from an investment particular to the early seventeenth century in reclaiming the Knights of Malta as templates for a chaste and restrained masculinity.

Imperial Alliance and Gentle Conquest: *The Travails of the Three English Brothers*

As I have suggested throughout this chapter, the stage's investment in knightly chastity addressed a need for a Christian masculinity anchored in bodily control, a need informed in part by sexual and reproductive anxieties generated by the threat of Islam. The vow of chastity not only guarded against racial contamination, but also addressed specific concerns about the unrestrained sexual practices of contemporary Christian privateers and their susceptibility to conversion through bodily temptation. The celebration of masculine chastity thus revealed an emerging sense of race linked to the sexual regulation of heritable somatic difference and pointed up the utility of Catholic models of resistance that were embodied and material, serving to bolster the otherwise ethereal notions of Christian spiritual faith and resistance. Thus, the stage's rehabilitation of the Knights of Malta signaled not merely a re-embracement of Protestantism's Catholic past, but rather a resignification of Catholic models as anchors for a *Christian* masculine identity against Islam. In addition, male chastity served as an instrument for restoring the Christian man's ability to direct his aggressions against the Turk by cultivating a clear, single-minded focus. The Spanish writer Bartholomew Leonardo de Argensola alludes to this quality when he describes Francis Drake's reluctance to attack Spanish possessions in the West Indies because doing so would mean crossing a Knight of Malta. Argensola characterizes Drake's Spanish adversary as "a Batchelor, nothing weakened with Womanish Affection, or the Care of Children; but watchful, and intent upon defending the Place, and so Resolute, that he would dye on the Spot before he would lose it."[67] In these terms, chastity simplifies a warrior's calling by severing all genealogical bonds. To be chaste, then, was to be a race of one.[68]

But male chastity also cemented bonds of fellowship between men and served as a model for pan-Christian alliances held together by a common cause and shared values of masculine self-restraint, temperance, and gentility. In important ways, this behavioral ideal addressed concerns about the class status of English privateers and adventurers. If, as Feerick has suggested, foreign contact unsettled class hierarchies based on blood lineage by making unlanded men eligible for social promotion, the stage assuaged class anxieties about male adventurers by cultivating

Christian crusaders who were also gentlemen in manners.[69] This model of gentility, expressed through behavior rather than inherited rank, began with the ability to exert control over one's body, and set a standard for the redemption of Christian renegades.

As a play like *The Maid of Honor* demonstrates, gentle masculinity was desirable not only in conflicts that demanded resistance, but also in contexts where the Christian Knight operated as an invader or imperial presence. The Knight of Malta's legendary identity as both defender of Christian territories and imperial crusader made him an apt model for a range of cross-cultural enterprises. I want to conclude by suggesting that this model of masculinity resonates in plays that feature Christian protagonists who are not necessarily Knights of Malta but who conquer others through their unwavering chastity, temperance, and mercy. Examples include John Fletcher's *The Island Princess* (1619–21) (for which Argensola's narrative served as a source); Fletcher and Massinger's *The Sea Voyage* (1622); and John Day, William Rowley, and George Wilkins's *The Travails of the Three English Brothers* (*c.*1607). Negotiating male rivalries and alliances across a variety of cross-cultural settings, these plays model masculinity tempered by civil, martial, and bodily restraint oriented around uncompromising cultural values, including the refusal to convert. In *The Island Princess*, two Portuguese suitors compete for the eponymous Moluccan princess while simultaneously staking a colonial claim to her island; the untested newcomer prevails by gently taming the pagan princess into submission (and eventually Christian conversion) through his superior example of sexual restraint, carefully directed force, and resolute commitment to his Christianity. Similarly, *The Sea Voyage* resolves a conflict among European colonists, this time French and Portuguese, through a love story that rewards innate gentility as expressed through bodily restraint, including the ability to maintain gentlemanly conduct while withstanding unbearable hunger.

While the European imperial contexts of *The Island Princess* and *The Sea Voyage* have led literary critics to insist on their differentiation from the "Turk" plays, their valorization of temperate but resolutely unconvertible Christian male protagonists suggests that resistance and conquest were not conceived as inherently distinct enterprises in the early modern period. In this regard, *The Travails of the Three English Brothers* is a particularly useful example because it relocates its Christian protagonists across a range of distinct eastern and European geographies, and in doing so illustrates the intertwined agendas of Christian conquest and resistance. Whereas Robert Shirley's stay in Persia explores the potential for Christian missionary efforts and a

Christian-Persian alliance in which Persia defers to Christianity's morally superior example, Anthony Shirley's capture by Turks in Kea and subjection to torture in Constantinople emphasize the utility of Christian resistance to a mightier imperial force.

In depicting the Shirleys' attempts to forge explicit alliances with both the Persian sophy and the Catholic pope, the play demonstrates just how far the stage will go in sanctioning alliances against the Turk. The Shirleys' open, even reverent attitude toward the pope is particularly striking given their English identities. Whereas the other plays discussed in this chapter model masculine redemption and Christian alliance through Sicilian, Neapolitan, Rhodian, Maltese, and otherwise Catholic characters, this play features protagonists who were native English Protestants. In scene five of the play, Anthony Shirley visits Rome and makes an appearance before the pope and his cardinals, saluting the pope thus: "Peace to the father of our Mother Church, / The stair of men's salvations and the key / That binds or looseth our transgressions" (5.38–40).[70] His recognition of the Catholic church as "our" (English Protestantism's) "Mother Church" is even more remarkable given the fairly recent memory of the Gunpowder Plot of 1605, which helped inspire Dekker's vehemently anti-Catholic *Whore of Babylon*, performed in the same year as *The Three English Brothers*. However, the Catholic sympathies identified in many of the plays discussed in this book help to make sense of this English identification with Rome, revealing how the common Muslim enemy compels an ecumenical alliance that is both politically advantageous and conceptually practical in terms of bolstering Protestant faith with tangible or embodied Catholic practices. Anthony acknowledges the Turkish impetus for his alliance with Rome, when, with the Persian Halibeck in tow, he appeals to the pope for the support of "Christian princes" to "lend level strength" to their league against the Turk (5.44). As Anthony Parr notes, the play's depiction of the papacy was so flattering that it was deemed suitable viewing for a Catholic family in 1609.[71]

Interestingly, the pope's support, which is contingent upon Anthony's learning a lesson from him in self-restraint, suggests that an alliance with Rome belies an imperial hierarchy that differs from the one between the Shirleys and the Persian sophy. Specifically, the pope chastises Anthony for striking his Persian traveling companion when Haliback attempts to accompany him onto the dais of the pope's throne:

> Refrain therefore! And whate'er you are,
> If you were kings as but king's ministers
> Thinking by privilege of your affairs
> Your outrage hath a freedom, you are deceived. (5.59–62)

The pope's reproach of Anthony, rather than Halibeck, makes clear who wields the ultimate authority among them – an authority that demands equal deference from both Protestant gentleman and Persian noble. Only after Anthony apologizes for the "heat of blood" that temporarily overcame him and made him forget his presence in a place "wherein all knees should stoop" does the pope authorize him to sign his name in an official register and promise to back him with the military support of other Christian princes (5.65, 67). Like Ferneze's alliance with Spain in *The Jew of Malta*, Anthony's alliance with the pope is both hierarchical and equivocal in nature.

In contrast to the respectful submission they show to the papal hierarchy, the Shirleys' alliance with the sophy reveals an imperial hierarchy that subjugates the Persians to English Protestantism. The Shirleys explain that they have come to Persia to aid in the wars against Turkey because they have been so successful in securing England that "war no more dares look upon our land" (1.141), rendering them "unactive" and in need of "employment" (1.144). In addition to extending the charity of their military support, the Shirleys enlighten the Persians about the virtues of gentle, Christian conquest. In the opening scene, they answer a mock battle staged by the Persians with their own mock battle in which they display their superior Christian methods. Whereas the Persians parade their victory over the Turks by mercilessly displaying their victims' heads on spears, the Shirleys model Christian clemency by sparing the lives of their Turkish prisoners. The sophy's response – "We never heard of honour until now" – conveys a sense of wonder that culminates later in the scene when, awed by the firing of an English canon, the sophy mistakes it for a "god" (1.111–17). Over the course of the play, the Shirleys indoctrinate the Persians as to their true, Christian God and establish a missionary presence in Persia, facilitated by Robert Shirley's romantic seduction of the Persian emperor's daughter, the baptism of their child, and the authorization of Robert's plans to erect a church and a Christian school. Though the Shirleys distinguish this kind of missionary work from raw imperial ambition, which they associate with Turkish tyranny, they impose a religious influence in Persia that is simply unimaginable in either Rome or the Ottoman empire. Both their alliances with Persia and Rome are oriented around a shared opposition to the Ottoman Turks; however, Anthony's alliance with the pope is expressed through reverence, whereas Robert's alliance with the sophy compels a recognition of English superiority.

When the real-life Robert Shirley traveled to Europe on his first embassy in 1609, he reputedly wore a turban decorated with a jeweled crucifix given to him by the pope (see Figure 4.4). The

Figure 4.4: Anthony van Dyck, *Sir Robert Shirley* (c.1622). Petworth House, The Egremont Collection (acquired in lieu of tax by H.M. Treasury in 1957 and subsequently transferred to The National Trust). ©NTPL/Derrick E. Witty.

crucifix demonstrates the use of a Catholic object to signal his Christian identity. While the turban symbolizes his successful integration into Persian culture, the crucifix seems to reflect his attempt to hold onto and insist upon the endurance of his Christian faith – a prospect made more difficult by Protestantism's invalidation of outward objects of faith.

The play suggests that one crucial key to sustaining the Shirleys' Christian identity in any geographical context – whether it be Persia, Turkey, Russia, Spain, or Italy – is their uncompromising commitment to brotherhood, a bond literalized through their familial relationship. When Thomas Shirley's Christian identity is put to the ultimate test in Constantinople, after he is abandoned by his crew, captured by Turks, and hoisted onto the rack, he refuses to reveal his "blood and parentage / And yield under the ransom" the Turks have assigned for his release (12.102–3). Rather than expose his brothers or his family name, he adopts a posture of unwavering resistance and a willingness to be martyred. Repeatedly pressured to convert to Islam, he staunchly refuses, answering, "First shall the sun melt from his restless seat / Ere that our name shall turn apostata" (12.113–14). Unbeknownst to him, his brother Robert has offered to free his Turkish prisoners in Persia in exchange for Thomas's release. Addressing the Persian sophy's objections to this offer, Robert invokes his sacred commitment to his brothers:

> We in all are three
> Sons of one father, branches of one tree.
> Should a rough hand but violently tear
> One scion from a tree, the rest must bear
> Share in the hurt. (11.163–7)

Combining the image of a family tree with that of the Christian trinity, which unites three persons in one God, Robert's metaphor suggests that the fraternal bond between brothers and the integrity of a Christian identity are mutually sustaining. This emphasis on brotherhood as the basis for Christian unity protects the integrity of the brothers' identities as they travel from country to country over the course of the play. Although they are physically separated by vast distances and individually seek alliances with other nations, they retain a central connection to one another. This connection is perhaps most powerfully illustrated in the play's epilogue, wherein the Chorus instructs the audience to imagine the stage divided "into three parts," representing Thomas safely returned to England, Anthony's induction in Spain into the Knights of the "Order of Saint Iago," and Robert's continued mission in Persia (Epilogue, l. 9, 17). The stage direction reveals a spectacle of the brothers united on one stage and further linked through the aid of a particular prop: "Enter three several ways the three brothers . . . Fame gives to each a prospective glass: they seem to see one another and offer to embrace." Separated by implied geographical distance but connected through their views of one another, the three brothers conclude the play with a reassuring symbolic gesture that conveys the unity of Christian values across the globe.

Like *The Jew of Malta*, *The Devil's Law-case*, and *The Maid of Honor*, *The Three English Brothers* was performed at the Red Bull Theatre and exhibits a number of affinities with the Knight of Malta plays through its modeling of Christian brotherhood. That it presented Protestant Englishmen as the representatives of this unified Christianity constituted a national fantasy for English audiences. However, the significance of the Shirley brothers in this role was not merely the fact of their Englishness, but also the fact that their real-life counterparts were notorious renegade adventurers who had fallen into disrepute and financial debt. As Parr notes, the Shirleys inspired a considerable production of laudatory pamphlets, despite their unpopularity "with people of influence in England."[72] The play acknowledges its agenda of redeeming these disgraced figures through Fame's parting plea to the audience: "Since [the Shirleys] in all places have found favourites, / We make no doubt of you: 'twere too hard doom / To let them want your liking here at home" (Epilogue, ll. 31–3). Crucial to the play's redemption of the Shirley brothers is its portrayal of them as paradigms of gentility and civil restraint.

This masculine ideal not only addressed the Shirleys' association with dishonorable, piratical activities and their questionable political allegiances, but also compensated for their insecure class status. Although Thomas and Anthony Shirley possessed the title of "Sir," they lacked both wealth and prestige. (Thomas lost all of his family money in the early 1600s and died in tremendous debt, and Anthony was forced by Elizabeth to relinquish his knighthood, which had been conferred on him by Henry IV of France.) Their debasement made them subject to the charges of monetary opportunism that the stage often attached to adventuring and colonial figures. As Parr notes, plays like *The Sea Voyage* mockingly exposed the opportunism of European adventurers and would-be colonists through its depiction of "feckless gallants . . . modeled on the younger sons of minor gentry who hoped to find in the colonies the wealth and status denied them at home."[73] In contradistinction to these figures, the stage also cultivated a new Christian hero whose inherent virtue was established not through his inherited class status but through his genteel behavior. To transform the Shirley brothers from figures of national embarrassment into gentlemen and legendary national heroes, *The Three Brothers* presented them as models of genteel behavior, temperance, and Christian fellowship.

I want to conclude by suggesting that in some sense the destabilization of class produced by geographical displacement and cross-cultural encounter helped make way for the consolidation of Christian identity around these behavioral qualities – qualities that ultimately comprised not just a religious but a racial distinction. Although the Shirley brothers were not Knights of Malta, their unwavering commitment to a male fellowship oriented around Christian temperance, restraint, and resistance accomplished similar goals to those of the Knight's vow of chastity. The multiple functions of this vow in the plays I have considered spoke to the ways in which emerging distinctions of race were constituted by both sexually regulated somatic differences and behavioral (or cultural) differences. Though in some ways distinct, these different manifestations of an early modern proto-racial logic were intimately linked and served a similar purpose. If *The Three English Brothers* and plays depicting the Knights of Malta extended the bounds of Christian fellowship across class and geographical boundaries, they also made clear how this fellowship worked in the service of a certain kind of uncompromising exclusion.

Turning Miscegenation into Tragicomedy (Or Not): Robert Greene's *Orlando Furioso*

Robert Greene's 1591 English stage adaptation of Ludovico Ariosto's *Orlando Furioso* (1516, rev. 1532) converts a sprawling and digressive epic romance into a unified plot centered on interfaith sexual union. Following just one of Ariosto's many interwoven storylines, Greene's play focuses on the rivalry among international suitors for the beautiful pagan princess, Angelica. In adapting this story for the stage, Greene crucially reverses the concluding events as presented in his source. In Ariosto's version, Angelica willingly marries the Saracen warrior Medor, sending his Christian rival Orlando into a fit of temporary madness, which he overcomes through the therapeutic slaughter of Saracens on the battlefield. In Greene's version, however, Angelica's preference for Medor turns out to be a false rumor and she winds up marrying Orlando. Thus, the triumph that produces the play's happy ending depends less on Orlando's battlefield prowess in Christian crusade than on his heroic rescue of the pagan princess from the literally unthinkable charge that she loved his Muslim rival. In effect, Greene's adaptation elevates the stakes of this potential sexual union by making its consummation or prevention the determining factor between a tragic or comic resolution.

If I have attempted throughout this book to expose the gendered and proto-racial stakes of Christian conversion to Islam, the following analysis considers how the adaptation of Ariosto's episodic plot into a dramatic stage play lays bare the cultural stakes that are necessary to produce a comic ending. My reading is intentionally schematic in order to emphasize the rigid logic that determines how a story of interfaith seduction, resistance, and redemption can play out in the genres of the stage. In some ways, Greene's *Orlando Furioso* differs from the other plays I discuss in this book. Though the plot is framed by Charlemagne's battles against the Saracen Turks, it foregrounds not a simple Christian-Muslim sexual union but a love triangle between a Muslim warrior, a Christian warrior, and a pagan princess. What interests me about the resolution of this love triangle is the way it links a happy ending with a comic coupling that is explicitly contrasted with the specter of a tragic one. While one way of looking at this is to say that the Christian hero's successful rescue of the pagan princess from Muslim clutches enables a comic resolution, I'd also like to approach this dynamic from the opposite angle by considering how generic considerations, informed by the effects of theatrical adaptation and performance, might shape Greene's depiction of the interfaith union. Thus, I want to consider how Greene's revision of Ariosto reflects the structural demands of making a narrative romance conform to a dramatic arc, revealing the revisions of content that are necessary to comically resolve a love triangle between a Christian hero, a Muslim villain, and a pagan princess. This approach also enables us to consider the significance of the theatrical medium in representing the dangers of interfaith unions by exposing the difference between what is possible in a live performance and in a narrative that is read. Furthermore, the fact that Greene's play can imagine no way to attach a happy ending to Ariosto's mutually desired union between Angelica and the Muslim Medor, other than to reveal it as utterly unfounded rumor, tells us something about the cultural logic of Muslim sexual contamination, its apparent irreversibility, and its inherent incompatibility with comic resolution.

In all of my discussions of plays throughout this book I have been implicitly engaged with questions of genre. I began with a most unlikely pairing of two of Shakespeare's plays: the tragedy of *Othello* and *The Comedy of Errors*, and ultimately argued that these two plays – one a tragedy of difference, and the other a comedy of sameness – have more in common than one might assume. In *Othello*, a Moor's tragic murder of his white wife and subsequent damnation convey the bodily limits of a spiritual Christian fellowship that professes to be universal. Conversely, in *The Comedy of Errors*, the confusions, violence, and misunderstanding that result from a lack of bodily distinction among two sets of identical twins reveals the risks of a Christian universalism that effaces differences. My second chapter, which suggests that Catholic models of virgin martyrdom underpin dramatic representations of resistance to Islam, offers an alternative model for figuring the relationship between bodily persistence and generic resolution. In Massinger's *The Virgin Martyr*, Henry Shirley's *The Martyred Soldier*, and the anonymous *Two Noble Ladies and the Converted Conjuror*, martyrdom converts the potential tragedies of Christian persecution into Christian triumph, resolving the tensions of Pauline fellowship by imposing an essential division between Christian and non-Christian identity.

Chapter 3 is also concerned with mediating conversion and resistance through the conventions of genre. Philip Massinger's *The Renegado*, a fully realized tragicomedy, sets out to redeem the inevitably tragic ending that results when a Christian refuses the path of martyrdom and succumbs instead to Islamic conversion. Ultimately, the play illustrates how the undoing of interfaith sexual seduction and conversion can only be possible for male Christian renegades; by contrast, if a Christian woman succumbs to sexual intercourse with a Muslim man and converts, she can never be brought back into the fold. In addition, *The Renegado* suggests that, even for male protagonists, Christian redemption relies upon embodied and material rituals that anchor the ethereal nature of spiritual faith in more tangible forms. My fourth chapter, on the portrayal of the Knights of Malta in five Renaissance plays, further exposes the links between comic resolution, Christian redemption, and Catholic models. In equating comic resolution with a Knight of Malta's re-embracement of his vow of celibacy, these plays invert the conventional marriage plot that normally structures comedy. I show how the specter of conversion compels an alignment of comic resolution with the cementing of male fellowship against the Muslim enemy. The plays that I examine throughout this book all carefully align the logic of conversion with the comic or tragic arcs of early modern dramatic genres.

While dramatic genre is one factor that shapes the kinds of stories that the stage produces around the threat of conversion to Islam, another important factor is the theatrical medium itself. The live performance of plays generated considerations about what could be believably enacted, what was possible and practical, and what could not be shown on stage because the presence of the actors' bodies made it too real. In addition, the prescribed time constraints on plays, as well as the material limitations of the early modern theater and the audience's expectations of what a stage play *should* do, underscored the virtues of retaining Aristotle's unities of time, place, and action. As I illustrate, the vast differences between Ariosto's sprawling narrative romance and Greene's five-act stage play reflect these considerations. In particular, in focusing on Greene's radical rewriting of the interfaith union between Angelica and the Muslim Medor, I hope to expose the stage's unique commitment to containing the threat of interfaith seduction and conversion. If I began this book by drawing attention to the stage's interplay with other popular forms of entertainment such as news pamphlets, I end it by considering what was unique about the stage's treatment of conversion to Islam.

Romance, Tragicomedy, and Theatrical Unity

Ariosto's epic romance is of course famous for its multiple, meandering storylines and its refusal of resolution. As Patricia Parker has demonstrated, one of the defining characteristics of narrative romance is its digressive proliferation of storylines that rarely lead to closure or collectively cohere.[1] Described by Parker as "a willful deviation from epic and its single path," Ariosto's narrative poem exemplifies romance's structural looseness. Nevertheless, romance provided English playwrights with a rich source of material, in part, as Cyrus Mulready has argued, because it fulfilled fantasies of faraway places and exotic peoples that were invigorated by England's nascent involvement in imperial trade and exploration.[2] By connecting the production of romances on the early modern stage to audience's interests in foreign places, Mulready makes visible a genealogy of stage romance that encompasses much more than the late plays of Shakespeare with which dramatic romance is typically associated. But the narrative conventions of romance did not lend themselves easily to the conditions and conventions of theatrical enactment. As Mulready observes, "In translating the elements of romance narrative (travel to foreign lands, feats of magic, fanciful creatures), dramatists stretched the representational capacity of the stage."[3] Sir Philip Sidney famously objected to the "gross absurdities" that resulted when playwrights transferred the disjointed plots and settings of narrative romance to the theater: romance's endless digressions and deferrals conflicted with the stage's demand for unity and closure.[4] Such digressions also interfered with the build-up of an audience's suspense and the catharsis provided by the resolution.

Part of what Sidney's critique points to are the particular conditions and contingencies of dramatic enactment, which require unique strategies to effect mimesis and verisimilitude. Mockingly describing the tendency of contemporary playwrights to disregard classical standards, Sidney complains,

> Now you shall have three ladies walk to gather flowers: and then we must believe the stage to be a garden. By and by we hear news of shipwreck in the same place: and then we are to blame if we accept it not for a rock. Upon the back of that comes out a hideous monster with fire and smoke: and then the miserable beholders are bound to take it for a cave. While in the meantime two armies fly in, represented with four swords and bucklers: and then what hard heart will not receive it for a pitched field?[5]

In capturing the material limitations of the stage, the meandering quality of romance, and romance's lack of verisimilitude when transferred to the stage, Sidney illustrates the inherent differences between narrative romance and dramatic enactment. Drawing on Aristotle and Horace, he suggests that playwrights should take pains to construct plots to meet the demands of the form. Whereas epic romance may be an appropriate medium for telling episodic stories that unfold across many places and times, the stage was not.

I want to suggest that the newly emergent genre of tragicomedy provided an answer to dramatists' challenge of reconciling the content of romance with the pressures of dramatic form. Whereas romance eschewed unity and coherence, tragicomedy forced them through its rigid structure. Influenced by Giambattista Guarini's *Il pastor fido*, performed in Italy in 1581, English dramatists began experimenting with this form in the early 1590s, though the word "tragicomedy" did not appear with any frequency on English title pages until the 1620s. Responding to contemporaries who viewed tragicomedy as an arbitrary and indecorous mixture of comic and tragic modes, in Sidney's words "mingling kings and clowns," practitioners such as Guarini and John Fletcher defended the form as achieving a complex unity through its subordination of the tragic to the comic, "taking from tragedy . . . its danger but not its death."[6] While neither Renaissance nor modern critics have been able to concur on a single definition for tragicomedy, we might agree that it follows a narrative arc in which there is the potential for tragedy, but eventually ends with a resolution that is ostensibly comic. Thus, it owes an important debt to the medieval stage, especially the Corpus Christi plays, which established a structural pattern of fall and redemption, death and resurrection, or of suffering transformed into joy through divine intervention. In the medieval tradition, the potential for tragedy and the triumphant resolution were not unrelated in a single play, but closely integrated. As Verna Foster explains, "Christian doctrine produces a drama whose comic conclusion is achieved not despite but because of the tragic suffering from which it arises."[7] Similarly, Valerie Forman deems tragicomedy particularly well suited for resolving economic anxieties about foreign expenditure because of the way that its own structural economy transforms losses into profits.[8] The structural unity of tragicomedy, while often overtly forced and mechanical, offered an opportunity for converting the disjointed plots of romance to the stage.

"Mongrel Tragi-comedy" Or "A Third Thing"?

Certainly, early modern tragicomedy was not without its early modern critics, chief among them Sidney and other neoclassicists who contended that tragicomic playwrights failed to attain coherent unity through their arbitrary mixing of genres and corresponding mixture of high and low characters. According to Sydney,

> their plays be neither right tragedies, nor right comedies, mingling kings and clowns, not because the matter so carrieth it, but thrust in the clown by head and shoulders, to play a part in majestical matters, with neither decency nor discretion, so as neither the admiration and commiseration, nor the right sportfulness, is by their mongrel tragi-comedy obtained.[9]

Somewhat similarly Jason Denores rejected pastoral and tragicomic drama in his *Discorso* (1586) for its lack of civic moral utility, a standard set for poetry by Aristotle in his *Poetics*. As Matthew Treherne observes, Denores's critique also emanates from his belief that "comedy and tragedy are fundamentally incompatible entities . . . and that the only way that tragicomedy could exist would be to have a plot which was double" and therefore lacking in Aristotelian unity.[10]

But in response to these critics, tragicomedy also had two important contemporary defenders in Guarini and John Fletcher, who sought to highlight the integrated and sophisticated relationship that tragicomedy negotiated between comedy and tragedy. Guarini countered Denores's view in his 1599 defense of his highly popular but controversial *Il pastor fido* by characterizing tragicomedy not as the yoking together of two separate genres but as "a third thing that will be perfect in its kind."[11] He compares the new form to the mating of a horse and an ass, which produces a mule, or to the mixing of tin and copper to make bronze.[12] He also emphasizes tragicomedy's complex mediation of comedy and tragedy in which the tragic is ultimately subordinated to the comic:

> [Tragicomedy] takes from tragedy its great persons but not its great action, its verisimilar plot but not its true one, its movement of the feelings but not its disturbance of them, its pleasure but not its sadness, its danger but not its death; from comedy it takes laughter that is not excessive, modest amusement, feigned difficulty, happy reversal, and above all the comic order.[13]

In describing tragicomedy as subsuming the tensions of tragedy ("its danger but not its death") under the "comic order," Guarini stresses its careful integration of tragic and comic conventions, its discrete integrity and its verisimilitude. Similarly, John Fletcher defended tragicomedy's unity in his epistle "to the reader," which was printed in the first edition of *The Faithful Shepherdess* (1608). Like Guarini, he emphasizes not an arbitrary mixing of tragedy and comedy, but the dramatic tension generated through its suspenseful aversion of death:

> A tragicomedy is not so called in respect of mirth and killing, but in respect it wants deaths, which is enough to make it no tragedy; yet brings some near it, which is enough to make it no comedy, which must be a representation of familiar people, with such kind of trouble as no life be questioned.[14]

Echoing Guarini, Fletcher describes tragicomedy as a kind of third thing. His observation that tragicomedy "wants [i.e. lacks] deaths . . . yet brings some near it" describes its structuring principle. Whether or not it was always successful in producing a unified plot, tragicomedy pursued coherence precisely through its "mingling" of tragedy and comedy, a mingling that was not haphazard but carefully orchestrated in terms of both plot structure and emotional impact.

Greene's Tragicomic Structure

Notably, Greene's play was billed as a "historie" on its 1594 title page – a particularly capacious and unstable generic marker that often encompassed episodic plots as well as early tragicomic structures. Critics have questioned the use of title pages to accurately reflect the ways that audiences understood the genres of early modern plays and to date the emergence of new genres.[15] Indeed, the inconsistent ways in which dramatic genres were recorded on title pages may lend insight into the instability of generic designation in and of itself in the early modern period. Nevertheless, Greene's play follows a clear tragicomic structure. It opens with the contest for Angelica's hand; turns toward tragedy in Act 2, when Orlando learns of Angelica's apparent sexual union with Medor and consequently descends into violent madness; shifts again through the recuperative tragicomic turn in Act 4, when Orlando is cured by a conjuring sibyl who reveals the union between Medor and Angelica to have been a villainous rumor; and concludes with Orlando defending Angelica's honor, winning her hand, and anticipating a victorious return to his native France. The particular way in which the central conflict of the play is resolved seems to adhere to Guarini's formula. Rather than overcome a sexual union between Angelica and Medor, the play insists that such a union has never taken place, thereby providing the potential for tragedy but not the outcome.

In addition, Greene's play exemplifies tragicomedy's characteristic "mingling" of high and low in that Orlando's class status makes him the least likely suitor for Angelica's hand. Though Orlando is one of Charlemagne's twelve peers, he is not equal in rank to the princess Angelica, daughter to the emperor of Africa, nor can he compete in status with Angelica's other royal suitors: the soldan of Egypt, the king of Cuba, the king of Mexico, and the king of the Isles. I suggest that the play's collapsing of class distinctions through the union of Orlando and Angelica in turn consolidates the religious and racial differences between Orlando and Medor, Christian and Muslim rivals. The identity markers that come to matter for Orlando are his Christianity and his whiteness, as well as his relationship to the ruler of much of western Europe. By contrast, in his 1591 English translation of Ariosto's romance (closely contemporary with Greene's play), John Harington relies on a rhetoric of class to construct a category of chivalric masculinity that trumps religious difference. More specifically, he justifies Medor's conquest of Angelica by calling attention to his honorable masculinity, attributed not to inherited nobility but to his loyal willingness to sacrifice his life for a male friend. Haringon says in the paratextual allegory that is appended to the end of book 19, "In Angelica's wedding with Medore I gather this Allegorie: Angelica is taken for honor, which brave men hunt after by blood and battells and many hardie feats and misse it, but a good servant with faith and gratefulnesse to his Lord gets it."[16] Importantly, the Lord to whom Medor is faithful is another man, his friend Clorindano, not the Christian God, revealing how Harington privileges a homosocial masculine code over religious affiliation.

Whereas Greene makes Orlando the central protagonist, Orlando figures as a relatively minor character in both Ariosto's original and Harington's version (despite the poem's title), playing a less significant role than Ruggiero, for example. After losing his mind to jealousy when Angelica runs away with Medor, Orlando reappears in the narrative only periodically. Eventually he regains his sanity through the aid of an English duke who locates his lost wits on the moon, and Orlando is then able to reoccupy his role in the crusades against the Muslim Turks. If Ariosto's story provides any sense of closure for Orlando, it is that he is cured of his unrequited love in order to return to the business of war. Reinforcing this dichotomy between love and war, Harington associates Orlando with the moral lesson that love, like idolatry, distracts a man from his main course. Though Greene departs from this theme, instead valuing Orlando's romantic conquest – and the commercial and colonial acquisitions that come with it – Shakespeare picks up on it in *Othello*. Like Ariosto, Shakespeare sets Christian crusade and matters of the heart at odds with one another: if the Turks hadn't drowned on the way to Cyprus, Othello would have been too busy trying to defeat them to become obsessed with his wife's fidelity. While Othello swears that "housewives" will never "make a skillet of [his] helm," his love for Desdemona does seem to dismantle his professional self-assurance, in effect converting him from a focused general to an insecure husband (1.3.273).[17] This dichotomy also resonates with the sultan's predicament in the popular story of the Sultan and the Fair Greek, mentioned above as a source for plays discussed in Chapters 2 and 4. Upon conquering Constantinople, the sultan takes possession of a beautiful Christian captive who in turn captivates his heart. When his advisors convince him that his love for Irene as well as the constant jealousy that consumes him are causing him to neglect the affairs of his empire, the sultan publicly beheads the fair Greek to prove them wrong. This popular story was appropriated not only by Shakespeare but also by Thomas Kyd in *Soliman and Perseda* (*c*.1589), George Peele in a lost play titled *The Turkish Mahomet and Hyrin the Fair Greek* (*c*.1594), Thomas Goffe in *The Courageous Turk* (*c*.1618), Lodovick Carlell in *Osmond the Great Turk* (*c*.1622), and Gilbert Swinhoe in *Unhappy Fair Irene* (1640). Notably, all of these plays are tragedies, pointing up how Greene's comic rendering requires that he substitute a Christian hero for a Muslim one and align, rather than oppose, romantic love and imperial objectives. It also requires that he depart crucially from his source – whether it be Ariosto's version or Harington's translation or both.

A discussion of genre that occurs in Kyd's *Soliman and Perseda* offers insight into how the interpretation of genre depends on a protagonist's subject position.[18] The play, whose Chorus consists of the allegorical figures of Love, Death, and Fortune, sustains an ongoing commentary about how its resolution will unfold and which genre will best describe it. At times this overarching metatheatrical awareness bleeds into the fiction of the play. After defeating Rhodes and executing his Christian rival for the Christian virgin Perseda, Soliman reflects on the play's course of events in terms of genre:

> Heere ends my deere Erastus tragedie,
> And now begins my pleasant Comedie;
> But if Perseda vnderstand these newes,
> Our seane will prooue but tragicomicall. (5.2.140–3)

While his use of the word "tragicomicall" may at first suggest Sidney's understanding of a "mongrel" mixing of tragedy and comedy, it also calls attention to the ways that genre is determined by a viewer's perspective. Whereas, from Soliman's point of view, Erastus's death opens up the potential for a comic ending, the possibility that Perseda might comprehend his scheme and thwart it would mix his comedy with tragedy. Indeed, the play's ultimate characterization as "The Tragedy of Soliman and Perseda" seems to speak to the fates of both Muslim persecutor and Christian virgin, reflecting the fact that they both wind up dead. As the same time, the play's title and all of its overt commentary about how things will conclude elide the fact that a "Comedy of Soliman and Perseda" is not possible on the early modern stage. The only way that this love triangle could be resolved through comedy would be for Erastus to survive and marry the Christian virgin. Thus, it is not so much Soliman's death as Erastus's that finally makes this play a tragedy, revealing the underlying ways that generic designations crucially privilege the perspective of the Christian male.

The Love Triangle

In addition to leaving aside numerous plotlines of Ariosto's narrative to focus on the story of Orlando, Angelica, and the Muslim rival, Medor, Greene's adaptation also reframes the love triangle in significant ways. Although both versions are set against the backdrop of war between Charlemagne and the Saracen Turks, the stage version relocates Angelica from Cathay (or India in Harington's version) to North Africa, where she is the daughter of the African emperor, with whom Charlemagne's paladins are united in warding off the Turks. Thus, Greene's play renders Angelica the subject of a colonial space over which both Turks and Europeans were vying for control. Greene reframes his narrative in terms of contested colonial geographies in other ways as well. Whereas in Ariosto, Angelica's suitors are eastern and African, in Greene's adaptation the same characters are identified with Cuba and Mexico. In addition, despite Angelica's ostensible African heritage, the play repeatedly emphasizes her "fair" skin and her pagan, rather than Muslim, religion: she is thus construed as a blank, capable of being reinscribed by her husband. She furthermore embodies virgin territory ready to be possessed: the man who marries Angelica also gains by contract her father's kingdom. At the end of the play, Orlando anticipates a triumphant return home to France with Angelica in a ship richly rigged with silks, ivory, cypress, and other commodities from Barbary. He announces to his fellow Christian warriors,

> So rich shall be the rubbish of our barks,
> Ta'en here for ballass to the ports of France,
> That Charles himself shall wonder at the sight.
> Thus, lordings, when our banquetings be done,
> And Orlando espoused to Angelica,
> We'll furrow through the moving ocean,
> And cheerily frolic with great Charlemagne. (5.2.1451–7)[19]

With these words, which conclude the play, Orlando references his imminent marriage and homecoming in terms that are explicitly comic. He looks forward to carefree "frolic[king]" with Charlemagne, who shall "wonder at the sight" of his richly rigged ship. In this way he imagines that his conquest of Angelica has promoted him in social status, as if closing the gap between the contrasting highs and lows that tragicomedy brings together.

But if comic resolution demands female conquest in which the native woman is reinscribed by her Christian husband, the heroine of Greene's play is not merely passive. Timothy Billings's exploration of the word "Catayan" and its association with deceptive seduction points to how this meaning may actually be informed by Angelica's role as a deceptive and ensnaring object of sensual desire.[20] Crucially, in both the play and Ariosto's poem, Angelica's husband is of her own choosing. In Ariosto and Harington, Angelica's preference for Medor is explicitly driven by sexual desire. After witnessing Medor being wounded in honorable combat, Angelica takes pity on him and nurses him back to health. According to Harington, taking "the juyse" from medicinal herbs "between her fingers bright" and "infus[ing]" it into Medor's "wound," Angelica "reviv[es] Medoros spright" (19.19). But in the process of healing him, "another dart" simultaneously "wound[s] her thoughts and hye conceits so deep"; healing Medor awakens in Angelica a wound of her own (19.22). She beseeches Medor to heal her in turn by taking her maidenhead: "though modestie a while did let her, / Yet now perforce no further she forbore / But plainly to Medoro told her griefe / And at his hands as plainly askt reliefe" (19.23). The desire that drives Angelica's choice of Medor is overt and palpable, and things progress fairly rapidly into marriage, sex, and finally the overflowing joy that prompts them to engrave their linked names on every wall, stone, or "shadie tree" (19.28).

In Harington's translation, the narrative progression of Medor and Angelica's coupling is depicted in a detailed engraving at the start of book 19 (Figure 5.1), emphasizing how it begins with Medor's loyalty to his male friend and ends with the newly wed Medor and Angelica riding off into the future and literally off the page. In the foreground, Medor comes to the aid of his wounded friend; he is himself wounded in the process; Angelica heals him; they are married; they have sex under the trees; and they ride off together toward to a ship in which they set sail for India at the end of book 19 out of 46, never again to reappear. Book 42 briefly invokes the couple when a sprite reports that Angelica "was to th'Indies gon, / With her Medoro, and was welnie there," thus indicating that the two have successfully returned to command the throne and live happily ever after. If there is anything transgressive about their union, it is, ironically, the sense of

Figure 5.1: Book 19 from Ludovico Ariosto (trans. John Harington), *Orlando Furioso* (London, 1591), Plate XVIIII. Reproduced by permission of the Massachusetts Center for Interdisciplinary Renaissance Studies.

Medor's unworthiness due to his low birth, particularly in Harington's interpretation. As we have seen, Greene assigns this (somewhat) lower status to Orlando, showing how his Christian identity compensates for his lesser nobility. By contrast, Harington in book 30.15 remarks of Medor "what a Lord / He grew, by matching with so great an haire, / Liuing with her in loue and, sweet accord, / (Although by byrth an vnfit matched paire)." In the genre of epic romance, Medor's identity as a Muslim and a Turk does not present an obstacle to winning the fair maiden's love and "living with her in love and sweet accord."

Mixing and Un-Mixing it Up

In the first scene of Greene's play Angelica decisively chooses Orlando, not Medor, to become her husband, employing the unequivocal words, "I choose Orlando, County Palatine" (1.1.161). If she had not, I want to suggest, she would have had to end up in a tragedy like Perseda and Desdemona. Rather than harboring a burning sexual desire, Greene's Angelica is resolutely chaste and innocent – a more suitable bride for a Christian. However, the mutual love between Angelica and Orlando is thwarted by a rival suitor named Sacripant, who sows the seeds of doubt in Orlando by carving Angelica and Medor's names on trees in the woods where Orlando strolls. Sacripant plots,

> I'll slyly have engrav'n on every bark
> The names of Medor and Angelica.
> Hard by, I'll have some roundelays hung up,
> Wherein shall be some posies of their loves,
> Fraughted so full of fiery passions
> As that [Orlando] shall perceive by proof
> Medor hath won his fair Angelica. (2.1.516–22)

Clearly the engravings and posies convey not only love but sexual passion, which is the real threat to Orlando; in this, they prefigure Cassio's ocular proof of Desdemona's infidelity. Orlando responds to the sexual implications of this evidence when he exclaims, "No name of hers / . . . / And yet her name! / for why Angelica; / But, mixed with Medor, not Angelica" (2.1.588, 591–4). As in Ariosto's romance, proof of Angelica's desire for another man drives Orlando out of his mind; only here (as later in *Othello*) his jealousy is completely unfounded. In making the villainous Sacripant, rather than Medor and Angelica, the agent who writes their names in the tree trunks, Greene *rewrites* romance into tragicomedy, reappropriating the romance trope of engraving to set up for a comic reversal, or *unmixing* of Medor and Angelica. In staging Sacripant's engraving of false rumors, the play in effect performs its own rewriting of Ariosto. This rewriting becomes necessary, I want to suggest, because of the story's adaptation to a theatrical medium. The sexual passion between Medor and Angelica, while tolerable in a written narrative or even a visual engraving, could not be enacted on the stage without tragic consequences. Both the physical presence involved in live performance and the theater's demand for unity and closure create the impossibility of a triumphal sexual union between Medor and Angelica.

Angelica's unwavering choice of Orlando over Medor, her chaste innocence, and the fact that the engravings are forged are necessary to produce a tragicomic conclusion from Ariosto's plot. In Ariosto, romance structure enables Orlando to go on after Angelica and Medor drop out of the plot; in Greene's adaptation, tragicomic structure demands not only that Orlando possess Angelica but also that she remain untainted by Medor. Despite their "mingling" of tragedy and comedy, high and low, tragicomedies are deeply invested in forestalling certain kinds of mixture. Sacripant's dying confession leaves unquestioned Angelica's chaste innocence. Although the structure of tragicomedy suggests a trajectory in which sexual and religious transgression might be followed by redemption, in Greene's *Orlando Furioso* comic resolution depends not on the heroine's redemption but on the revelation that her transgression never actually took place. This elision in turn reveals the early modern stage's inability to imagine a recuperation of a female body after it has been contaminated by a Muslim.

Notably, the potential tragedy that is averted in Greene's play is the possibility that Orlando will believe Sacripant's false rumors and be consumed by jealousy. He does, in fact, lose his mind temporarily, and commits several acts of violence. Mistaking a shepherd for Medor, he cuts off the shepherd's leg, abuses his servant, beats a clown who cross-dresses as Angelica, and kills Brandimart, king of the Isles. But he is miraculously cured of his madness in Act 4 by an "enchantress" named Melissa. In this way, the plot turns on the conjuring of a sibyl. But just as significant as the sibyl's power to turn Orlando's mind are the implied limitations of her power: whereas she can restore Orlando to sanity, she could not undo a sexual union between Medor and Angelica. Her powers work in the service of Christian conquest. Crucially, as I've mentioned, Orlando is cured of his madness not so that he can return to his military duties but so that he can marry Angelica. On the stage, the romantic seduction does the work of the military conquest – a substitution that lends itself to the emotional and practical aspects of dramatic enactment.

If tragicomedy consciously reins in the unwieldiness of romance narratives, it also forces them into alignment with the structures of a cultural hierarchy. Thus, it enables us to isolate the interesting questions of what can constitute tragic potential and what can constitute resolution, which kinds of transgressions can be redeemed and what it takes to redeem them in convincing ways. The structural necessity of resolving a potentially tragic crisis with a happy ending forces a kind of nailing down of one's cultural investments. As Greene's play suggests, it was much more acceptable to dramatize the romantic triumph of a white Christian than of a Muslim Turk. Kyd and Shakespeare adapt the triumph of a Muslim lover to a tragic plotline. Just as interesting was what one could not see on the Renaissance stage: for example, comedies about English gentlemen who turned Turk or about Muslim tyrants who turned Christian. For certain, one thing you definitely could not see on the Renaissance stage was a play about a Muslim Turk who stole a fair pagan maiden from a Christian hero and lived happily ever after. That was simply no way to end a play.

Notes

Notes to Introduction

1 Robert Daborne, *A Christian Turned Turke*, in *Three Turk Plays from Early Modern England*, ed. Daniel Vitkus (New York: Columbia University Press, 2000), 6.442–3.

2 For a history of Britons taken captive between 1600 and 1850, see Linda Colley, *Captives: Britain, Empire, and the World, 1600–1850* (New York: Pantheon Books, 2002).

3 John Rawlins, *The famous and wonderfull recoverie of a ship of Bristoll, called the Exchange, from the Turkish pirates of Argier* (London, 1622), B1v-2r.

4 Ibid., B2r.

5 Alain Grosrichard, *The Sultan's Court: European Fantasies of the East*, trans. Liz Heron (New York: Verso, 1998).

6 Shakespeare and other playwrights employ the phrase "serve my turn" in ways that make clear its sexual connotations. See, for example, the exchange between Costard and the King of Navarre in *Love's Labor's Lost* 1.1. Instead of admitting that he was caught having sex with a virgin, Costard says, "I deny her virginity: I was taken with a maid." In objecting to this paradox, the King of Navarre replies, "This 'maid' will not serve your turn, sir." But Costard assures him that, indeed, "This maid will serve my turn, sir."

7 Jonathan Burton, *Traffic and Turning: Islam and English Drama, 1579–1624* (Newark: University of Delaware Press, 2005), 11.

8 Harold Jenkins, ed., *Hamlet*, Arden Shakespeare (London: Methuen, 1982).

9 This revisionist understanding of the Reformation has been influentially argued by Eamon Duffy as well as by literary critics such as Stephen Greenblatt, both of whom emphasize the vigor of late medieval Catholicism and the ways in which its remembered traditions continued to haunt the early modern imagination after the Reformation. See Duffy, *The Stripping of the Altars: Traditional Religion in England, 1400–1580* (New Haven: Yale University Press, 1992); and Greenblatt, *Hamlet in Purgatory* (Princeton: Princeton University Press, 2001). Other works that paved the way for revisionist histories of the Reformation include

Christopher Haigh, ed., *The English Reformation Revised* (Cambridge: Cambridge University Press, 1987), and Patrick Collinson, *The Birthpangs of Protestant England: Religious and Cultural Change in the Sixteenth and Seventeenth Centuries* (New York: St. Martin's Press, 1988).

10   Elizabeth Williamson, *The Materiality of Religion in Early Modern English Drama* (Farnham: Ashgate, 2009).

11   Ibid., 5.

12   "The Turn to Religion in Early Modern English Studies," *Criticism*, 46.1 (Winter 2004): 167–90.

13   For Jackson and Marotti's discussion of "alterity" as a central methodological concern of New Historicist criticism, as well as their sense of New Historicism's neglect of both the philosophical roots of alterity and the alterity of early modern religion, see ibid., 175–9.

14   Michael O'Connell, *The Idolatrous Eye: Iconoclasm and Theater in Early Modern England* (Oxford: Oxford University Press, 2000), 18.

15   Anthony Dawson, "Shakespeare and Secular Performance," in *Shakespeare and the Cultures of Performance*, eds. Paul Yachnin and Patricia Badir (Aldershot: Ashgate, 2008), 83–97, 87.

16   Studies include Andre Gunder Frank, *ReOrient: Global Economy in the Asian Age* (Berkeley: University of California Press, 1998); Kenneth Pomeranz and Steven Topik, *The World That Trade Created: Society, Culture, and the World Economy, 1400-Present* (Armonk, NY: M. E. Sharpe, 1999); Robert Brenner, *Merchants and Revolution: Commercial Change, Political Conflict, and London's Overseas Traders, 1550–1653* (Princeton: Princeton University Press, 1993); and Gerald Maclean, ed., *Re-Orienting the Renaissance: Cultural Exchanges with the East* (New York: Palgrave Macmillan, 2005).

17   On developments in English overseas commerce, see especially Brenner, *Merchants and Revolution*; and David Loades, *England's Maritime Empire: Seapower, Commerce, and Policy, 1490–1690* (New York: Longman, 2000). Literary critics who have addressed England's shifting position in the global market include Jonathan Gil Harris, *Sick Economies: Drama, Mercantilism, and Disease in Shakespeare's England* (Philadelphia: University of Pennsylvania Press, 2004); and Valerie Forman, *Tragicomic Redemptions: Global Economics and the Early Modern English Stage* (Philadelphia: University of Pennsylvania Press, 2008).

18   For a history of the rise of the joint stock companies, see Brenner, *Merchants and Revolution*. For a discussion of the East India Company's reorientation of trade around imports and re-exports, rather than English exports, see K. N. Chaudhuri, *The English East India Company: The Study of an Early Joint-Stock Company, 1600–1640* (New York: August Kelley, 1965).

19   Pierre d'Avity, *The estates, empires, & principalities of the world*, trans. E. Grimstone (London, 1615), 936.

20   Edward Said, *Orientalism* (New York: Pantheon Books, 1978).

21   Richmond Barbour, *Before Orientalism: London's Theatre of the East, 1576–1626* (Cambridge: Cambridge University Press, 2003). See also Lisa Jardine and Jerry Brotton's *Global Interests* (Ithaca, NY: Cornell University Press, 2000), whose exploration of a different archive – that of Renaissance

art, medals, tapestries, and equestrian images - reveals not a western "othering" of the Orient, but a culture of mutual East-West exchange. Ottoman historian Daniel Goffman considers the "societal commingling and cultural blending that accompanied the infusion of Ottoman civilization into Europe" in *The Ottoman Empire and Early Modern Europe* (Cambridge: Cambridge University Press, 2002), 6. Destabilizing western pre-eminence in a different way, Barbara Fuchs illuminates the dynamics of cultural mimesis that undermined Spain's and England's constructions of their imperial identities, and exposes the collective threat represented by the Ottoman empire. See *Mimesis and Empire: The New World, Islam, and European Identities* (Cambridge: Cambridge University Press, 2001).

22 Barbour, Vitkus, and Burton build upon the pioneering work of Nabil Matar, who, in bringing to light a new archive of English travel narratives, news pamphlets, and sermons, concluded that prose writings provided a relatively balanced assessment of Turks, whereas the stage perpetuated inaccurate negative stereotypes. See Nabil Matar, *Islam in Britain, 1558–1685* (Cambridge: Cambridge University Press, 1998), and *Turks, Moors, and Englishmen in the Age of Discovery* (New York: Columbia University Press, 1999), which draw connections between English representations of Muslims and Native Americans. In turn, Daniel Vitkus (2003) and Jonathan Burton (2005) respond to Matar by calling attention to the many complex and nuanced portrayals of Turks on the stage, which ranged from laudatory to debased and thus reflected England's ambivalence toward the more powerful Ottoman empire. In addition, Burton seeks to rectify the "unidirectional" orientation of previous studies by attempting to access "Muslim self-representations" in translated Ottoman narratives (14–15). See Daniel Vitkus, *Turning Turk: English Theater and the Multicultural Mediterranean, 1570–1630* (New York: Palgrave Macmillan, 2003) and Burton, *Traffic and Turning*.

23 Dimmock's study of Elizabethan drama closely aligns plays produced between 1581 and 1591 with corresponding political developments and expresses caution about the applicability of Said's theories in this period. He continues to complicate Matar's one-dimensional assessment of the stage by arguing that the portrayal of Turkish characters during this ten-year period "achieved an articulacy and a variety that . . . would not be superseded" in later periods (6). See *New Turkes: Dramatizing Islam and the Ottomans in Early Modern England* (Aldershot: Ashgate, 2005).

Linda McJannet's (2006) study extends Burton's methodology: she addresses whether "the Sultan can speak" by examining dialogue in English plays about Ottoman history in conjunction with Continental and Turkish chronicles. Resisting a reading of the plays as "orientalist," she warns against "exaggerat[ing] the sense of western 'anxiety' or 'panic' regarding Islam or the Ottoman empire" (6). See *The Sultan Speaks: Dialogue in English Plays and Histories about the Ottoman Turks* (New York: Palgrave Macmillan, 2006).

Benedict Robinson's exploration of early modern rewritings of medieval chivalric romances, in which the conflict between Christendom and Islam was central, provides a nuanced discussion of how early modern writers appropriated romance in order to grapple with the changes in their own expanding world. See *Islam and Early Modern English Literature: The Politics of Romance from Spenser to Milton* (New York: Palgrave Macmillan, 2007).

Bernadette Andrea's much-needed study is unique in its focus on writings by women and how Anglo-Ottoman relations impinged upon questions of female agency. See *Women and Islam in Early Modern English Literature* (Cambridge: Cambridge University Press, 2008).

24 Robinson, 12.

25 R. A. Foakes, ed., *Henslowe's Diary*, 2nd ed. (New York: Cambridge University Press, 2002), 318, 319.

26 James Shapiro, *Shakespeare and the Jews* (New York: Columbia University Press, 1996); Julia Reinhard Lupton, "*Othello* Circumcised: Shakespeare and the Pauline Discourse of Nations," *Representations*, 57 (Winter 1997): 73–89; Janet Adelman, "Her Father's Blood: Race, Conversion, and Nation in *The Merchant of Venice*," *Representations*, 81 (Winter 2003): 4–30.

27 McJannet, *The Sultan Speaks*, 197, fn. 4.

28 See, for example, Donusa's mocking of her Turkish suitor's "wainscot face" and "tadpole-like complexion" in Philip Massinger, *The Renegado*, in Vitkus, *Three Turk Plays from Early Modern England*, 3.1.48 and 50. I discuss these lines in Chapter 3.

29 Burton and Loomba, eds., *Race in Early Modern England: A Documentary Companion* (New York: Palgrave Macmillan, 2007), 2.

30 According to the *Oxford English Dictionary* (hereafter OED), early modern "race" was understood in terms of "a group of people belonging to the same family and descended from a common ancestor; a house, family, kindred" (n[6] I.1.a); "the offspring or posterity of a person; a set of children or descendants" (n[6] I.2.a); and "stock, family, or class" (n[6] I.4.a.). *OED Online*, 2nd ed., 1989.

31 Jean Feerick, *Strangers in Blood: Relocating Race in Renaissance Literature* (Toronto: University of Toronto Press, 2010). Many thanks to Jean for sharing her then unpublished manuscript with me. See also Feerick, "'Divided in Soyle': Plantation and Degeneracy in *The Tempest* and *The Sea Voyage*," *Renaissance Drama*, 35 (2006): 27–54.

32 Feerick, *Strangers in Blood*, 17.

33 See Kim Hall, *Things of Darkness: Economies of Race and Gender in Early Modern England* (Ithaca, NY: Cornell University Press, 1995); Joyce Green MacDonald, *Women and Race in Early Modern Texts* (Cambridge: Cambridge University Press, 2002); Mary Floyd-Wilson, *English Ethnicity and Race in Early Modern Drama* (Cambridge: Cambridge University Press, 2003); and Lara Bovilsky, *Barbarous Play: Race on the Renaissance Stage* (Minneapolis: University of Minnesota Press, 2008). For an analysis of the cultural mythologies of skin color in early modern England, see Sujata Iyengar, *Shades of Difference: Mythologies of Skin Color in Early Modern England* (Philadelphia: University of Pennsylvania Press, 2004). For a thirty-year overview of scholarship on race and Renaissance literature, see Floyd-Wilson, "Moors, Race, and the Study of English Renaissance Literature: A Brief Retrospective," *Literature Compass*, 3.5 (June 2006): 1044–52.

Other influential studies of race and early modern English drama include *Women, "Race," and Writing in the Early Modern Period*, eds. Margo Hendricks and Patricia Parker (London: Routledge, 1994); Michael Neill, "'Mulattos,' 'Blacks,' and 'Indian Moors': *Othello* and Early Modern Constructions of Human Difference," *Shakespeare Quarterly*, 49.4 (Winter 1998): 361–74; Emily Bartels, *Speaking of the Moor: From Alcazar to Othello* (Philadelphia: University of Pennsylvania Press, 2008); Bartels, "Making More of the Moor: Aaron, Othello, and Renaissance Refashionings of Race," *Shakespeare Quarterly*, 41.4 (Winter 1990): 433–54; Bartels, "*Othello* and Africa: Postcolonialism Reconsidered," *William and Mary Quarterly*, 3rd ser., 54.1 (January 1997): 45–64; and Benjamin Braude, "The Sons of Noah and the Construction of Ethnic and Geographical Identities in the Medieval and Early Modern Periods," *William and Mary Quarterly*, 3rd ser., 54. 1 (January 1997): 103–42.

34 Dympna Callaghan, "'Othello was a white man': Properties of Race on Shakespeare's Stage," in *Shakespeare Without Women: Representing Race and Gender on the Renaissance Stage* (New York: Routledge, 2000), 75–96; Virginia Mason Vaughan, *Performing Blackness on English Stages, 1500–1800* (Cambridge: Cambridge University Press, 2005); Andrea Stevens, "'*Assisted by a Barber*': The Court Apothecary, Special Effects, and *The Gypsies Metamorphosed*," *Theatre Notebook*, 61.1 (2007): 2–11; and Stevens, "Mastering Masques of Blackness," *English Literary Renaissance*, 39.2 (Spring 2009): 396–426.

35 Anthony Nixon, *Newes from the sea, of two notorious pyrats Ward the Englishman, and Danseker the Dutchman* (London, 1609); Andrew Barker, *A true and certaine report of the beginning, proceedings, ouerthrowes, and now present state of Captaine Ward and Danseker* (London, 1609).

36 For discussions of the play's moral investments and its utility as a "cautionary lesson," see Vitkus, *Turning Turk*, 158, and Matar, *Islam in Britain*, 58.

37 Burton, *Traffic and Turning*, 94.

38 Burton, "English Anxiety and the Muslim Power of Conversion: Five Perspectives on 'Turning Turk' in Early Modern Texts," *Journal for Early Modern Cultural Studies*, 2 (2002): 35–67.

39 Rawlins, *Famous and wonderfull recoverie*, E3r.

40 Ludovico Cortano, *Good newes to Christendome . . . discovering a wonderfull and strange apparition, visibly seene for many dayes togither in Arabia, ouer the place, where the supposed tombe of Mahomet (the Turkish prophet) is inclosed* (London, 1620).

41 Ibid., C3r. The phrase "rayning of blood" is part of the full title of the pamphlet.

42 On the rich and sacred significance of Christ's blood as an object of veneration, dating from fifteenth-century Catholic practices, see Caroline Walker Bynum, *Wonderful Blood: Theology and Practice in Late Medieval Northern Germany and Beyond* (Philadelphia: University of Pennsylvania Press, 2007). For an interesting discussion of the spectacle of Christ's blood as a sign of resistance, informed by the Corpus Christi plays, see

Claire Sponsler's chapter on "Violated Bodies" in *Drama and Resistance: Bodies, Goods, and Theatricality in Late Medieval England* (Minneapolis: University of Minnesota Press, 1997).

43 Cortano, *Good newes*, A3.

44 Ibid., F4r–v.

45 Nathaniel Butter, publisher and bookseller from 1604 to 1664, published a variety of books, including sermons, plays, practical works, and travel narratives, but he is best known for publishing scores of cheap news pamphlets in the 1620s and 1630s. For more on Butter and newsbooks, see Folke Dahl, *A Bibliography of English Corantos and Periodical Newsbooks, 1620–1642* (London: Bibliographical Society, 1952), and Joad Raymond, *Pamphlets and Pamphleteering in Early Modern Britain* (Cambridge: Cambridge University Press, 2003), 132–4.

46 On the sensational aspects of virgin martyr legends, see Karen Bamford, *Sexual Violence on the Jacobean Stage* (New York: St. Martin's Press, 2000).

47 For a study of the romance narrative form as a vehicle for imagining Christian-Muslim encounter, see Robinson, *Islam and Early Modern English Literature*.

48 See, for example, Geraldine Heng's discussion of sexual seduction and conversion in *The Man of Law's Tale* and other versions of the Constance story. *Empire of Magic: Medieval Romance and the Politics of Cultural Fantasy*, esp. "Beauty and the East, a Modern Love Story" (New York: Columbia University Press, 2002).

49 See, for example, Exodus 34.12–16, where God commands Moses, "Take hede to thy self, that thou make no compact with the inhabitants of the land whither you goest, lest thei be the cause of ruine among you . . . And lest thou take of their daughters vnto thy sonnes, and their daughters go a whoring after their gods, and make thy sonnes go a whoring after their gods." Geneva Bible [*The Bible and Holy Scriptures . . .*] (London, 1560).

50 For a historical overview of Reformation debates and developments, see Peter Marshall, *Reformation England, 1480–1642* (Oxford: Oxford University Press, 2003); Anthony Milton, *Catholic and Reformed: The Roman and Protestant Churches in English Protestant Thought, 1600–1640* (Cambridge: Cambridge University Press, 1995); Nicholas Tyacke, *Aspects of English Protestantism c.1530–1700* (Manchester: Manchester University Press, 2002); and David Cressy, ed., *Religion and Society in Early Modern England: A Sourcebook* (New York: Routledge, 1996).

51 For James I's injunction against piracy, see *By the King. A proclamation against pirats* (London, 1608 [i.e., 1609]); STC 8426.

52 In his *Religious Controversies of the Jacobean Age: A Survey of Printed Sources* (Lincoln: University of Nebraska Press, 1977), Peter Milward summarizes two debates that fueled a Calvinist resurgence in the second decade of the seventeenth century: ongoing debates between Calvinists and Catholic polemicists and the beginnings of the Arminian controversy. For the shifting contours of Jacobean anti-Catholicism, see Milton, *Catholic and Reformed*, esp. 31–59; for useful lists of many of the polemical works involved, see Milward, *Religious Controversies*, 72–131. For the early Arminan controversy, see ibid., 33–44. According to Milward, English

Calvinists responded to the theological attacks of Jacobus Arminius with polemical tracts of their own. The Calvinist backlash to Arminianism gained strength in 1612 in attacks on Konrad Vorst, successor to Arminius and an alleged Socinian. English responses to Vorst were swift and critical; they included a pamphlet by James I, entitled *His Maiesties declaration concerning his proceedings with the states generall of the United Provinces of the Low Countreys, in the cause of D. Conradus Vorstius* (London, 1612).

53 For other critical discussions that explore the play in relation to Arminianism, see Robinson, *Islam and Early Modern English Literature*, ch. 4; and Michael Neill, "Turn and Counterturn: Merchanting, Apostasy and Tragicomic Form in Massinger's *The Renegado*," in *Early Modern Tragicomedy*, eds. Subha Mukherji and Raphael Lyne (Cambridge: D. S. Brewer, 2007), 154–74.

54 W. B. Patterson, *King James VI and I and the Reunion of Christendom* (Cambridge: Cambridge University Press, 1997).

55 Michael C. Questier, *Conversion, Politics, and Religion in England, 1580–1625* (Cambridge: Cambridge University Press, 1996).

56 See Molly Murray, *The Poetics of Conversion: Verse and Change from Donne to Dryden* (Cambridge: Cambridge University Press, 2009); Murray, "'Now I am a Catholique': William Alabaster and the Early Modern Catholic Conversion Narrative," in *Catholic Culture in Early Modern England*, eds. Ronald Corthell, Frances Dolan, Christopher Highley, and Arthur Marotti (Notre Dame, IN: Notre Dame University Press, 2007), 189–215; and Holly Crawford Pickett, "Motion Rhetoric in Serial Conversion Narratives: Religion and Change in Early Modern England," in *Redrawing the Map of Early Modern English Catholicism*, ed. Lowell Gallagher (Toronto: University of Toronto Press, forthcoming). On the performance of conversions between Catholicism and Protestantism, see also Arthur Marotti, "Performing Conversion," in *Religious Ideology and Cultural Fantasy: Catholic and Anti-Catholic Discourses in Early Modern England* (Notre Dame, IN: University of Notre Dame Press, 2005), 95–130.

57 For critical studies that illustrate Protestant England's continued reliance on religious materiality, see James Kearney, *The Incarnate Text: Imagining the Book in Reformation England* (Philadelphia: University of Pennsylvania Press, 2009); William A. Dyrness, *Reformed Theology and Visual Culture: The Protestant Imagination from Calvin to Edwards* (Cambridge: Cambridge University Press, 2004); Ramie Targoff, *Common Prayer: The Language of Public Devotion in Early Modern England* (Chicago: University of Chicago Press, 2001); and Tessa Watt, *Cheap Print and Popular Piety, 1550–1640* (Cambridge: Cambridge University Press, 1991). Protestant denunciations of Catholic forms of materiality are extremely abundant; see for example the Church of England, *Certain sermons or homilies appointed to be read in churches in the time of Queen Elizabeth of famous memory and now reprinted for the use of private families, in two parts* (London, 1687); the frontispiece to John Foxe, *Acts and Monuments* (London, 1563); Thomas Williamson, *The sword of the spirit to smite in pieces that antichristian Goliah* (London, 1613) (see Chapter 3 for an image taken from this text); *The popes pyramides* (London, 1624);

and Jean de Chassanion, *The merchandises of popish priests* (London, 1629).

58 Samuel Hieron, *The baptizing of the eunuch in three sermons vpon Acts. 8. 36. 37. 38* (London, 1613). For another contemporary sermon discussing these biblical passages, see Charles Sonibancke, *The eunuch's conversion* (London, 1617), 21.

59 Ibid., 22.

60 E. A. J. Honigmann, ed., *The Arden Shakespeare Othello*, 3rd ed. (London: Thomas Nelson and Sons, 1996).

61 For one of many news stories published on Lindh in 2001, see Daniel Klaidman, Michael Isikoff, et al., "Walker's Brush With Bin Laden," *Newsweek* (December 31, 2001): 20.

Notes to Chapter 1

1 Biblical quotations throughout the chapter are taken from the Geneva Bible [*The Bible and Holy Scriptures . . .*] (London, 1560).

2 Julia Reinhard Lupton, *Citizen-Saints: Shakespeare and Political Theology* (Chicago: University of Chicago Press, 2005), 42.

3 A range of sermons explicating Paul's reference to "circumcision of the heart" include John Donne's commemoration of the Feast of the Circumcision (1624); William Attersoll, *The Badges of Christianity* (London, 1606); William Perkins, *A commentarie or exposition, vpon the fiue first chapters of the Epistle to the Galatians* (London, 1604); Francis Bunny, *A comparison betweene the auncient fayth of the Romans, and the new Romish religion* (London, 1595); and Henry Smith, *A preparatiue to marriage* (London, 1591).

4 R. T. Kendall, *Calvin and English Calvinism to 1649* (Oxford: Oxford University Press, 1979), 1.

5 The doctrine of predestination was first outlined in England in Article XVII of the Thirty-Nine Articles of the Church of England (1563). It was then more explicitly defined in the Lambeth Articles, devised by Archbishop John Whitgift in 1596. See the Lambeth Articles, as quoted by H. C. Porter, *Reformation and Reaction in Tudor Cambridge* (Cambridge: Cambridge University Press, 1958), 371.

6 For history on the debates, see in addition to Kendall, Porter, *Reformation and Reaction in Tudor Cambridge*; Peter Milward, *Religious Controversies of the Jacobean Age: A Survey of Printed Sources* (Lincoln: University of Nebraska Press, 1977); Peter Lake, *Moderate Puritans and the Elizabethan Church* (Cambridge: Cambridge University Press, 1982); Nicholas Tyacke, *Anti-Calvinists: The Rise of English Arminianism c.1590–1640* (Oxford: Clarendon Press, 1987); Peter White, *Predestination, Policy and Polemic* (Cambridge: Cambridge University Press, 1992); Anthony Milton, *Catholic and Reformed: The Roman and Protestant Churches in English Protestant Thought, 1600–1640* (Cambridge: Cambridge University Press, 1995); and Michael Questier, *Conversion, Politics and Religion in England, 1580–1625* (Cambridge: Cambridge University Press, 1996).

7 Tyacke, *Anti-Calvinists*, 9.

8   John Coolidge, *The Pauline Renaissance: Puritanism and the Bible* (Oxford: Clarendon Press, 1970).

9   Several influential historical studies detail England's expanding commercial relations in the eastern Mediterranean during the early modern period. Chief among these are Robert Brenner, *Merchants and Revolution: Commercial Change, Political Conflict, and London's Overseas Traders, 1550–1653* (Princeton: Princeton University Press, 1993); Kenneth Andrews, *Trade, Plunder and Settlement: Maritime Enterprise and the Genesis of the British Empire 1480–1630* (Cambridge: Cambridge University Press, 1984); and Ralph Davis, *English Overseas Trade, 1500–1700* (London: Macmillan, 1973). For a discussion of Mediterranean commerce in relation to the emergence of European capitalism, see Fernand Braudel, *The Mediterranean and the Mediterranean World in the Age of Philip II*, trans. Siân Reynolds, 2 vols. (London: Collins, 1972).

10 On maritime trade and the threat of conversion, see Nabil Matar, *Islam in Britain, 1558–1685* (Cambridge: Cambridge University Press, 1998); and Daniel Vitkus, *Turning Turk: English Theater and the Multicultural Mediterranean, 1570–1630* (New York: Palgrave Macmillan, 2003). Vitkus argues that anxieties associated with expanding Mediterranean commerce directly informed the popular stage's preoccupation with "Turks" and the phenomenon of "turning Turk."

11 See *The policy of the turkish empire* (London, 1597) for a theological interpretation of Islam from the English perspective. For a critical analysis of the threatening theological links between Islam and Christianity, see Julia Reinhard Lupton, "*Othello* Circumcised: Shakespeare and the Pauline Discourse of Nations," *Representations*, 57 (Winter 1997): 73–89.

12 Lupton, *Citizen-Saints*, and Gregory Kneidel, *Rethinking the Turn to Religion in Early Modern English Literature: The Poetics of All Believers* (New York: Palgrave Macmillan, 2008). Other critics who have influentially traced Paul's influences in early modern literature include Janet Adelman, *Blood Relations: Christian and Jew in* The Merchant of Venice (Chicago: University of Chicago Press, 2008), and Lisa Lampert, *Gender and Jewish Difference from Paul to Shakespeare* (Philadelphia: University of Pennsylvania Press, 2004). For an excellent overview of critical reassessments of St. Paul's legacy, see Lupton, "The Pauline Renaissance," forthcoming in *The European Legacy*. Many thanks to Julia Lupton for sharing her then unpublished manuscript with me as well as for her invaluable help in framing my discussion of St. Paul.

13 Lupton, *Citizen-Saints*, 30.

14 Kneidel, *Rethinking the Turn to Religion*, 3.

15 Ibid., 16, 13. As Kneidel notes, his use of the term "struggling universality" is indebted to Slavoj Žižek, *The Puppet and the Dwarf: The Perverse Core of Christianity* (Cambridge: MIT Press, 2003), 109.

16 Alain Badiou, *Saint Paul: The Foundation of Universalism*, trans. Ray Brassier (Stanford: Stanford University Press, 2003), and Giorgio Agamben, *The Time That Remains: A Commentary on the Letter to the Romans*, trans. Patricia Dailey (Stanford: Stanford University Press, 2005). Other theorists with whom Badiou and Agamben (and by extension Lupton and Kneidel) are in dialogue with about St. Paul's thought

include Slavoj Žižek, Jacques Derrida, and Walter Benjamin. Other scholarship emphasizing the continuities between Paul's rabbinic education and his writings include Daniel Boyarin, *A Radical Jew: Paul and the Politics of Identity* (Berkeley: University of California Press, 1994); Jacob Taubes, *The Political Theology of Paul* (Stanford: Stanford University Press, 2004); and Paula Fredriksen, *Augustine and the Jews: A Christian Defense of Jews and Judaism* (New York: Doubleday, 2008).

17 Badiou, *Saint Paul*, 35.
18 Ibid., 43.
19 Ibid., 59, 73.
20 Agamben, *The Time That Remains*, 62.
21 Ibid., 35.
22 Ibid., 18.
23 Kneidel, *Rethinking the Turn to Religion*, 17.
24 Kim Hall, *Things of Darkness: Economies of Race and Gender in Early Modern England* (Ithaca, NY: Cornell University Press, 1995), 114.
25 Henry Smith, *Foure Sermons Preached by Master Henry Smith* (London, 1599): sig. H4v. (STC 22748)
26 Thomas Rymer, *The Critical Works of Thomas Rymer*, ed. Curt Zimansky (New Haven: Yale University Press, 1956), 134.
27 Samuel Taylor Coleridge, *Shakespearean Criticism*, ed. Thomas M. Raysor (London: J. M. Dent, 1960); first pub. 1930.
28 All quotations from *Othello* are taken from E. A. J. Honigmann, ed., *The Arden Shakespeare Othello*, 3rd ed. (London: Thomas Nelson and Sons, 1996).
29 The title of an article by Karen Newman alludes to this connection, though it focuses not on Othello but on Desdemona and how her subversive femininity is aligned with "blackness and monstrosity." See Newman, "'And wash the Ethiop white': Femininity and the Monstrous in *Othello*," in *Shakespeare Reproduced*, eds. Jean Howard and Marion O'Connor (London and New York: Methuen, 1987), 143–62.
30 Parker, *Literary Fat Ladies: Rhetoric, Gender, Property* (London and New York: Methuen, 1987), 79.
31 For a discussion of the complex set of cultural and religious resonances attached to Shakespeare's Ephesus, especially the Hellenic resonances, see Randall Martin, "Rediscovering Artemis in *The Comedy of Errors*," in *Shakespeare and the Mediterranean: Selected Proceedings of the International Shakespeare Association World Congress, Valencia, 2001*, eds. Tom Clayton, Susan Brock, and Vicente Fores (Newark: University of Delaware Press), 363–79.
32 Wayne Meeks, ed., *The Writings of St. Paul: A Norton Critical Edition, Annotated Text and Criticism* (New York: Norton, 1972), 122.
33 Patricia Parker, "Anagogic Metaphor: Breaking Down the Wall of Partition," in *Centre and Labyrinth: Essays in Honor of Northrop Frye*, eds. Eleanor Cook, et al. (University of Toronto Press, 1983), 38–58. Reading *The Comedy of Errors* in relation to St. Paul's epistles, Parker analyzes the interplay between the play's internal structure and its Pauline references to divorce, division, and the middle wall of partition. She argues that the play occupies a symbolic "space of dilation" that corresponds structurally

to the "anagogic relationship" between Paul's breaking down of Jewish barriers and the Apocalypse, a gap that is ultimately resolved through the convergence of doom and nativity at the play's conclusion. Parker briefly revisits this discussion in *Literary Fat Ladies*, where she links the "chiasmic placing" of Egeon's family on the mast of the ship to the reunion of divided sides in Paul's Epistle. For a broader discussion of the multiple biblical echoes operating in *The Comedy of Errors*, see Parker's "Shakespeare and the Bible: *The Comedy of Errors*," *Recherches Semiotiques/Semiotic Inquiry*, 13.1 (1993): 47–71.

34 Linda McJannet, "Genre and Geography: The Eastern Mediterranean in *Pericles* and *The Comedy of Errors*," in *Playing the Globe: Genre and Geography in English Renaissance Drama*, eds. John Gillies and Virginia Mason Vaughan (London: Associated University Press, 1998), 86–106; and Jonathan Gil Harris, *Sick Economies: Drama, Mercantilism, and Disease in Shakespeare's England* (Philadelphia: University of Pennsylvania Press, 2004).

35 Harris, *Sick Economies*, 31.

36 All quotations from *The Comedy of Errors* are taken from T. S. Dorsch, *The New Cambridge Shakespeare The Comedy of Errors*, updated ed. (Cambridge: Cambridge University Press, 2004).

37 Arthur Kinney, "*The Comedy of Errors*: A Modern Perspective," in *The New Folger Library Edition: The Comedy of Errors* (New York: Washington Square Press, 2004), 179–96, esp. 185. See also Kinney, "Shakespeare's *Comedy of Errors* and the Nature of Kinds," *Studies in Philology*, 85.1 (Winter 1988): 29–52.

38 See indexes of *Calendar of State Papers, Domestic Series*, ed. Mary Anne Everett Green (London, HMSO, 1858).

39 *Notes Concerninge Trade Collected by Robr Williams, 1631–54* (University of Pennsylvania, MS Codex 207).

40 Vitkus, *Turning Turk*, 162.

41 Harris, *Sick Economies*, 30.

42 Valerie Forman, *Tragicomic Redemptions: Global Economics and the Early Modern English Stage* (Philadelphia: University of Pennsylvania Press, 2008).

43 Jackson, *The converts happines* (London, 1609), 4.

44 Stephen Greenblatt, "Shakespeare's Leap," *New York Times Magazine* (September 12, 2004): 52.

45 Queen Elizabeth to the Lord Mayor et al., 11 July 1596 and 18 July 1596, and in *Acts of the Privy Council of England*, n.s., 26 (1596–7), ed. John Roche Dasent (London: Mackie, 1902), 16–17, 20–1.

46 In the *OED*, see "part" 12; "title" 7; and "perfect" 4. *OED Online*, 2nd ed., 1989.

47 Charles Lamb, "On the Tragedies of Shakespeare, Considered with Reference to their Fitness for Stage Representation," in *Lamb as Critic*, ed. Roy Park, Routledge Critics Series (Lincoln: University of Nebraska Press, 1980), 97. The essay was first published in 1812.

48 Huston Diehl, *Staging Reform, Reforming the Stage: Protestantism and Popular Theater in Early Modern England* (Ithaca, NY: Cornell University Press, 1997), 125–55.

49 Ibid., 136.
50 Robert N. Watson, "*Othello* as Protestant Propaganda," in *Religion and Culture in Renaissance England*, eds. Claire McEachern and Debora Shuger (Cambridge: Cambridge University Press, 1997), 234–57.
51 For a reading of *Othello* in relation to the protagonists of early modern adventure plays, see Jean Howard "Gender on the Periphery," in *Shakespeare and the Mediterranean*, eds. Clayton et al., 344–62.
52 John Leo Africanus, *A geographical historie of Africa*, ed. John Pory (London, 1600). For a discussion of Leo Africanus's narrative as a source for *Othello* and the significance of the differences between the two texts, see Jonathan Burton, "'Bondslaves and pagans shall our statesmen be': *Othello*, Leo Africanus, and Muslim Ambassadors to Europe," in *Traffic and Turning* (Newark: University of Delaware, 2005), 233–56. As a point of contrast, see also Lois Whitney, "Did Shakespeare Know Leo Africanus?" *PMLA*, 37 (1922): 470–83.
53 For a variety of critical views on the significance of Moors in early modern England, see G. K. Hunter, "Elizabethans and Foreigners," *Shakespeare Survey*, 17 (1964): 37–52; Anthony Barthelemy, *Black Face, Maligned Race* (Baton Rouge: Louisiana State University Press, 1987); Emily Bartels, "Imperialist Beginnings: Richard Hakluyt and the Construction of Africa," *Criticism*, 34.4 (Fall 1992): 517–38; Hall, *Things of Darkness*; Michael Neill, "'Mulattos,' 'Blacks,' and 'Indian Moors': *Othello* and Early Modern Constructions of Human Difference," *Shakespeare Quarterly*, 49.4 (Winter 1998): 361–74; Ania Loomba, "Outsiders in Shakespeare's England," in *The Cambridge Companion to Shakespeare*, eds. Margreta de Grazia and Stanley Wells (Cambridge: Cambridge University Press, 2001), 147–66; and Bartels, *Speaking of the Moor: From Alcazar to Othello* (Philadelphia: University of Pennsylvania Press, 2008).

    According to the *OED*, in 1604 "Moor" could refer to (1) people indigenous to Mauritania in northwestern Africa; (2) people of a mixed Berber and Arab race, Muslim in religion; (3) "Negroes," dark-skinned people who differ from lighter-skinned "tawny Moors"; and (4) generically, Muslims, particularly those from the Indian subcontinent, thus a separate group called "Indian Moors." *OED Online*, 2nd ed., 1989.
54 Bartels, *Speaking of the Moor*, 5.
55 A sampling of Renaissance plays that depict Moors in diverse ways include Shakespeare's *Titus Andronicus* and *The Merchant of Venice*; Thomas Dekker's *Lusts Dominion*; Thomas Middleton's *All's Lost By Lust*; John Fletcher, Philip Massinger, and Nathan Field's *The Knight of Malta*; Thomas Heywood's *The Fair Maid of the West, Parts I and II*; George Peele's *The Battle of Alcazar*; and John Webster's *The White Devil*.
56 On Moors in the romance tradition, see Barbara Fuchs, *Romance* (New York: Routledge, 2004). On the association of African Moors with wisdom and nobility in the classical tradition of writers like Diodorus, see Mary Floyd-Wilson, *English Ethnicity and Race in Early Modern Drama* (Cambridge: Cambridge University Press, 2003). For a reading of Othello as a Morisco, see Barbara Everett, "'Spanish' Othello: The Making of Shakespeare's Moor," *Shakespeare Survey*, 35 (1982): 101–12.

57 The title of the play given in the 1623 folio catalogue is "Othello, the Moore of Venice," and in the 1622 quarto, "The Tragedy of Othello, the Moor of Venice."

58 Lupton, "*Othello* Circumcised"; and Daniel Vitkus, "Turning Turk in *Othello*: The Conversion and Damnation of the Moor," *Shakespeare Quarterly*, 48 (1997): 145–76.

59 Ibid., 78.

60 Loomba, *Shakespeare, Race, and Colonialism* (Oxford and New York: Oxford University Press, 2002), 92.

61 Burton, *Traffic and Turning*, 252.

62 Callaghan, "'Othello was a white man': Properties of Race on Shakespeare's Stage," in *Shakespeare Without Women: Representing Race and Gender on the Renaissance Stage* (New York: Routledge, 2000), 75–96, esp. 79.

63 Lupton, *Citizen-Saints*, 32.

64 Burton, *Traffic and Turning*, 251.

65 "Richard Eden to the reader," Peter Martyr d' Anghiera, *The decades of the Newe Worlde*, trans. Richard Eden (London, 1555), sig. c3v.

66 Meredith Hanmer, *The baptizing of a Turke. A sermon preached at the hospitall of Saint Katherine the 2 of October, 1586* (London, 1586), title page. (STC 12744) For a brief discussion of Hanmer's sermon that interprets his argument for converting Turks as anti-Catholic polemic, see Matar, *Islam in Britain*, 126–9.

67 Matar, *Islam in Britain*, 126.

68 John Foxe, *Actes and Monuments* (1583), vol. 1, 719. (STC 11225)

69 Hanmer, sig. [A]3r-v.

70 Ibid., sig. f4r.

71 Ibid., sig. f4r.

72 See Porter, *Reformation and Reaction*, 371.

73 Ibid.

74 Reprinted from BL MS. Lansdowne No. 80, art. 65, in *Cambridge University Transactions During the Puritan Controversies of the 16th and 17th Centuries*, collected by James Heywood and Thomas Wright, vol. II (London: Henry G. Bohn, 1854), 94.

75 For a reading of *Othello* as an allegorical commentary on the predestination debates, see Maurice Hunt, "Predestination and the Heresy of Merit in *Othello*," *Comparative Drama*, 30.3 (Fall 1996): 346–76. Hunt argues that the injustice of Desdemona's "non-election" to heaven casts the doctrine of predestination in an "unfavorable light" (369).

76 Valerie Traub has similarly called attention to the way Desdemona's dead body objectifies her chastity, but for Traub, this objectification is oppressive in its move to contain the erotic threat of female sexuality. See Traub, *Desire and Anxiety: Circulations of Sexuality in Shakespearean Drama* (London: Routledge, 1992), ch. 1.

77 As Mary Floyd-Wilson has shown, the association between coldness and chastity also assumed a particular racial valence under the terms of geohumoralism, a climatic explanation of color and disposition grounded in the composition of the body's humors. Inherited from classical and medieval traditions, geohumoralism associated England's northern climate with "intemperate" bodies, a culture that was "borrowed and belated," and a

"barbarous" nature (4), but as Floyd-Wilson has argued, the early modern period marked a "discursive rearrangement of [this] inherited knowledge" in reorienting the intemperate coldness and pallid complexion of the northern climate with qualities of fairness, civility, and self-control (13). See Floyd-Wilson, *English Ethnicity and Race.*

78 Other heroines who sustain their sexual chastity and their faith against the pressures of lustful Turks and Moors include Perseda in Thomas Kyd's *Soliman and Perseda* (*c.*1589); Bess in Thomas Heywood's *The Fair Maid of the West, Part I* (*c.*1604); Alizia in Robert Daborne's *A Christian Turned Turke* (*c.*1610), Ariana in John Fletcher's *The Knight of Malta* (*c.*1618); and Paulina in Philip Massinger's *The Renegado* (*c.*1624).

79 Vitkus, *Turning Turk*, 99.

80 This story was widely disseminated through William Painter's *Palace of Pleasure* (1566), Henry Wotton's *A courtlie controuersie of Cupids cautels* (1578), Richard Knolles's *Generall historie of the Turks* (1603), and William Barksted's poem *Hiren or The Faire Greeke* (1611). It was adapted on the stage in Thomas Kyd's *Soliman and Perseda* (*c.*1589), George Peele's (now lost) *Turkish Mahomet and Hyrin the Fair Greek* (*c.*1594), Thomas Goffe's *The Courageous Turk* (1618), Lodowick Carlell's *Osmond the Great Turk* (1622), and Gilbert Swinhoe's *Unhappy Fair Irene* (1640).

81 For a history of Cyprus, see George Hill, *A History of Cyprus: The Ottoman Province, the British Colony, 1571–1948*, vol. 4 of 5 (Cambridge: Cambridge University Press, 1952).

82 Horace Howard Furness, ed., *A New Variorum of Shakespeare* (New York: AMS Press, 1965).

83 Jones, "*Othello, Lepanto* and the Cyprus Wars," *Shakespeare Survey*, 21 (1968): 47–52.

84 Richard Hakluyt, *The principall nauigations, voiages and discoueries of the English nation* (London, 1589), 1:218.

85 Ibid., 2:130–1.

86 Burton, *Traffic and Turning*, 252.

87 See, for example, Richard S. Veit, "'Like the base Judean': A Defense of an Oft-Rejected Reading in *Othello*," *Shakespeare Quarterly*, 26.4 (Autumn 1975): 466–9; and Edward Snow, "Sexual Anxiety and the Male Order of Things in *Othello*," *English Literary Renaissance*, 10 (1980): 384–412.

88 Lupton, *Citizen-Saints*, 93.

89 Kneidel, *Rethinking the Turn to Religion*, 148.

90 Ibid., 16.

91 Lupton, *Citizen-Saints*, 105.

92 Agamben, *The Time that Remains*, 62.

93 Badiou, *Saint Paul*, 43.

Notes to Chapter 2

1 G. E. Bentley identifies 1620 as the earliest performance date with some degree of certainty, on the basis of a sizable licensing fee paid to Sir George

Buck, Master of the Revels, on October 6, 1620. See *The Jacobean and Caroline Stage*, 7 vols. (Oxford: Clarendon Press, 1956), 4:754. In this, Bentley refutes F. G. Fleay's speculation that Dekker first wrote the play in 1612 and that it appears in Henslowe's records as the lost *Dioclesian*, later to be revised by Massinger and retitled *The Virgin Martyr*. For this view, see Fleay's *A Biographical Chronology of the English Drama, 1559–1642* (London, 1891), 212–13.

2   All quotations from the play are based on Phillip Massinger and Thomas Dekker, *The Virgin Martir, A Tragedie* (London, 1622), STC 17644. Line numbers correspond to Fredson Bowers's critical edition of the play in *The Dramatic Works of Thomas Dekker*, 4 vols. (Cambridge: Cambridge University Press, 1966).

3   On the suppression of medieval biblical drama and the complexly achieved secularization of the theater in post-Reformation England, see Michael O'Connell, *The Idolatrous Eye: Iconoclasm and Theater in Early Modern England* (Oxford: Oxford University Press, 2000); Patrick Collinson, *The Birthpangs of Protestant England* (New York: St. Martin's Press, 1988); Lawrence Clopper, *Drama, Play, and Game: English Festive Culture in the Medieval and Early Modern Period* (Chicago: University of Chicago Press, 2001); Paul White, *Theatre and Reformation* (Cambridge: Cambridge University Press, 1993); Harold Gardiner, *Mysteries' End* (New Haven: Yale University Press, 1946); and Glynne Wickham, *Early English Stages 1300–1660* (London: Routledge, 1980). Recently, studies like Clopper's seek to complicate the view that biblical drama was unilaterally suppressed in England, especially prior to the 1570s, and offer evidence of the ways in which it persisted.

4   The record of the fee is made in Sir Henry Herbert's office-book, which contains some extracts from the otherwise scant records of George Buck, Herbert's predecessor as Master of the Revels. As Bentley notes, the specific amount of the fee indicates that it was paid for the licensing of a new play which required revision, probably due to "censorable matter" (*The Jacobean and Caroline Stage*, 3:265–6). Presumably, the play's alignment of the martyred heroine with certain Protestant sensibilities and her pagan enemies with Marian persecutors constituted enough of a concession to get the play past the censors.

5   I quote from Jose M. Ruano de la Haza, "Unparalleled Lives: Hagiographical Drama in Seventeenth-Century England and Spain," in *Parallel Lives: Spanish and English National Drama 1580–1680*, eds. Louise Fothergill-Payne and Peter Fothergill-Payne (Lewisburg: Bucknell University Press, 1991), 257.

Clubb argues that the play bears an essential affinity to the Italian genre of *tragedia sacra*, a product of the Continental Counter-Reformation, and suggests that it appealed to Roman Catholics in England who could identify with the persecuted Roman heroine. See *"The Virgin Martyr and the Tragedia Sacra," Renaissance Drama*, 7 (1964): 103–26. Other critics who align the play with the Counter-Reformation include Uve Christian Fischer, "Un drama martirologico barocco: *The Virgin Martyr* di Philip Massinger," *Siculorum Gymnasium*, 16 (1963): 1–19; Cyrus Hoy, *Introductions, Notes, and Commentaries to Texts in The Dramatic*

Works of Thomas Dekker, 4 vols. (Cambridge and New York: Cambridge University Press, 1980–3), 3:181–8; and Walter Cohen, *Drama of a Nation: Public Theater in Renaissance England and Spain* (Ithaca, NY: Cornell University Press, 1985), 375.

By contrast, Julia Gasper reads the play as Protestant propaganda; see "*The Virgin Martyr* and the War in Germany," in *The Dragon and the Dove: The Plays of Thomas Dekker* (Oxford: Clarendon Press, 1990), 136–65. Champion also rejects Clubb's reading of play as Catholic; see "Disaster With My So Many Joys: Structure and Perspective in Massinger and Dekker's *The Virgin Martyr*," *Medieval and Renaissance Drama in England*, 1 (1984): 199–204, 200. More recently, Susannah Monta has concurred with Gasper's Protestant reading of the play, but also argues that its depiction of a Catholic virgin martyr demonstrates the flexibility of competing martyrological conventions in the early seventeenth century. See *Martyrdom and Literature in Early Modern England* (Cambridge: Cambridge University Press, 2005), 194–216.

Critics who argue that the play's religious content is superficial include De la Haza; George Price, *Thomas Dekker* (New York: Twayne, 1969), 95–6; and Peter Mullany, "Religion in Massinger's and Dekker's *The Virgin Martyr*," *Komos*, 2 (1970): 89–97.

6   As discussed in the Introduction, notions of racial difference were in a nascent state of development and highly unstable in the early modern period. Though not yet signified by the term "race," a set of differences was emerging that eventually came to comprise the modern category. Thus, when I refer to "race" in the early modern period, I am referring to an evolving and slippery notion of difference that was sometimes distinguished by skin color or taxonomies of darkness and fairness, sometimes by humoral compositions dictated by geography and climate, sometimes by the effects of diet, exercise, or cosmetics, sometimes by physical marks like circumcision, and sometimes by a certain relationship between internal temperament and external complexion. For a useful discussion of how religious and bodily differences were complexly interrelated in the early modern period, see Ania Loomba, "Religion, Colour, and Racial Difference," in *Shakespeare, Race, and Colonialism* (Oxford and New York: Oxford University Press, 2002), 45–74.

7   Figure 2.1 is a well-known early modern map from the first Geneva Bible (1560); it appears in the *Newe Testament* just after the *Actes of the Apostles* and depicts countries and places that are mentioned in that book. According to Lloyd Berry's introduction to *The Geneva Bible: A Facsimile of the 1560 Edition* (Madison: University of Wisconsin Press, 1969), "A good case has been made for Thomas Dekker's preference for the *Geneva Bible*" (19).

8   Thomas Noble and Thomas Head, eds., *Soldiers of Christ: Saints and Saints' Lives from Late Antiquity and the Early Middle Ages* (University Park, PA: Penn State University Press, 1995), xxi.

9   See Kirsten Wolf, "The Legend of Saint Dorothy: Medieval Vernacular Renderings and their Latin Sources," *Analecta Bollandiana*, 114 (1996): 41–72. See also Julia Gasper, "The Sources of *The Virgin Martyr*," *Review of English Studies*, 42.165 (1991): 17–31.

10 Karen Winstead, *Virgin Martyrs: Legends of Sainthood in Late Medieval England* (Ithaca, NY: Cornell University Press, 1997).

11 For more detailed discussion of Dorothy's legend in each of these sources, see Wolf, "The Legend of Saint Dorothy," and Gasper, "The Sources of *The Virgin Martyr*."

12 See Theodora Jankowski's *Pure Resistance: Queer Virginity in Early Modern English Drama* (Philadelphia: University of Pennsylvania Press, 2000) on the subversive (or "queer") signification of virginity in the early modern period. Jankowski draws a clear distinction between premarital virginity in a Protestant context and the Catholic validation of vowed virginity. Reading *The Virgin Martyr* in the former context, she argues that the Protestant mandate against celibacy and the early modern valorization of the patriarchal family rendered virginity a highly subversive choice in the early modern period. For a broader theoretical discussion of the implications of virginity in early modern England, particularly with respect to questions of agency, see Kathryn Schwartz, "The Wrong Question: Thinking Through Virginity," *differences*, 13.2 (2002): 1–34. For a consideration of early modern dramatic representations of virginity in relation to contemporary medical discourses, see Marie Loughlin, *Hymeneutics: Interpreting Virginity on the Early Modern Stage* (Lewisburg: Bucknell University Press, 1997). Loughlin's study focuses mainly on the plays of Beaumont and Fletcher and does not consider the plays discussed in this chapter.

13 Reflecting a similar method of analysis, Linda McJannet has suggested that the classical settings of Shakespeare's *Pericles* and *The Comedy of Errors* are partly informed by their contemporary resonance with the Ottoman empire, which occupies the same geographical territory. See Linda McJannet, "Genre and Geography: The Eastern Mediterranean in *Pericles* and *The Comedy of Errors*," in *Playing the Globe: Genre and Geography in English Renaissance Drama*, eds. John Gillies and Virginia Mason Vaughan (London: Associated University Press, 1998), 86–106. A similar recognition of how the Old World is partially reinscribed by the contemporary significance of its Mediterranean geography is reflected in discussions of *The Tempest* and its setting. See for example Jerry Brotton, "'This Tunis, sir, was Carthage': Contesting Colonialism in *The Tempest*," in *Post-Colonial Shakespeares*, eds. Ania Loomba and Martin Orkin (London: Routledge, 1998), 23–42.

14 Brenner's *Merchants and Revolution: Commercial Change, Political Conflict, and London's Overseas Traders, 1550–1653* (Princeton: Princeton University Press, 1993) offers a detailed history of the factors that enabled England's penetration of the eastern markets and the rise of the joint stock companies.

15 The volume of the *Calendar* covering the years 1611–18 lists fifty-four discrete entries under Turkish "Piracies" or "Pirates" (680). That number jumps to ninety-six in the next volume covering the years 1619–23, including substantial increases under the categories of "contributions for the suppression of pirates" and "expeditions against pirates" (695). See indexes of *Calendar of State Papers, Domestic Series, of the Reign of James I, 1611–18* and *1619–23*, ed. Mary Anne Everett Green (London: HMSO, 1858).

16 *Calendar of State Papers*, 1619–23: 393.
17 Daniel Vitkus, *Turning Turk: English Theater and the Multicultural Mediterranean, 1570–1630* (New York: Palgrave Macmillan, 2003), esp. "Scenes of Conversion: Piracy, Apostasy, and the Sultan's Seraglio," 107–62. See also Jonathan Gil Harris, *Sick Economies: Drama, Mercantilism, and Disease in Shakespeare's England* (Philadelphia: University of Pennsylvania Press, 2004), for an analysis of how the rapid rise of global trade fostered English anxieties about foreign agents that were manifested in discourses of bodily disease.
18 Jean Howard, "Gender on the Periphery," in *Shakespeare and the Mediterranean: The Selected Proceedings of the International Shakespeare Association World Congress, Valencia, 2001*, eds. Tom Clayton, Susan Brock, and Vicente Forés (Newark: University of Delaware Press, 2004), 344–62.
19 Barbara Fuchs, *Mimesis and Empire: The New World, Islam, and European Identities* (Cambridge: Cambridge University Press, 2001), 125.
20 For a related argument, see Jean Howard, "An English Lass Amid the Moors: Gender, Race, Sexuality, and National Identity in Heywood's *The Fair Maid of the West*," in *Women, "Race," and Writing in the Early Modern Period*, eds. Margo Hendricks and Patricia Parker (London: Routledge, 1994), 101–17.
21 See Daniel Vitkus, ed., *Piracy, Slavery, and Redemption: Barbary Captivity Narratives from Early Modern England* (New York: Columbia University Press, 2001); see also Nabil Matar, *Turks, Moors, and Englishmen in the Age of Discovery* (New York: Columbia University Press, 1999).
22 The conflation between castration and the cut of circumcision associated with Muslims and Jews is a running joke on the early modern stage. Jonathan Burton has argued that circumcision/castration and conversion in the drama are almost always displaced onto clown figures as a way to disavow the true allure and power of Islam, which he argues receives more accurate representation in non-dramatic texts of the period. See "English Anxiety and the Muslim Power of Conversion: Five Perspectives on 'Turning Turk' in Early Modern Texts," *Journal for Early Modern Cultural Studies*, 2 (2002): 35–67. In *Shakespeare and the Jews* (New York: Columbia University Press, 1996), James Shapiro offers an historical analysis of the common conflation of circumcision and castration in early modern representations of Jews and Jewish conversion; see esp. 114–17. For an insightful discussion of the typological links between Jews and Muslims, see Julia Reinhard Lupton, "*Othello* Circumcised: Shakespeare and the Pauline Discourse of Nations," *Representations*, 57 (Winter 1997): 73–89.
23 Holly Pickett, "Dramatic Nostalgia and Spectacular Conversion in Dekker and Massinger's *The Virgin Martyr*," *SEL, 1500–1900*, 49.2 (Spring 2009), 437–62, esp. 440 and 441.
24 Monta, *Martyrdom and Literature*, 194–216, esp. 196.
25 Foxe identifies his source for the primitive church as Eusebius's *Ecclesiastical History*. Foxe overtly rejects the Catholic sources, such as Jacobus's *Legenda aurea*, through which stories of early Christian martyrs had been widely disseminated in the Middle Ages.

26   *Actes and Monuments* (1570), 1:273.
27   John R. Knott offers a detailed analysis of Foxe's use of the persecution of the primitive church as a precedent for contemporary narratives of martyrdom. See Knott, "Heroic Suffering," in *Discourses of Martyrdom in English Literature, 1563–1694* (Cambridge: Cambridge University Press, 1993), 33–83. James Knapp has also discussed Foxe's reliance on historical precedent and specifically the chronicles of Eusebius to provide an "analogue to the current strife in the Christian world." See Knapp, "Stories and Icons: Reorienting the Visual in John Foxe's *Acts and Monuments*," in *Illustrating the Past in Early Modern England: The Representation of History in Printed Books* (Aldershot: Ashgate, 2003), 124–206, esp. 131. On the illustrations in Foxe and early modern print culture, see John N. King, *Foxe's Book of Martyrs and Early Modern Print Culture* (Cambridge: Cambridge University Press, 2006).
28   Huston Diehl, *Staging Reform, Reforming the Stage: Protestantism and Popular Theater in Early Modern England* (Ithaca, NY: Cornell University Press, 1997). Diehl's argument on this point may be seen to concur with Eamon Duffy's influential claim that English Protestantism was largely based on Catholic forms and that more continuities exist between Catholicism and Protestantism than we typically acknowledge. Duffy, *The Stripping of the Altars: Traditional Religion in England, 1400–1580* (New Haven: Yale University Press, 1992).
29   Diehl, *Staging Reform, Reforming the Stage*, 45.
30   *Actes and Monuments* (1570), 3:1418–19.
31   Caroline Walker Bynum has written of the "peculiarly bodily" nature of medieval spirituality: the saint was defined not by overcoming but by harnessing her body – by enduring illness, by self-flagellation, by fasting. See "The Female Body and Religious Practice in Later Middle Ages," in *Fragments for a History of the Human Body I*, eds. Michel Feher, Ramona Naddaff, and Nadia Tazi (New York: Zone, 1989), 161–219. See also Bynum's discussion of the late medieval "heightened concern with matter, with corporeality, with sensuality" and the accompanying emphasis on the Eucharist as sufferance and bleeding flesh, and on the "bodiliness of Christ's humanity," in *Holy Feast and Holy Fast* (Berkeley: University of California Press, 1987), esp. 250–9.
32   Reprinted in Elaine V. Beilin, ed., *The Examinations of Anne Askew* (Oxford: Oxford University Press, 1996). Despite overall congruity between Bale's (1546, 1547) and Foxe's editions, Bale's introduction was omitted from the first edition of *Actes and Monuments* and all subsequent editions. For a detailed analysis of the editorial differences between Bale's and Foxe's treatment of Askew, see Thomas Freeman and Sarah Wall, "Racking the Body, Shaping the Text: The Account of Anne Askew in Foxe's *Book of Martyrs*," *Renaissance Quarterly*, 54 (2001): 1165–96.
33   Beilin, *The Examinations of Anne Askew*, 11.
34   Knapp, *Illustrating the Past in Early Modern England*, 134, 160.
35   "Martyr," n. 2.a. OED Online, 2nd ed., 1989.
36   Antonio Gallonio, *Trattato de gli instrumenti di martirio, e delle varie maniere di martoriare vsata da' gentili contro christiani, descritte et intagliate in rame* (Rome, 1591). The original copper plates for these images

featured the designs of Giovanni de Guerra, painter to Pope Sixtus V, and were engraved by Antonio Tempesta. Following the original Italian edition, a Latin edition of Gallonio's text was printed in Rome in 1594 and in Antwerp in 1600. The first English translation was prepared by A. R. Allison under the title *Tortures and Torments of the Christian Martyrs* (New York: Walden, 1939). A newly illustrated edition based on Allison's translation was published by the alternative Feral House and marketed as erotica (*Tortures and Torments of the Christian Martyrs: The Classic Martyrology* [Los Angeles, 2004]).

37   Another popular Counter-Reformation martyrology was Richard Verstegan's *Theatre des cruautes des heretiques de notre temps* (Antwerp, 1587). Available in numerous editions throughout the early seventeenth century and marketed as a "theatre" of (Protestant) heretical cruelty, Verstegan's book contained similarly graphic depictions of different methods of bodily penetration and other tortures, each image a kind of stage vignette.

38   "Habitation" refers to a physical "place of abode or residence" (n., 2) and the related "habit," denoting "bodily apparel or attire" (n., 1.a.), suggests material worn on the outside of the body that both defines and conforms to its external contours. *OED Online*, 2nd ed., 1989. For a discussion of clothing and its material construction of early modern subjecthood, see Ann Rosalind Jones and Peter Stallybrass, *Renaissance Clothing and the Materials of Memory* (Cambridge: Cambridge University Press, 2000).

39   As described in Allison's English translation of Gallonio, the brazen bull was "a most exceeding cruel sort of punishment in use among the Ancients, into the which . . . anyone that was to be tortured was cast by an opening or door that was in its side. Then the door being shut to again, a fire was lighted about the bull, causing those imprisoned therein to suffer unexampled agonies, and by their lamentations and cries to imitate the bellowing of a bull" (123).

40   Claire Sponsler also links these acts of violence in discussing the medieval spectacle of violated bodies and how it opened a space of resistance to contemporary ideologies of social wholeness. See "Violated Bodies: The Spectacle of Suffering in Corpus Christi Pageants," in *Drama and Resistance: Bodies, Goods, and Theatricality in Late Medieval England* (Minneapolis: University of Minnesota Press, 1997), 136–60.

41   On the trope of ineffective or clownish torturers in the medieval Corpus Christi pageants, see V. A. Kolve, *The Play Called Corpus Christi* (Stanford: Stanford University Press, 1996), 175–205.

42   See Nova Myhill, "Making Death a Miracle: Audience and the Genres of Martyrdom in Dekker and Massinger's *The Virgin Martyr*," *Early Theatre*, 7.2 (2004): 9.

43   See Karen Bamford, *Sexual Violence on the Jacobean Stage* (New York: St. Martin's Press, 2000), for a reading of *The Virgin Martyr* as "sadomasochistic pornography," 53. Other critics have discussed the erotic appeal of medieval virgin martyr legends and mystery passion plays, also comparing them to pornography. See for example Karen Winstead, *Chaste Passions: Medieval English Virgin Martyr Legends* (Ithaca, NY: Cornell University Press, 2000), 3. Sheila Delany seeks to complicate the association of

medieval martyrology with pornography or "masculinist voyeuristic sadism" in "Last Things and Afterlives," in *Impolitic Bodies* (Oxford: Oxford University Press, 1998), 186.

44 See Andrew Gurr, *The Shakespearean Stage*, 3rd ed. (Cambridge: Cambridge University Press, 1996), for a discussion of how the large, open amphitheater of the Red Bull lent itself to "lavishly staged plays" and battle scenes in the vein of *Tamburlaine* (190). See also Gurr's *Playgoing in Shakespeare's London* (Cambridge: Cambridge University Press, 1987) on the Red Bull's reputation for low theatrical standards, its less than respectable location, and its appeal to "citizens, and the meaner sort of people" (185).

45 The quotation from *The Renegado* comes from *Three Turk Plays from Early Modern England*, ed. Daniel Vitkus (New York: Columbia University Press, 2000), 4.2.49–50.

46 Edward Kellet and Henry Byam, *A retvrne from Argier: A semon preached at Minhead in the county of Somerset the 16 of March, 1627 at the re-admission of a relapsed Christian into our chvrch* (London, 1628), 76; Charles Fitzgeoffrey, *Compassion towards captives chiefly towards our brethren and country-men who are in miserable bondage in Barbarie. Vrged and pressed in three sermons on Heb. 13.3. Preached in Plymouth, in October 1636* (Oxford, 1637); and William Gouge, *A Recovery from apostacy. Set out in a sermon preached in Stepny church neere London at the receiving of a penitent renegado into the church, Oct. 21, 1638* (London, 1639).

47 Christopher Angelos, *Christopher Angell, A Grecian, who tasted of many stripes inflicted by the Turkes* (Oxford, 1617), A4r.

48 Ibid., A4v.

49 Ibid.

50 Ibid.

51 Francis Knight, *A relation of seaven yeares slaverie under the Turkes of Argeire, suffered by an English captive merchant* (London, 1640).

52 Ibid., 6.

53 Similar accounts of torture inflicted by Turks include those of John Rawlins in *The famous and wonderfull recoverie of a ship of Bristoll* (London, 1622), and Sir Henry Blount, *A voyage into the Levant* (London, 1636), esp. 52.

54 Mundy's manuscript, entitled *Itinerarium Mundii*, records the author's travels between 1608 and 1667 and includes an account of his stay in Constantinople from 1617 to 1620.

55 Bynum, "The Female Body," 175.

56 A large body of criticism explores the importance and function of virginity in the Middle Ages. These studies have uncovered the ways in which virgin martyr legends provided moral guidance for both anchoresses and lay readers and how celibacy offered medieval women a means of autonomy that was at once empowering and disabling. See, for example, Katherine Lewis, "Model Girls? Virgin-Martyrs and the Training of Young Women in Late Medieval England," in *Young Medieval Women*, eds. Katherine Lewis, Noel James Menuge, and Kim M. Phillips (New York: St. Martin's Press, 1999), 25–46; Jocelyn Wogan-Browne, "The

Virgin's Tale," in *Feminist Readings in Middle English Literature*, eds. Ruth Evans and Lesley Johnson (London: Routledge, 1994), 165–94; Sarah Salih, *Versions of Virginity in Late Medieval England* (Cambridge: D. S. Brewer, 2001); Julie Hassel, *Choosing Not to Marry: Women and Autonomy in the Katherine Group* (New York and London: Routledge, 2002); and Ruth Evans, "Virginities," in *The Cambridge Companion to Medieval Women's Writing*, eds. Carolyn Dinshaw and David Wallace (Cambridge: Cambridge University Press, 2003), 21–39.

57 Monta, *Martyrdom and Literature*, 211.

58 Ibid., 208.

59 Loomba, *Shakespeare, Race, and Colonialism*, 32.

60 John Barclay, *The mirrour of mindes, or, Barclays Icon animorum* (London, 1631), rpt. 1633; first published in Latin, 1614; 289. The reference appears in ch. 9, "Turkes and Iewes."

61 Lynda Boose, "'The Getting of a Lawful Race': Racial Discourse in Early Modern England and the Unrepresentable Black Woman," in Hendricks and Parker, *Women, "Race," and Writing in the Early Modern Period*, 33–54, 45.

62 This description comes from its manuscript flyleaf (v). Though apparently popular as a performance piece, the play was never printed in the seventeenth century. My quotations are based upon Rebecca G. Rhoads's Malone Society edition (Oxford: Oxford University Press, 1930).

63 Elizabeth Williamson, *The Materiality of Religion in Early Modern English Drama* (Farnham: Ashgate, 2009), esp. ch. 4; and James Kearney, *The Incarnate Text: Imagining the Book in Reformation England* (Philadelphia: University of Pennsylvania Press, 2009).

64 Kearney, *The Incarnate Text*, 2, 3.

65 See, for example, the debate between John Salkeld, *A treatise of angels* (London, 1613), and John Boys, *An exposition of the festivall epistles and gospels . . . the third part* (London, 1615). Salkeld, a Jesuit-trained writer who later converted to Protestantism, offers a full-blown celebration of Thomistic angelology, particularly with regard to "assisting and protecting angels," whereas Boys cites John Calvin's rejection of personal angels and argues further that the Bible does not substantiate any belief in personal angels. For Calvin's objection to the divinity of angels, see *The institution of Christian religion, wrytten in Latine by maister Ihon Calvin, and translated into Englysh according to the authors last edition*, trans. Thomas Norton (London, 1561), I.xiv.3, fol. 44r. For a modern critical discussion of the idolatrous associations of angels, see Alexandra Walsham, "Angels and Idols in England's Long Reformation," in *Angels in the Early Modern World*, eds. Peter Marshall and Alexandra Walsham (Cambridge: Cambridge University Press, 2006), 134–67.

66 Holly Crawford Pickett, "Angels in England: Idolatry and Wonder at the Red Bull Playhouse," in *Thunder at a Playhouse: Proceedings from the Fourth Blackfriars Conference*, eds. Peter Kanelos and Matt Kozusko (Selinsgrove, PA: Susquehanna University Press, 2010), 175–99. Many thanks to Holly for sharing her insightful essay with me before it went to press.

67   For a broader discussion of male heroism in the seventeenth century that argues that it was redefined to privilege endurance over action, see Mary Beth Rose, *Gender and Heroism in Early Modern England* (Chicago: University of Chicago Press, 2002).

Notes to Chapter 3

1   See Malieckal, "'Wanton Irreligious Madness': Conversion and Castration in Massinger's *The Renegado*," *Essays in Arts and Sciences*, 31 (October, 2002): 18–36; Fuchs, *Mimesis and Empire: The New World, Islam, and European Identities* (Cambridge: Cambridge University Press, 2001), ch. 5; Harris, *Sick Economies: Drama, Mercantilism, and Disease in Shakespeare's England* (Philadelphia: University of Pennsylvania Press, 2004), ch. 6; Burton, *Traffic and Turning: Islam and English Drama, 1579–1624* (Newark: University of Delaware Press, 2005), chs. 2 and 3; Vitkus, *Turning Turk: English Theater and the Multicultural Mediterranean, 1570–1630* (New York: Palgrave Macmillan, 2003), ch. 5; and Valerie Forman, *Tragicomic Redemptions: Global Economics and the Early Modern English Stage* (Philadelphia: University of Pennsylvania Press, 2008), ch. 5.

2   Critics who focus on the Catholic elements of *The Renegado* and/or argue for Massinger's Catholicism include William Gifford, "Introduction," in *The Plays of Philip Massinger*, 4 vols. (London, 1805); Frederick Boas, *An Introduction to Stuart Drama* (Oxford: Oxford University Press, 1946), 308; Maurice Chelli, *Le Drame de Massinger* (Lyon: M. Audin, 1923), 328; Alfred Cruickshank, *Philip Massinger* (New York: Frederic A. Stokes, 1920), 3; and Thomas Dunn, *Philip Massinger: The Man and the Playwright* (London: Thomas Nelson, 1957), 191. For a succinct overview of these findings, concluding that Massinger's use of religion simulates the serious tone of Fletcherian tragicomedy, see Peter Mullany, "Massinger's *The Renegado*: Religion in Stuart Tragicomedy," *Genre*, 5.1 (1972): 138–52. For a reading that argues in opposition that the play is anti-Catholic, presenting the Muslim characters as stand-ins for demonized Catholics, see Claire Jowitt, *Voyage Drama and Gender Politics, 1589–1642: Real and Imagined Worlds* (Manchester: Manchester University Press, 2003), esp. 175–84.

3   All citations of the play are from *Three Turk Plays from Early Modern England*, ed. Daniel Vitkus (New York: Columbia University Press, 2000). This edition is based on the first printed edition of the play, published in 1630.

4   While Francisco's wearing of the cope fell within the mandates of the established church, the prop also cited a history of controversy over vestments and represented a Protestant concession to an older Catholic tradition. Debate over vestments emerged during Queen Elizabeth's reign, with one side arguing for uniformity in the wearing of Eucharistic vestments and the other side objecting to them because of their association with "popish" ceremonies. For an overview of the controversy, see Patrick Collinson, "That Comical Dress" and "The People and the Pope's Attire"

in *The Elizabethan Puritan Movement* (1967; repr., Oxford: Clarendon Press, 1990), 71–83 and 92–7. James's injunction of 1604 concerning the use of the cope reveals the enduring Catholic stigma that made some clergy reluctant to conform in the wearing of vestments. See Canon 24, *Constitvtions and canons ecclesiasticall, treated vpon by the bishop of London* (London, 1604).

5 Metzger's discussion of Jessica's conversion to Christianity in *The Merchant of Venice* offers interesting anticipations of the gender dynamics that I observe in *The Renegado*; see Mary Janell Metzger, "'Now by My Hood, a Gentle and No Jew': Jessica, *The Merchant of Venice*, and the Discourse of Early Modern English Identity." *PMLA*, 113.1 (January 1998): 52–63. Although I resist any direct equation between Jewish-Christian conversion and Muslim-Christian conversion, I perceive strong parallels between the two plays in their representations of the colluding logics of gender, religious difference, and race that influence the terms of conversion. Drawing upon earlier work by Kim Hall and Lynda Boose, Metzger argues that Jessica is crucially distinguished from Shylock as a candidate for conversion, particularly by her whiteness and female gender, which "make possible her reproduction as a Christian" through Lorenzo's choice to marry her (57). For a subsequent discussion of the play that expands upon Metzger's argument and also departs from it by emphasizing the limitations of Jessica's conversion, see Janet Adelman, "Her Father's Blood: Race, Conversion, and Nation in *The Merchant of Venice*," *Representations*, 81 (Winter 2003): 4–30.

6 Other plays in which conversion to Islam is presented as a sexual threat include Thomas Kyd's *Soliman and Perseda* (*c.*1589); Thomas Dekker's *Lust's Dominion, or The Lascivious Queen* (*c.*1600); John Mason's *The Turk* (*c.*1607); Robert Daborne's *A Christian Turned Turke* (*c.*1610); and John Fletcher, Nathan Field, and Massinger's *The Knight of Malta* (*c.*1618).

7 See Gifford, "Introduction," xliv. For a useful overview of Massinger's Spanish sources, see Warner Rice, "The Sources of Massinger's *The Renegado*," *Philological Quarterly*, 11.1 (1932): 65–75. *The Renegado* is loosely based on Cervantes's "Story of the Captive" in *Don Quixote* (1605), part i, book IV, chs. 12–14, and on his play *Los Baños de Argel* (1615).

8 Michael Neill, "Turn and Counterturn: Merchanting, Apostasy and Tragicomic Form in Massinger's *The Renegado*," in *Early Modern Tragicomedy*, eds. Subha Mukherji and Raphael Lyne (Cambridge: D. S. Brewer, 2007), 154–74, 174. Many thanks to Michael Neill for sharing his then unpublished essay with me as I was completing the final version of this chapter.

9 Benedict Robinson, "The Turks, Caroline Politics, and Philip Massinger's *The Renegado*," in *Localizing Caroline Drama*, eds. Adam Zucker and Alan Farmer (New York: Palgrave Macmillan, 2006), 213–38. A revised version of his essay appears in his *Islam and Early Modern English Literature: The Politics of Romance from Spenser to Milton* (New York: Palgrave Macmillan, 2007), 117–43.

10 Jean Howard, "Gender on the Periphery," in *Shakespeare and the Mediterranean: The Selected Proceedings of the International Shakespeare*

Association World Congress, Valencia, 2001, eds. Tom Clayton, Susan Brock, and Vicente Forés (Newark: University of Delaware Press, 2004), 344–62, 349.

11   Robert Daborne, *A Christian Turned Turke: or, The tragicall lives and deaths of the two famous pirates, Ward and Dansiker* (London, 1612). The plays have other similarities as well: both are set in the city of Tunis, and both include a priestly counselor named Francisco.

12   As discussed in Chapter 1, this doctrine held that all souls were pre-divided between election to heaven and reprobation to hell, and that both fates were completely reliant on the will of God, impervious to good works or individual will. The doctrine of predestination was first outlined by the English Church in Article XVII of the Thirty-Nine Articles of the Church of England (1563). It was then more explicitly defined in the Lambeth Articles, devised by Archbishop John Whitgift in 1596.

13   Vitkus, *Three Turk Plays,* 41–2, and *Turning Turk,* 159. For a related discussion of how *The Renegado* "rewrites/rerights" *A Christian Turned Turke,* see Patricia Parker, "Preposterous Conversions: Turning Turk and its 'Pauline' Rerighting," *Journal for Early Modern Cultural Studies,* 2.1 (2002): 21–7.

14   See especially Nabil Matar, *Islam in Britain, 1558–1685* (Cambridge: Cambridge University Press, 1998); Vitkus, *Turning Turk;* and Fuchs, *Mimesis and Empire.*

15   Whereas Elizabeth implicitly sanctioned English privateering and the plundering of Spanish galleys on the Barbary coast, James proclaimed an official suspension of English privateering in June of 1603. See "A Proclamation Against Pirates," issued January 8, 1609, reprinted in *Stuart Royal Proclamations,* eds. James Larkin and Paul Hughes, 3 vols. (Oxford: Clarendon Press, 1973), 1:203–6. For an account of James's attempt to combat Barbary piracy, see David Hebb, *Piracy and the English Government, 1616–42* (Aldershot: Scolar Press, 1994). See also Kenneth Andrews, *Trade, Plunder and Settlement: Maritime Enterprise and the Genesis of the British Empire, 1480–1630* (Cambridge: Cambridge University Press, 1984), and Godfrey Fisher, *Barbary Legend: War, Trade, and Piracy in North Africa, 1415–1830* (Oxford: Clarendon Press, 1957).

16   Burton suggests that early modern plays represented castration in comedic ways in order to assuage English anxieties about the emasculation of English men and the serious threat posed by Christian conversion to Islam. See his "English Anxiety and the Muslim Power of Conversion: Five Perspectives on 'Turning Turk' in Early Modern Texts," *Journal for Early Modern Cultural Studies,* 2 (2002): 35–67.

17   This is not to suggest that Protestants never translated the threat of Catholicism into sexual and embodied terms; indeed, the metaphor of the Whore of Babylon did powerful work in associating Catholics with pathologies such as syphilis, also known as the "Romish sickness" or the "French pox." Nevertheless, the Whore of Babylon, and Catholics more generally, were typically not associated with entrapping potential con- verts through sexual seduction, as were Muslim Turks. Thomas Dekker's *Whore of Babylon* (1606) offers a clear dramatic example of how the

Catholic Whore of Babylon functions as a figurative rather than a literal "whore."

18 John Stradling, *Beauti pacifici* (London, 1623).

19 Ibid., 18.

20 Francisco is identified as "a Jesuite" under the Dramatis Personae in the earliest edition of the play (1630).

21 See, for example, John Gee, *The foot out of the snare* (London, 1624), which vehemently argued for the banning of Jesuits from England. In response to the controversy, King James issued a royal proclamation banning Jesuits on May 6, 1624; see *Stuart Royal Proclamations*, 1:591–3. For an overview of the events associated with the royal Proclamation, see Thomas Cogswell, *The Blessed Revolution: English Politics and the Coming of War, 1621–1624* (Cambridge: Cambridge University Press, 2005), esp. 288–9. See also Alison Shell, *Catholicism, Controversy, and the English Literary Imagination, 1558–1660* (Cambridge: Cambridge University Press, 1999), esp. 113–18.

22 See Burton, "English Anxiety and the Muslim Power of Conversion."

23 Drawing upon Alain Grosrichard's discussion of the "absurd economy" of non-convertible commodities in early modern European fantasies of the Orient (*The Sultan's Court: European Fantasies of the East*, trans. Liz Heron [London: Verso, 1998], 68), Harris links Carazie's impotence with the pathological hoarding of treasure that disrupts the healthy circulation of trade. See Harris, *Sick Economies*, 156–61. Forman similarly focuses on the economic dimensions of *The Renegado*'s threat of castration, arguing that the eunuch is a figure for the complete obstruction of trade, which the play resolves through its redemptive embracing of a restrained and ethical form of circulation; see Forman, *Tragicomic Redemptions*. I thank Valerie Forman for sharing her then unpublished manuscript with me while I was completing revisions for this chapter.

24 Catholic relics (as well as icons and images) and their denunciation in post-Reformation England are the subjects of an extensive critical discourse. See, for example, Margaret Aston, *England's Iconoclasts* (Oxford: Clarendon Press, 1988); Hans Belting, *Likeness and Presence: A History of the Image Before the Era of Art*, trans. Edmund Jephcott (Chicago: University of Chicago Press, 1994); John Phillips, *The Reformation of Images: Destruction of Art in England, 1535–1660* (Berkeley: University of California Press, 1973); and Robert Whiting, *The Blind Devotion of the People: Popular Religion and the English Reformation* (Cambridge: Cambridge University Press, 1989).

25 Frances Dolan, *Whores of Babylon: Catholicism, Gender, and Seventeenth-Century Print Culture* (Ithaca, NY: Cornell University Press, 1999), 27.

26 See, for example, Andreas Vesalius, *Epistola rationem modumque propinandi radicis Chynae decocti* (*Letter on the China Root*; Basel, 1546), and *De humani corporis fabrica* (Basel, 1543). Vesalius's anatomical illustrations informed a number of subsequent medical texts published in England, including Thomas Geminus's *Compendiosa totius anatomiae delineatio* (London, 1545) and Helkiah Crooke's *Microcosmographia: A description of the body of man* (London, 1615). For a discussion of anxieties surrounding the existence and function of the hymen in these

and other texts, see Marie Loughlin, *Hymeneutics: Interpreting Virginity on the Early Modern Stage* (Lewisburg: Bucknell University Press, 1997), esp. 27–52.

27 "Maidenhead," n[1] 1.a. *OED Online*, 2nd ed., 1989.

28 As Vitkus glosses, Manto's reference to passing as "current" draws an analogy between passing for a virgin and passing for a "genuine coin." See *OED Online*, "current" 5.

29 See Arjun Appadurai, "Introduction: Commodities and the Politics of Value," in *The Social Life of Things: Commodities in Cultural Perspective*, ed. Arjun Appadurai (Cambridge: Cambridge University Press, 1986), 3–63; Jonathan Gil Harris, "Shakespeare's Hair: Staging the Object of Material Culture," *Shakespeare Quarterly*, 52.4 (Winter 2001): 479–91.

30 As Ania Loomba has argued, the stage's propensity to Christianize Muslim women and marry them to Christian men is fostered by England's political interests in mastery and colonialism. See Loomba, "'Delicious Traffick': Racial and Religious Difference on Early Modern Stages," in *Shakespeare and Race*, eds. Catherine Alexander and Stanley Wells (Cambridge: Cambridge University Press, 2000), 203–15, and "'Break her will, and bruise no bone, sir': Colonial and Sexual Mastery in Fletcher's *The Island Princess*," *Journal for Early Modern Cultural Studies*, 2.1 (2002): 68–108.

31 For a related argument that *The Renegado* uses the rescue of a Muslim princess to help assuage domestic anxieties about threatened masculinity in the early modern period, see Burton, *Traffic and Turning*, chs. 2 and 3. Burton contends that Islam and women produced parallel anxieties for English men in the period.

32 For a detailed overview of post-Reformation debates about baptism in England, see David Cressy, *Birth, Marriage, and Death: Ritual, Religion, and the Life-Cycle in Tudor and Stuart England* (Oxford: Oxford University Press, 1997), 97–194.

33 For a reading that relates this scene to the topos of washing the Ethiope white, see Anston Bosman, "'Best Play with Mardian': Eunuch and Blackamoor as Imperial Culturegram," *Shakespeare Studies*, 34 (2006): 123–57, 147.

34 See John Whitgift, *The defense of the aunswere to the admonition against the replie of T.C.* (London, 1574). For a summary of reformers' objections to lay baptism argued at the Hampton Court Conference, see William Barlow, *The summe and substance of the conference* (London, 1604), esp. 14–20. King James adopted a middle position that condoned baptisms outside of the church in cases of dire necessity, but restricted the performance of baptisms to lawful ministers (Barlow, *Summe and substance*, 8). For an overview of the debate, see Cressy, *Birth, Marriage, and Death*, 117–23.

35 At the Hampton Court Conference, several bishops argued that "the administration of baptism, by women, and lay-persons, was not allowed in the practice of the Church" because it suggested a popish practice (Barlow, *Summe and substance*, 14). For earlier debate on the subject, see Whitgift, *The defense of the aunswere to the admonition*, 29, 504, 509, 516, 793. I am grateful to Joseph Black for drawing my attention to these passages

in Whitgift's polemical exchange with Thomas Cartwright. For a critical discussion of the cultural role of the midwife in performing baptisms and other duties, see Caroline Bicks, *Midwiving Subjects in Shakespeare's England* (Aldershot: Ashgate, 2003), esp. 127–60.

36 Robinson identifies this allusion to Tasso in "The 'Turks,' Caroline Politics, and Philip Massinger's *The Renegado*," 229.

37 *The Statutes of the Realm from the Beginning to the End of the Reign of King Henry VIII (A.D. 1509–10 to A.D. 1545)*, vol. 3 (London, 1817), ch. 24, 778.

38 Malieckal, "'Wanton Irreligious Madness,'" 25–6. Intended to redeem thousands of Christian captives who had been captured and enslaved by Barbary corsairs, the attack was thwarted by bad weather and a second attempt was supported by Ottoman forces. For a historical account of the attack, see Fisher, *Barbary Legend*, 114. For a contemporary report of the mission, led by Sir Robert Mansell, see John Button, *Algiers voyage, in a journall or briefe reportary of all occurrents* (London, 1621).

39 Richard Montagu, *Appello Caesarem* (London, 1625), 152. Even earlier, there is evidence of theologians advocating a *via media* between Protestantism and Catholicism. Richard Hooker pushed for acknowledging the legitimate status of the Catholic church, arguing that by drawing near to Islam "we should be spreaders of a worse infection . . . than any we are likely to draw from papists by our conformity with them in ceremonies"; see *The Lawes of Ecclesiastical Polity*, book IV, ch. vii, in *The Folger Library Edition of the Works of Richard Hooker*, ed. W. Speed Hill, 6 vols. (Cambridge, MA: Harvard University Press, 1977–98), 1:297.

40 On James's support of Laud's early career, see Charles Carlton, *Archbishop William Laud* (London and New York: Routledge, 1987), esp. 27. On the history of the rise of Arminianism (the religious doctrine of the Dutch theologian Jacobus Arminius) in England, see Nicholas Tyacke, *Anti-Calvinists: The Rise of Arminianism c.1590–1640* (Oxford: Clarendon Press, 1987); Patrick Collinson, *The Religion of Protestants: The Church in English Society 1559–1625* (Oxford: Oxford University Press, 1982); Peter White, "The Rise of English Arminianism Reconsidered," *Past and Present*, 101 (1983): 34–54; and Peter Lake, "Calvinism and the English Church, 1570–1635," *Past and Present*, 114 (1987): 32–76.

41 Tyacke, *Anti-Calvinists*.

42 In a similar vein, Pauline Croft argues that the breakdown of Calvinism was not just accomplished through the high church clerical cabal, but was also carried out by laymen such as Robert Cecil, first earl of Salisbury; see Croft, "The Religion of Robert Cecil," *Historical Journal*, 34.4 (1991): 773–96.

43 For this line of thinking I am indebted to Debora Shuger's thoughtful response to a panel I organized along with Elizabeth Williamson for the Modern Language Association conference in 2003. The panel was titled "Contested Objects: Religious Upheaval, Catholic Idols, and Body Parts on the Renaissance Stage."

44 For a historical study of the use of blackface on English stages between 1500 and 1800, see Virginia Mason Vaughan, *Performing Blackness on English Stages, 1500–1800* (New York: Cambridge University Press, 2005).

45 Lynda Boose, "'The Getting of a Lawful Race': Racial Discourse in Early Modern England and the Unrepresentable Black Woman," in *Women, "Race," and Writing in the Early Modern Period*, eds. Margo Hendricks and Patricia Parker (London: Routledge, 1994), 33–54, 45.

46 Reprinted in Daniel Vitkus, ed., *Piracy, Slavery, and Redemption: Barbary Captivity Narratives from Early Modern England* (New York: Columbia University Press, 2001), appendix 5.

47 Edward Kellet and Henry Byam, *A returne from Argier* (London, 1628), opposite title page.

48 Ibid., 43, 41, 44.

49 Ibid., 42.

50 See Stephen Greenblatt, *Hamlet in Purgatory* (Princeton: Princeton University Press, 2001); and Eamon Duffy, *The Stripping of the Altars: Traditional Religion in England, 1400–1580* (New Haven: Yale University Press, 1992).

51 I am especially grateful to the students in my graduate seminar on "Tragicomedy" at the University of Massachusetts Amherst who helped me to reach new conclusions about the significance of this scene.

52 Anthony Dawson, "Shakespeare and Secular Performance," in *Shakespeare and the Cultures of Performance*, eds. Paul Yachnin and Patricia Badir (Aldershot: Ashgate, 2008), 83–97, 88.

53 Ibid., 87–8.

54 Ibid., 84.

55 Ken Jackson and Arthur Marotti, "The Turn to Religion in Early Modern English Studies," *Criticism*, 46.1 (Winter 2004): 167–90, 167.

Notes to Chapter 4

1 *The Statutes of the Realm from the Beginning to the End of the Reign of King Henry VIII (A.D. 1509–10 to A.D. 1545)*, vol. 3 (London, 1817), ch. 24, 778.

2 Thomas Fuller, *The historie of the holy warre* (London, 1639), 47.

3 In addition to appearing in the five plays I discuss here, the Knights of Malta make a brief appearance in John Webster's *The White Devil* (1612), when they take part in the ceremony of electing a new pope. There is also an appearance of a Knight of Rhodes in the play-within-a-play of Thomas Kyd's *The Spanish Tragedy* (1587); the scene in question corresponds to a story portrayed quite differently in Kyd's *Soliman and Perseda*.

4 On pan-Christian alliance and the rhetoric of the "common corps of Christendom," see Franklin Baumer, "England, the Turk, and the Common Corps of Christendom," *American Historical Review*, (1945): 27–8; and Molly Greene, "Beyond the Northern Invasion: The Mediterranean in the Seventeenth Century," *Past and Present*, 174 (2000): 42–71.

5 One exception is Peter Mullany, who notes the popularity of the Knights of Malta on the English stage and briefly discusses these plays. See "The Knights of Malta in Renaissance Drama," *Bulletin of the Modern Language Society*, 74 (1973): 297–301. Mullany attributes the appearance

of the Knights to "considerable interest in the East as well as to [their] historical importance" (297).

6 See Raphael Holinshed, "The First Book of the History of England," *Chronicles*, vol. 1 of 4 (London, 1587). As Margreta de Grazia has observed, the first volume of Holinshed's *Chronicles*, a crucial source of history for many early modern playwrights, organizes British history into four periods of foreign rule. See *Hamlet Without Hamlet* (Cambridge: Cambridge University Press, 2007), 57. De Grazia persuasively argues that this understanding of British history meant that "in 1600, England could still consider itself in the Fourth or Norman Rule, and its submission to a fifth was not unimaginable" (57).

7 See Jean Howard, *Theater of a City: The Places of London Comedy, 1598–1642* (Philadelphia: University of Pennsylvania Press, 2006); Jonathan Gil Harris, *Sick Economies: Drama, Mercantilism, and Disease in Shakespeare's England* (Philadelphia: University of Pennsylvania Press, 2004); and Amanda Bailey, "Custom, Debt, and the Valuation of Service in Early Modern England," in *Working Subjects in Early Modern English Drama*, eds. Michelle M. Dowd and Natasha Korda (Aldershot: Ashgate, 2010), 304–36. On London immigration and racial anxieties, see Emily Bartels, "Too Many Blackamoores: Deportation, Discrimination, and Elizabeth I," *SEL*, 46.2 (Spring 2006): 305–22. Bartels usefully illustrates how restrictions on the immigration of racialized subjects were intertwined with other foreign political relationships.

8 There have been many historical treatments of the Knights of Malta. See for example Helen Nicholson, *The Knights Hospitaller* (Woodbridge: Boydell Press, 2001); Jonathan Riley-Smith, *Hospitallers: The History of the Order of St. John* (London: Hambledon Press, 1999); Anthony Luttrell, *The Hospitallers of Rhodes and Their Mediterranean World* (Aldershot: Ashgate, 1992); and Henry J. A. Sire, *The Knights of Malta* (New Haven: Yale University Press, 1994).

9 Palmira Brummett, "The Overrated Adversary: Rhodes and Ottoman Naval Power," *Historical Journal*, 36.3 (1993): 517–41.

10 Brian Blouet, *A Short History of Malta* (New York: Frederick A. Praeger, 1967), 53.

11 For a history of Malta that emphasizes the formation of a Maltese national identity not shaped exclusively through the Knights, see Carmel Cassar, *Society, Culture, and Identity in Early Modern Malta* (Msida: Mireva, 2000).

12 Aaron Kitch, "Shylock's Sacred Nation," *Shakespeare Quarterly*, 59.2 (Summer 2008): 131–55, 144. See also Ernle Bradford, *The Great Siege: Malta, 1565* (New York: Harcourt, Brace, and World, 1961).

13 For a bibliography of primary and secondary sources relating to English responses to the siege of Malta, see Helen Vella Bonavita, ed., *Caelius Secundus Curio, His Historie of the Warr of Malta, Trans. Thomas Mainwaringe (1579)*, Medieval and Renaissance Texts and Studies vol. 339 (Tempe, AZ: MRTS, 2007). For an informative discussion of many of these sources that extends Bonavita's analysis of the early modern discursive construction of Malta, see Bernadette Andrea, "From Invasion to Inquisition: Mapping Malta in Early Modern England," in *Remapping the*

Mediterranean World in Early Modern English Writings, ed. Goran V. Stanivukovic (New York: Palgrave *Macmillan*, 2007), 245–71.

14   For a thoroughly documented history of the English *langue* of the Knights of Malta, see Gregory O'Malley, *The Knights Hospitaller of the English Langue, 1460–1565* (Oxford: Oxford University Press, 2005).

15   *Statutes of the Realm*, 3:780–1.

16   Andrea, "From Invasion to Inquisition," 250.

17   Fuller, *Historie of the holy warre*, 239.

18   Ibid., 254.

19   For an extended passage on the Knights' superstitions about relics, see ibid., 128. Fuller cites as one of many examples of the Knights' basis in superstition the well-known story of their mythological origins involving a Frenchman named Peter the Hermit, who assembled an army under the pope and won a decisive battle at Antioch by virtue of a bloody lance believed to be the same spear that wounded Christ on the cross. In a mocking tone, Fuller goes on to indulge a "merry digression" about a chest of relics that King Richard redeemed from the Turks in Palestine. Marveling at their mysterious propensity to multiply, "so that the head of the same Saint is shewed at several places" and the only possible explanation could be "synecdoche," Fuller sarcastically demonstrates how the relic's reproduction reveals its forgery and the profitable business behind it.

20   Ibid., 47.

21   William Davies, *A true relation of the travailes and most miserable captiuitie of William Dauies, barber-surgion of London* (London, 1614), D3v.

22   George Sandys, *Relations of Africa . . . obserued in his iourney, begun Ann. 1610*, as excerpted in Samuel Purchas, *Purchas his pilgrimes* (London, 1625), STC 20509. Sandys's description of Malta appears in vol. 2:915–20.

23   Sandys, *Relations of Africa*, 919.

24   Melissa Sanchez discusses a similar dynamic in Edmund Spenser's *The Faerie Queene*, in which the "feminine, private quality of Chastity" serves as a model for masculine virtue, friendship, and a just state. See "Fantasies of Friendship in *The Faerie Queene*, Book IV," *English Literary Renaissance*, 37.2 (Spring 2007): 250–73, 250.

25   Quotations from *Soliman and Perseda* are taken from *The Tragedye of Solyman and Perseda*, ed. John Murray (New York: Garland, 1991).

26   Lisa Celovsky, "Early Modern Masculinities and *The Faerie Queen*," *English Literary Renaissance*, 35.2 (Spring 2005): 210–47. Celovsky's exploration of the gendered category of knighthood in *The Faerie Queen* offers an excellent explication of the conventions of knighthood, as established through the epic and romance traditions. The plays I examine appropriate and refigure these conventions in order to grapple with contemporary threats of religious and racial difference.

27   Arthur Ferguson, *The Indian Summer of English Chivalry: Studies in the Decline and Transformation of Chivalric Idealism* (Durham, NC: Duke University Press, 1960). See also Ferguson's *The Chivalric Tradition in Renaissance England* (Cranbury, NJ: Associated University Presses, 1986). For other discussions of chivalry in the Renaissance and its medieval legacy, see Alex Davis, *Chivalry and Romance in the English*

Renaissance (Cambridge: D. S. Brewer, 2003); Sydney Anglo, ed., *Chivalry in the Renaissance* (Woodbridge: Boydell Press, 1990); and Maurice Keen, *Chivalry* (New Haven: Yale University Press, 1984).

28 Lukas Erne, *Beyond the Spanish Tragedy: A Study of the Works of Thomas Kyd* (Manchester: Manchester University Press, 2001), 193. In ch. 8, Erne offers an extended analysis of the ways in which Kyd's play departs from its primary source.

29 For a more general discussion of the blazon as an act of male violence and possession, see Nancy J. Vickers, "Diana Described: Scattered Woman and Scattered Rhyme," *Critical Inquiry*, 8 (Winter 1981): 265–79. Kim Hall plays off of Vickers's discussion of the blazon to draw a connection between Petrarchan imagery and the construction of whiteness; see *Things of Darkness: Economics of Race and Gender in Early Modern England* (Ithaca, NY: Cornell University Press, 1995), esp. ch. 2.

30 The probability that Soliman was performed in dark makeup is supported by the depiction of a figure in blackface on the title page of Kyd's *The Spanish Tragedy*, wherein *Soliman and Perseda* constitutes a play-within-the-play.

31 Queen Elizabeth actively pursued trade and diplomatic intercourse with the Ottoman empire. Having opened formal trade relations with the Ottoman Porte in 1578, she granted a charter to the Levant Company in 1592. In addition, she sought naval aid from the Turks against the pressing Spanish threat. In 1582, she dispatched an embassy to Sultan Murad II in the hopes of establishing an alliance with the Ottomans against Spain. For an analysis of shifting Anglo-Ottoman relations under Elizabeth and corresponding dramatic representations of the Turk, see Matthew Dimmock, *New Turkes: Dramatizing Islam and the Ottomans in Early Modern England* (Aldershot: Ashgate, 2005).

32 Henry Wotton, *A courtlie controuersie of Cupids cautels* (London, 1578), K2r.

33 Daniel Vitkus, *Turning Turk: English Theater and the Multicultural Mediterranean, 1570–1630* (New York: Palgrave Macmillan, 2003), 126.

34 For a discussion of the dating of *Soliman and Perseda* and *The Jew of Malta* in relation to one another, see Erne, *Beyond the Spanish Tragedy*, 159. Erne suggests, on the basis of *The Jew of Malta*'s allusion to the siege of Rhodes as a battle that the Christians refused to surrender – an interpretation that replicates Kyd's play – *The Jew of Malta* likely post-dated *Soliman and Perseda*. Erne dates *Soliman and Perseda*'s composition in 1588 or 1589, and *The Jew of Malta*'s composition in 1589 or 1590.

35 Emily Bartels, "Malta: *The Jew of Malta*, and the Fictions of Difference," *English Literary Renaissance*, 20 (1990): 1–16. Aaron Kitch also reads Ferneze's willingness to submit to Spain as a sign of his "religious and political hypocrisy," which is motivated by his economic interest in avoiding payment of tribute to Spain. See "Shylock's Sacred Nation," 144.

36 Bartels, "Malta," 8.

37 Quotations from *The Jew of Malta* are taken from *Christopher Marlowe: Doctor Faustus and Other Plays*, eds. David Bevington and Eric Rasmussen (Oxford: Oxford University Press, 1995), 247–322.

38 From this reference, Mark Hutchings argues that Ithamore is "a victim of the Ottoman policy of recruiting by force Christian boys from the Balkans and converting them to Islam to serve in either the Turkish military or the Ottoman government" (*Notes and Queries*, 47.4 [December 2000]: 428–30, esp. 429).

39 Julia Reinhard Lupton, *Citizen-Saints: Shakespeare and Political Theology* (Chicago: University of Chicago Press, 2005), 63.

40 Phyllis Rackin, "The Lady's Reeking Breath," in *Shakespeare and Women* (Oxford: Oxford University Press, 2005).

41 Quotation from *The Merchant of Venice* is taken from *The Complete Works of Shakespeare*, ed. David Bevington, 5th ed. (New York: Longman, 2004).

42 Stevie Simkin, *A Preface to Marlowe* (Harlow: Pearson Education, 2000), 158.

43 Zachary Lesser, "Tragical-Comical-Pastoral-Colonial: Economic Sovereignty, Globalization, and the Form of Tragicomedy," *ELH*, 74 (2007): 881–908, 883.

44 Dena Goldberg argues that Barabas is in fact sacrificed solely to save Malta from Turkish domination, thus contributing to a larger sacrifice motif that runs throughout the play; see "Sacrifice in Marlowe's *The Jew of Malta*," *SEL*, 32.2 (1992): 233–45. Similarly, David Riggs argues that "Marlowe's Antichrist [Barabas] literally perishes for the common good. His stolen wealth ransoms the Maltese Christians from the Turk; his sacrificial death in Act Five redeems Malta from the pagan [sic] foe that holds it in bondage"; see "Double Agents," in *The World of Christopher Marlowe* (New York: Henry Holt, 2004), 250–73, esp. 266.

45 On the dating of *The Knight of Malta*'s earliest performance, see G. E. Bentley, *The Jacobean and Caroline Stage*, 7 vols. (Oxford: Clarendon Press, 1956), 3:352–3. Bentley bases his estimate on the cast list printed in the 1679 folio, which includes Nathan Field and Richard Burbage. The performance date must fall between 1616, when Field joined the King's Men, and 1618, when Burbage died.

46 For more a detailed discussion of James's foreign policies and their religious implications, see James Doelman, *King James I and the Religious Culture of England* (Cambridge: D. S. Brewer, 2000).

47 Quotations from *The Knight of Malta* are taken from *The Dramatic Works in the Beaumont and Fletcher Canon*, ed. George Walton Williams, gen. ed. Fredson Bowers, 10 vols. (Cambridge: Cambridge University Press, 1966), 8:360–465.

48 For a broader discussion of the cultural function of the duel in early modern England, see Jennifer Low, *Manhood and the Duel: Masculinity in Early Modern Drama and Culture* (New York: Palgrave Macmillan, 2003). Surveying a range of plays and other textual representations of dueling, Low argues that the duel functioned as "an overdetermined sign of masculine identity that helped to stabilize significantly volatile notions of both rank and gender" (3).

49 Bertha Hensman, *The Shares of Fletcher, Field and Massinger in Twelve Plays of the Beaumont and Fletcher Canon*, Salzburg Studies in English

Literature, Jacobean Drama Studies 6 (Salzburg: University of Salzburg, 1974), 71–5.

50 Ania Loomba "'Delicious Traffick': Racial and Religious Difference on Early Modern Stages," in *Shakespeare and Race*, eds. Catherine Alexander and Stanley Wells (Cambridge: Cambridge University Press, 2000), 216.

51 William Segar, *Honor military, and ciuill contained in foure bookes* (London, 1602), book 2, ch. 20, 96.

52 Segar, *Honor military, and ciuill*, 97.

53 Elizabeth Williamson, *The Materiality of Religion in Early Modern English Drama* (Farnham: Ashgate, 2009). This important study explores the significance of religious stage properties on the English public stage. See especially ch. 3 on crosses and crucifixes.

54 In fact, by the end of the play, it is revealed that Lucinda has already undergone Christian conversion in Constantinople and married a Christian husband, who turns out to be the disguised Angelo. For further discussion of the distinction between Zanthia and Lucinda, see Bindu Malieckal, "'Hell's Perfect Character': The Black Woman as the Islamic Other in Fletcher's *The Knight of Malta*," *Essays in Arts and Sciences*, 28 (1999): 53–68. See also Suzy Beemer, "Masks of Blackness, Masks of Whiteness: Coloring the (Sexual) Subject in Jonson, Cary, and Fletcher," *Thamyris*, 4.2 (Autumn, 1997): 233–47. Beemer argues that the black/white binary in the play trumps the Christian/Turk binary.

55 Jean Feerick, *Strangers in Blood: Relocating Race in Renaissance Literature* (Toronto: University of Toronto Press, 2010).

56 Ibid., 15.

57 Hall, *Things of Darkness*, 160–6.

58 Quotations from *The Devil's Law-case* are taken from *The Works of John Webster*, eds. David Gunby, David Carnegie, and MacDonald Jackson, vol. 2 (Cambridge: Cambridge University Press, 2007), 76–167.

59 Fuller, *Historie of the Holy Warre*, 47.

60 Richard Jones, *Booke of honor and armes* (London, 1590), 55.

61 Segar, *Honor military, and ciuill*, 98.

62 Edward Grimstone, *The estates, empires, & principallities of the world* (London, 1615), 1145.

63 Barbara Fuchs, *Mimesis and Empire: The New World, Islam, and European Identities* (Cambridge: Cambridge University Press, 2001), 100. On Spain's attempt to construct itself as a homogeneous nation, see also Fuchs, *Passing for Spain: Cervantes and the Fictions of Identity* (Urbana: University of Illinois Press, 2003).

64 Fuchs, *Passing for Spain*, 2.

65 Quotations from *The Maid of Honor* are taken from *The Plays and Poems of Philip Massinger*, eds. Philip Edwards and Colin Gibson, vol. I (Oxford: Clarendon Press, 1976), 104–97.

66 *The Maid of Honour*, ed. Eva Bryne (London, 1927), xxviii–xxxi.

67 I quote from the earliest English translation, *The discovery and conquest of the Molucco and Philippine islands* (London, 1708), 146; first published in Spanish in 1609, by Bartholomew Leonardo de Argensola.

68 I am grateful to Jean Feerick for bringing this passage to my attention and for offering insight into its analysis.

69 See Feerick's central argument in "'Divided in Soyle': Plantation and Degeneracy in *The Tempest* and *The Sea Voyage*," *Renaissance Drama*, 35 (2006): 27–54.

70 Quotations from *The Travails of the Three English Brothers* are taken from *Three Renaissance Travel Plays*, ed. Anthony Parr (Manchester: Manchester University Press, 1995), 55–134.

71 Parr, "Introduction," in *Three Renaissance Travel Plays*, 10. Parr also suggests that the fact that Anthony had converted to Catholicism during his early travels may have been known to the playwrights and influenced their decision to "present the pope as a dignified and credible spiritual leader" (10).

72 Parr, "The Shirley Brothers and the 'Voyage of Persia,'" in *Travel and Drama in Shakespeare's Time*, eds. Jean-Pierre Maquerlot and Michele Willems (Cambridge: Cambridge University Press, 1996), 14–31, 18.

73 Ibid., 20, 21.

Notes to Epilogue

1   Patricia Parker, *Inescapable Romance: Studies in the Poetics of a Mode* (Princeton: Princeton University Press, 1979).

2   Cyrus Mulready, "'Asia of the One Side, Affric of the Other': Sidney's Unities and the Staging of Romance," in *Staging Early Modern Romance: Prose Fiction, Dramatic Romance, and Shakespeare*, eds. Valerie Wayne and Mary Ellen Lamb (London: Routledge, 2008), 47–71.

3   Ibid., 49.

4   Philip Sidney, "The Defense of Poesy," in *Sir Philip Sidney: The Major Works*, ed. Katherine Duncan-Jones (Oxford: Oxford University Press, 2002), 243.

5   Ibid., 243.

6   Giambattista Guarini, *The Compendium of Tragicomic Poetry* (*Compendio della poesia tragicomica*), trans. Allan H. Gilbert, in *Literary Criticism from Plato to Dryden* (Detroit: Wayne State University Press, 1962), 511.

7   Verna Foster, *The Name and Nature of Tragicomedy* (Aldershot: Ashgate, 2004), 35.

8   Valerie Forman, *Tragicomic Redemptions: Global Economics and the Early Modern English Stage* (Philadelphia: University of Pennsylvania Press, 2008).

9   Sidney, "The Defense of Poesy," 244.

10 Matthew Treherne, "The Difficult Emergence of Pastoral Tragicomedy: Guarini's *Il pastor fido* and its Critical Reception in Italy, 1586–1601," in *Early Modern Tragicomedy*, eds. Subha Mukherji and Raphael Lyne (Cambridge: D. S. Brewer, 2007), 28–42, 36.

11 Guarini, *Compendium of Tragicomic Poetry*, 507.

12 Ibid., 509–10.

13 Ibid., 511.

14 John Fletcher, "To The Reader," in *The Faithful Shepherdess* (London, 1608).

15 See for example Peter Berek, "Genres, Early Modern Theatrical Title Pages, and the Authority of Print," in *The Book of the Play: Playwrights, Stationers, and Readers in Early Modern England*, ed. Marta Straznicky (Amherst: University of Massachusetts Press, 2006), 159–75.

16 Ludovico Ariosto, *Orlando Furioso*, trans. John Harington (London, 1591), ed. Robert McNulty (Oxford: Clarendon Press, 1972), 218. Subsequent references to Harington's translation of the poem will cite it parenthetically by book and stanza.

17 E. A. J. Honigmann, ed., *The Arden Shakespeare Othello*, 3rd ed. (London: Thomas Nelson and Sons, 1996).

18 Thanks to Michael Neill for drawing this discussion to my attention in his response to an early version of this chapter presented at the 2008 conference of the Renaissance Society of America.

19 Quotations from Greene's *Orlando Furioso* are taken from *The Historie of Orlando Furioso, One of the Twelve Pieres of France*, in *The Plays and Poems of Robert Greene*, vol. I, ed. J. Churton Collins (Oxford: Clarendon Press, 1905).

20 Timothy Billings, "Caterwauling Cataians: The Genealogy of a Gloss," *Shakespeare Quarterly*, 54.1 (Spring 2003):1–28, esp. 7 and 20–3.

Index